The New

Now

and Z_EN

Epicure

The New
Now
and Zen
Epicure

Gourmet Vegan Recipes
for the
Enlightened Palate

Miyoko Nishimoto Schinner

Book Publishing Company
Summertown, Tennessee

© 2001 Miyoko Nishimoto Schinner

Cover and interior photos: Dan McGarrah
Food styling: Miyoko Nishimoto Schinner, Michael Cook
Cover design: Warren Jefferson, Cynthia Holzapfel
Interior design: Gwynelle Dismukes

Printed in Canada
Book Publishing Company
415 Farm Road
P.O. Box 99
Summertown, TN 38483
888-260-8458

Pictured on the front cover (from left): Tri-Colored Pepper & Quinoa Charlotte, page 130, Sushi Crêpes, page 62, Shiso Steaks with Shiitake Béarnaise Sauce, page 165

Pictured on the back cover: Chocolate Almond Raspberry Torte, pages 188-89, Portobello & Polenta Lasagne, pages 136-37

ISBN 1-57067-114-1

09 08 07 06 05 04 03 02 01   1 2 3 4 5 6 7 8 9

Library of Congress Catalog-in-Publication Data
Schinner, Miyoko Nishimoto, 1957-
    The new now and Zen epicure : gourmet vegan recipes for the enlightened palate /
    Miyoko Nishimoto Schinner.
        p. cm.
    Includes index.
    ISBN 1-57067-114-1 (alk. paper)
    1. Vegetarian cookery. 2. Cookery, Japanese. I Title.
    TX837.N57 2001
    641.5'636--dc21   2001029513

Calculations for the nutritional analyses in this book are based on the average number of servings listed with the recipes and the average amount of an ingredient if a range is called for. Calculations are rounded up to the nearest gram. If two options for an ingredient are listed, the first one is used. Not included are fat used for frying (unless the amount is specified in the recipe), optional ingredients, or serving suggestions.

Table of Contents

Foreword   vii

Preface   ix

Ingredients & Their Uses   1

Breakfast   21

Appetizers   35

Sauces   67

Soups   89

Entrées   115

Vegetable Dishes &
          Salads   171

Desserts   187

Mail Order Sources   234

Index   235

FOREWORD

The Now and Zen Epicure grew out of recipes I created over a period of time when I threw dinner parties nearly every Friday night in order to create and test new dishes on willing friends and other subjects. The new recipes in this updated edition feature favorite dishes from my restaurant, as well as others created in a more leisurely fashion between working and raising a family.

Like many of my readers, every aspect of my life in the last ten years has become busier and more complex. A husband, Michael, and three children—Aki, Seraphina, and Camellia—all vegetarian, for starters. Naturally, raising children and running businesses do not leave much time for creative escapades in the kitchen. But one thing still draws me to savor a complete cooking experience: food is still an utter celebration of life, something that is best shared with friends or family, a ritual whose meaning goes beyond the nourishment of body to the soul itself. Because it is an affirmation of life, I continue to believe that it is unnecessary to take life—the life of animals—in order to affirm it, especially in light of the abundance of plant foods to be enjoyed. As I hope to show again in this new edition, these plant-based foods present endless possibilities for preparation and transformation into exciting dishes. And I still love to prove exactly that—to students in my classes, my friends, and my family.

Over the years, I have had many folks call me to thank me for writing the original *Now and Zen Epicure*. With this book, too, my original intent remains the same: I truly hope that I can continue to inspire people to cook delicious, healthful, compassionate meals, and thereby encourage them (or their friends or family) to take steps toward a vegetarian diet.

PREFACE

I have met a few stoics in my life who ate mainly for sustenance, but I believe most of us have had a lifelong love affair with food. My own interest began at the age of twelve when, for reasons not fully understood even to myself, I became a vegetarian. Our seventh grade class had gone on a camping trip. We had been divided into several groups, each with its own focus on particular foods, and prepared our own meals with those foods. I got stuck in the vegetarian group, along with the teacher and the only two vegetarians in the class. I didn't know how I would manage to get through those three days without the meat I loved and thought necessary for stamina, but I kept thinking of it as an experiment and challenge, and thus survived. However, to my surprise, I was unable to eat the pork chops my mother placed in front of me for dinner when I returned home. I decided to give vegetarianism another week's try, again simply to see if I could make it.

Of course, my parents protested loudly. They were certain that their darling, albeit rebellious, daughter would die of malnutrition, and the arguments did not cease for several weeks. Finally, my mother, seeing my resolve and the fact that I was getting no skinnier, gave up arguing… as well as cooking for me. So, I was on my own. Armed with a few recipes from one of my vegetarian schoolmates (her whole family was vegetarian and had pictures of some guru hanging all over their house), I braved the pots and stove and diligently read Adele Davis to ensure that I was getting enough protein. Thus the experiments in cooking began.

It was the late sixties, so I made a lot of the "organic type" food for which vegetarianism got a bad name—carob brownies, soy burgers, and lentil casseroles. It was good down-home food, but nothing fancy. Then, at a graduation party at Ernie's in San Francisco (the only time I have ever been to this fine restaurant), I was served a special vegetarian plate of the most deliciously prepared vegetables I have ever eaten. I discovered French cuisine and spent the next few years at college reading Julia Child.

Although I had adamantly refused to eat sugar as a vegetarian child, I began to use it freely, along with heavy cream, butter, rich cheeses, and refined flours. I threw fancy dinner parties. My roommates gladly let me have the run of the kitchen. I was eating and serving wonderful things, but was probably no kinder to the body than the average meat eater.

I realized this several years later while living in Japan. I wanted to go back to a more natural diet but did not want to sacrifice the richness and taste I had learned to love. There was no cookbook available that could show me how to do this, as most gourmet vegetarian cookbooks relied heavily on dairy products and eggs. I had to set about experimenting all over again. Eventually, with the help of my ex-husband and friends who participated in week- ly "taste-testing parties," I was able to develop a new and unique cuisine that allowed one to indulge while remaining perfectly healthy and completely vegetarian.

Many of the recipes in this book reflect this new cuisine. From them you can make delicious creations that will impress the fussi- est dinner guest. He or she will never even think about whether it is vegetarian or not because the "good-for-you" food will be so good. So, throw away your fears about serving a somewhat off- beat dinner to your boss, because he will only be impressed by the wonderful things you set before him. I have fallen out of the habit of telling unsuspecting dinner guests that the fare they are about to be served is purely vegetarian. In many cases telling them is tantamount to giving them a warning:

Beware!
The food you are about to be served may endanger
your palate. Eat at your own risk!

They will often be predisposed, and negatively, to the meal. So I suggest that you create several of the recipes given in this book and serve them without any fanfare. Then sit back and listen to the "ooh's" and "aah's" as the guests marvel.

One of my greatest cooking influences has been Japanese "Kaiseki" cuisine, a highly sophisticated and formal style of food with its cultural roots in Buddhism and tea ceremony. In Kaiseki cuisine, a wide array of beautifully arranged dishes is served in tiny portions over a range of courses called "mountain," "sea," "land," etc., denoting where the ingredients are from. Although I do not adhere to the true tenets of Kaiseki cuisine in my cooking, I have tried to simulate the atmosphere of it by devising menus and dishes that are served in small portions with numerous courses arranged to achieve a balance of flavors, colors, and textures. It is a fun way to eat, and guests are always intrigued by what will come next. Unlike the American way of serving voluminous amounts of some main dish accompanied by a couple of side dishes, eating "Kaiseki style" will provide a unique dining experience for all.

People become vegetarians for a variety of reasons, ranging from health considerations to environmental and humanitarian issues. The purpose of this book is not to convert everyone to vegetarianism, but simply to offer recipes for fine dining and home cooking. The emphasis here is on good taste and artful presentation, because food is a celebration of life, not just sustenance for stoics. Food should nourish both the body and spirit. For it to nourish the former, it must please and satisfy the latter. Herein lies one of the key factors to good health. Relax. Enjoy. Moderation is the motto. Eat as naturally as you can, maintaining a low-fat diet rich in fiber and complex carbohydrates, but don't be afraid to indulge once in a while. A little rich food will occasionally do wonders for a person's soul, especially if they are the dishes in this book. The Greeks had a god of wine named Dionysus (Bacchus to the Romans) who punished those who were too strict with themselves and would not join in the revelry. So, don't be afraid. Go ahead and pour that libation to Dionysus. Then pour some for yourself and have it with something wonderful like French Moussaka, Pâté en Croûte, or Strawberry Almond Tart.

And many happy hours of discovery to you in the kitchen!

Ingredients
&
Their Uses

Agar, or "kanten" in Japanese, is a seaweed product that can replace gelatin in most recipes. Unlike gelatin, agar will set at room temperature in 30 to 60 minutes and become a bit firmer when refrigerated. It is available in bar, flake, or powdered forms. The bar form, which is the most prevalent in Japan, is the least processed. It can be found in Asian markets and some natural food stores; otherwise, the flakes or powder are more commonly found.

AGAR

Unlike gelatin, agar will only set if it is completely dissolved by boiling or simmering. Lemon juice and ingredients containing oxalic acid (such as spinach) will require more than the usual amount of agar to set properly, although a small amount of lemon juice will not be a problem. Although agar will never become rubbery like gelatin, too much of it will produce a very stiff, unappetizing product. Thus the amount used is crucial to producing a dish with the proper texture and firmness. I have found that in mousses and bavarians where a delicate, gelatinous texture is desired, a combination of agar and arrowroot (or better yet, kuzu or kudzu powder—see page 5) produces a very similar effect.

Aside from its jelling powers, agar has many other uses. Cooked along with rice, agar will provide a sheen and luscious texture. It also lends a creamy texture when used in frozen desserts and ice cream. It has no calories and is among the highest in fiber of any plant product known. Of the three types of agar—bar, powder, and flakes—the powder is the easiest to use, dissolving quickly in water as it boils. Flakes should be soaked in water for a few minutes before bringing to a boil. Bars are also easy to use, but must be soaked for a few minutes, shredded, and simmered a bit longer to dissolve.

When substituting flakes for powder, use these proportions:

1 teaspoon of agar powder = ¼ cup of agar flakes

Depending on the ingredients being used, the amount of liquid and solid matter, and the degree of firmness desired, the amounts will seem to vary from recipe to recipe. If you find that a recipe does not harden enough or is too hard for you, simply increase or decrease the amount of agar the next time you use it. And be sure to follow the directions for dissolving agar; it will not set if it is not dissolved properly. It is actually a very simple process, less tricky than gelatin, and one that will become second nature to you once you learn it.

AGAR

How to Use Agar

Bars: Run the bar under cold water to moisten it, making it soft and pliable enough to fit in a bowl to soak. Cover with water for at least 5 minutes (longer if desired—up to 24 hours). Remove the bar from the bowl, and squeeze it to extract the water. The longer you soak it, the softer and less solid it becomes, so if you have left it soaking for several hours, be sure you get all of it out. Shred it into little pieces, and add it to the liquid called for in the recipe. Bring it to a boil in a small, covered saucepan. (Covering is especially important if only a small amount of liquid—a half cup or so—is being used.) Lower the heat and stir frequently, letting it simmer on medium to medium-high heat for 2 to 3 minutes until it is completely dissolved. It must be added to the other ingredients in the recipe while it is still hot or it will set right there in the pan as it cools.

Powder or flakes: The soaking process can be skipped with these two forms, making them less fussy to use, although the flakes will dissolve faster if soaked for a couple of minutes. Otherwise, the directions are the same as for bars: add it to the liquid called for in the recipe, whisk well, cover, and bring to a boil, then allow to simmer on medium to medium-high heat for 2 to 3 minutes, stirring frequently.

When adding dissolved agar to the other ingredients in a recipe (as in mousses, terrines, bavarians, etc.), it is a good idea to add it while the blender or food processor is running. If it is not mixed or blended adequately, you will find little pieces of hardened agar in your creamy mousse, and this, to say the least, will not be pleasant. If you are not using a blender or food processor, add it in a steady stream while whisking rapidly and continuously so that it is uniformly incorporated. Make sure that the mixture to which you are adding the agar is close to room temperature or warm (not cold); if the mixture is cold, the agar could congeal in little bits immediately.

A note on purchasing agar: Agar powder or flakes can be extremely expensive if purchased in natural food stores, where they are usually sold in small quantities. Japanese stores usually carry both the powder and bars at more reasonable prices. However, I have found some wholesale herb and spice distributors who sell powdered or flaked agar by the pound at a much more reasonable price. Check the Internet for possible sources for bulk purchase.

Arrowroot is a substance that thickens like cornstarch. It is derived from the root of a plant that is considered highly nutritious. If a large quantity is used, it will produce a texture that is considerably more gelatinous than cornstarch. Arrowroot is available in natural food stores.

ARROWROOT

Carob, or St. John's Bread (what St. John supposedly ate in the desert), is a highly nutritious pod. When ground, it becomes a cocoa-like substance and can be substituted for chocolate in most recipes. Although it looks and tastes like chocolate, it has less than half the fat of cocoa and contains no caffeine, theobromine, or oxalic acid, substances that can make chocolate undesirable for many people. Because of its naturally high sugar content (40%), carob desserts can be made with only a minimum amount of sweetener. (Cocoa, on the other hand, is extremely bitter if left

CAROB

unsweetened.) Carob contains protein, B vitamins, and calcium, making it a very wholesome treat for young and old. Although some chocolate aficionados object to the more "homely" flavor of carob, I find that most people rarely know the difference if a carob dessert is prepared and flavored properly with the addition of natural grain coffee, vanilla, and/or various spirits or liqueurs.

CAROb

Carob powder can be purchased either raw or lightly toasted. The recipes in this book use the lightly toasted variety, so if only raw carob is available, toast it by spreading it on a baking sheet and baking it in an oven at 150°F for 10 to 15 minutes. You can also dry-roast it in a skillet over a low flame. Be careful that it does not burn.

The block carob or carob chips that are available in some natural food stores can be used like chocolate bars or baking chocolate in most recipes. They may or may not be sweetened. Since carob is naturally sweet, I find that the unsweetened variety is preferable since it allows me to control the amount of additional sweetener in the recipe. If only the sweetened kind is available, check to see what sweetener has been used. The most nutritious brands are those sweetened with date sugar or barley malt. Otherwise the carob may contain white or brown sugar, fructose, or corn syrup, which are less desirable. There is no carob equivalent to bitter-sweet or unsweetened baking chocolate because of carob's naturally high sugar content, but this does not usually pose a problem in most recipes where substitutions are made. Simply decrease the amount of sweetener called for if you are using carob in place of unsweetened baking chocolate. If block carob is unavailable, mix 3 tablespoons of carob powder in 1 tablespoon of water and 2 teaspoons of margarine, oil, or shortening for each 1 ounce square of chocolate or block carob. Vegans should look for dairy-free carob which is available in most natural food stores.

Carob chips can be used in the same way as block carob and should be melted in a double boiler over low heat as you would with chocolate. Be sure that all the utensils used with carob are completely dry since even a drop of water can cause the carob to become grainy. Should this happen, the addition of a tablespoon or two of cocoa butter, coconut oil, or vegetable shortening will restore its smoothness and capacity to melt. Also, carob burns as easily as chocolate and will refuse to melt if the heat is too high. If you find this to be a problem, turn off the heat and let it sit for awhile over hot water, stirring occasionally.

Coconut milk is a purée of coconut meat and water; it is not the watery liquid found inside the coconut. It can be purchased in cans both in regular and reduced-fat varieties. Also, the more adventuresome cook can easily make this at home, especially if canned coconut milk is not available. Combine grated, shredded, or flaked coconut with twice the amount of boiling water (in volume, not weight) in a blender, and whip for 3 or 4 minutes. Strain through cheesecloth or a fine wire mesh, pressing as much milk out of the pulp as possible. The amount of hot water can be increased or decreased according to the consistency of the milk or "cream" desired. Coconut milk can give a tropical flair to drinks, desserts, ice creams, and cakes, and can lend a wonderful depth and subtle sweetness to curries.

Kuzu-ko or Kudzu is a high-quality starch or thickening agent derived from the root of the kuzu plant, which has been touted for its medicinal powers in Asia for ages. It comes in small, rock-like pieces which dissolve easily in water. Although it is used like arrowroot or cornstarch, you need much less to thicken and bind; when substituting kuzu, use only half as much as the arrowroot or cornstarch called for in a recipe. Unlike cornstarch and other highly refined starches, kuzu is is natural and unprocessed.

Although kuzu is more expensive than cornstarch or arrowroot, I prefer the smooth and subtle texture it lends to mousses and other dishes; arrowroot can become too gelatinous.

Mirin is a sweet Japanese sake (rice wine) that is often used in cooking to add sweetness, roundness, or mellowness to a dish. The alcohol will evaporate entirely in cooking, leaving only its flavor.

Although it was originally made from only glutinous sweet rice and "kohji" (an enzyme used in the fermentation of sake and miso), mass production has introduced the use of sugar, distilled alcohol, and sometimes dextrose or other starches as ingredients to expedite the fermentation and production. The alcoholic content can be an indication of how natural the product is; the higher the content (10% to 12%), the "truer" it probably is. Mirin that contains sugar and other ingredients will only have a minimal alcoholic content (2% to 3%). Reading the label closely will help you select a natural brand, but mirin is used in such small quantities that even the less pure types are acceptable. Asian markets, natural food stores, and even some supermarkets stock mirin.

Miso is a fermented paste made primarily from soybeans, salt, and "kohji," an enzyme. It can also be made from rice, barley, or other grains and beans, and will vary greatly in flavor and character according to the substance used. It is a "living" product full of enzymes and friendly bacteria that aid digestion and keep the colon happy. In fact, the Japanese Ministry of Health and Welfare advises the Japanese to drink a bowl of miso soup daily for this reason. Traditionally, a day in Japan starts with a bowl of this simple brew.

Although miso has been an integral part of Japanese cuisine for centuries, I find that it adapts easily to Western cooking, adding depth and flavor to many vegetarian dishes. Miso comes in various colors and shades from light to dark; lighter, golden-colored miso has a milder, less salty flavor, and dark brown miso has a saltier, more prominent flavor. I prefer a mellow, reddish-brown type called sweet kohji miso, which I find to be neither too salty nor light in flavor. There are as many varieties of miso as wine, and each family in Japan will usually subscribe to a particular brand that they like. Japanese and Asian markets carry a fair selection. You may want to try several kinds in order to find one you particularly prefer. The type of miso you incorporate in your recipes is not so crucial if you're using it in place of salt or as a flavoring, and not as the main ingredient, as in miso soup. Simply

MISO

choose one that is neither too light nor dark in color. The grains or beans used to make the miso will affect its flavor, with barley or barley mixtures considered the tastiest by some. But here again, I find that all of this depends on the length of time the miso was allowed to ferment, its salt content, and other factors peculiar to each manufacturer, making even the same type of miso widely varying in flavor.

Like peanut butter, miso comes in both smooth and chunky styles. Both are acceptable in miso soup, although the former is better for flavoring most dishes. (Speaking of peanut butter, I once had an American friend in Tokyo who told me of all the huge vats of peanut butter in his local supermarket. I told him they probably contained miso. Undeterred, he bought himself a pound of it, and later told me about his very salty peanut butter-and-jelly sandwich!)

Aside from the recipes in this book that use miso as a flavoring agent, do go ahead and try it in place of salt in spaghetti or tomato sauces, stir-fried vegetables, and casseroles; you will find it lends a meaty and satisfying depth to your cooking.

Nut milks made from cashews, almonds, or sesame seeds can be tasty and nutritious substitutes for dairy milk or soymilk in cooking. They are easily made by blending blanched raw nuts with water in a blender or food processor. Although nuts are high in fat, they are also high in magnesium, calcium, essential fatty acids, and other valuable minerals, and can lend a richness and depth to many dishes and sauces. The Chinese have a delicious custard-like dessert made from almond milk that has a subtle sweetness and flavor that can not be achieved with either dairy milk or soymilk. This book contains many recipes that call for either cashew or almond milk.

NUT milks

To make cashew milk, combine ¼ to ½ cup cashews with 1 cup of water in a blender for 2 to 3 minutes until absolutely smooth. The more cashews you add, the richer the resulting milk or cream will be. Straining is not necessary. *To make almond milk*, start with blanched almonds. You can remove the skins by plunging the whole raw almonds in boiling water for a few minutes. The skins will slip off easily. Follow the directions for cashew milk, but strain it to remove the remaining pulp since almonds are harder to purée as smoothly as cashews. Hulled sesame seeds are used to make milk in the same way as cashews and almonds.

Brazil nuts are excellent for a rich cream, as are cashews, and both can be flavored with vanilla or a liqueur to produce a delicious dessert topping or sauce.

NUTRITIONAL YEAST

Nutritional yeast is a vitamin- and mineral-packed food substance that is available in flake or powder forms in natural food stores. Unlike brewer's yeast, which is almost offensive in flavor, nutritional yeast is delicious. It adds great fullness, richness, and depth if used in combination with other ingredients and is thus used profusely throughout this book.

OKARA

Okara is the leftover pulp of the soybean that results from making soymilk or tofu. It is thus the "other half" of the soybean, containing all its fiber and a considerable amount of protein, while being much lower in fat than tofu. It is a white, fluffy, moist substance that, despite its nutritional value, is so lacking in flavor that 99.9% of the okara produced in Japan is either fed to hogs or used as fertilizer. Although tons of it are produced daily, it is rarely available to consumers in Japan; one has to arrive at a neighborhood tofu shop practically at dawn to get any before it is all carted away. I have had to run around to six or seven shops before finding one that had kept even a pound or two for sale. To make this easier for you, there is a recipe for making a small amount of okara at home on page 189.

In all the centuries of tofu production in Japan, okara has traditionally been used in basically one dish called "U No Hana," a tasty blend of vegetables and okara seasoned with soy sauce, mirin, and stock. However, it is a versatile ingredient that can be used to bind or fill croquettes, dumplings, and nut or bean loaves, or used to replace some of the flour in cakes and pastries.

If you make your own tofu and end up with mounds of okara you do not know what to do with, try adding it to burgers and loaves. Or you can partly dry it in a nonstick frying pan over low heat, stirring almost constantly, and use it in cakes or cookies, or to replace bread crumbs in coating croquettes for frying. Cookies made with okara do tend to absorb a lot of moisture, so it is best to use it in a soft cookie.

To make semidried okara, place it in a dry skillet and cook over very low heat, stirring almost constantly, until most of the moisture evaporates. It will look fluffy and light, and will not clump up. As it dries, it will increase in volume; to get 1 cup of dried okara start with ½ to ⅔ cup wet okara. It should take about 10 to 15 minutes to dry in a skillet.

Sake, or Japanese rice wine, is as wonderful to use in cooking as it is to drink on a nippy winter night. It is used extensively in Japanese cuisine and in several recipes in this book. Sake comes in various grades, and a dry sake is preferable to a sweet one for both cooking and drinking. In cooking, dry sherry or a dry vermouth can be substituted if sake is not available.

SAKE

If you are going to drink the sake, warm it up by pouring it into a small ceramic pitcher or bottle, and place in simmering water for a few minutes. Do not let the sake boil—it should be hot but not scalding. Enjoy!

Shimeji (oyster) mushrooms grow in clumps and have a delicate texture and flavor. They can be found in Japanese food stores as well as some supermarkets. Although more expensive than regular button mushrooms, they can add a wonderful contrast and flavor to many dishes.

SHIMEJI (OYSTER) MUSHROOMS

Shiitake (black) mushrooms are perhaps the best known of all Oriental mushrooms and are used extensively in both Chinese and Japanese cooking. They have a rich, deep, meaty flavor and texture and lend themselves well to everything from stocks to being stuffed as an appetizer. They are available either fresh or dried and in either case will be very expensive if purchased in a

SHIITAKE (BLACK) MUSHROOMS

natural food store or supermarket. If there is a Chinatown or Chinese market where you live, it is definitely worth a trip to purchase a pound bag of dried shiitake mushrooms, since they will be considerably less expensive. Although some dishes call for fresh shiitake mushrooms, some work better with the dried ones which are meatier and more flavorful. They are also high in vitamin D and have been used as an ingredient in Chinese herbal therapy for centuries.

The best method for reconstituting dried mushrooms is soaking in tepid water for several hours or overnight; this gives you a nice stock that can be used to flavor Asian dishes such as stir-fry vegetables and sauce. If you are pressed for time, the soaking can be expedited by using hot water, but the resulting stock will not be as flavorful. Since mushrooms vary in size and thickness, it is hard to give the exact amount of water to use, but 1 cup of water for 3 to 4 large mushrooms should reconstitute the mushrooms and yield a flavorful stock. I find it helpful to keep a large jar of mushrooms soaking in liquid in the refrigerator so I can use them anytime. They will keep for a week or two under refrigeration.

Once again, shiitake mushrooms come in various grades, with the thick "donkoh shiitake" being the best variety. When buying dried shiitake, try to find ones that are thick with a crinkled, cracked surface; they will be much more flavorful and have a silkier, superior texture. In fact, a good shiitake mushroom is so good that a light grilling or sautéing with soy sauce and lemon juice is all that it needs.

Soymilk: There are so many varieties of soymilk on the natural food market today that it both baffles and delights someone like myself who has had to make it from scratch most of her life. Soymilk—and very good soymilk—can be made at home fairly easily, especially with the new countertop soymilk makers that produce fresh milk from soaked beans in less than half an hour. However, there are also a number of excellent commercial brands available today. What one wants to avoid with soymilk is the

soymilk

"beany" taste. A number of these brands have managed to eliminate this with a minimum of adulteration. Some have added oil to produce a rich and creamy product suitable for use as "cream" or half-and-half in dairy-free recipes. Others have blended in kombu (a type of seaweed) and barley malt to produce a lighter, though still creamy, tasty product. Some brands of soymilk now come in aseptic packaging, allowing you to store it without refrigeration. Chinese and Japanese food stores also carry soymilk, but be sure to purchase a brand that does not contain sugar. If you are using pure, unblended soymilk made from only soybeans and water, you can eliminate the beany taste by adding a very small amount of salt and maple syrup. This gives it a creamier consistency, especially if the soymilk is thick rather than thin and watery.

SOY CREAM

A slightly richer soy cream can be produced by blending in 2 to 3 tablespoons of oil per cup of unblended soymilk, along with the tiny amount of salt and sweetener. If you want to keep your fat intake to a minimum, use a commercial, blended brand that does not contain any additional oil.

SOY SAUCE

Soy sauce has become a household word in America, although I remember a time when the only soy sauce available was a strange sweet and salty substance with caramel coloring that came on your table in Chinese restaurants. Today, many fine brands are available in not only Asian and natural food stores, but supermarkets as well. A one-gallon can will be considerably cheaper than little bottles, and you will find that it is an indispensable ingredient in many of the recipes in this book. Soy sauce can be used in place of salt in soups, sauces, casseroles, and other dishes (Western as well as Asian) and will not be overpowering in flavor.

There are many brands of soy sauce. The best contain only soybeans, salt, and wheat, and have been aged slowly. They will be rich and deep in color and absolutely delicious over chilled fresh tofu with grated ginger and green onions. But here again, as with miso, soy sauce manufacturers have compromised quality for quantity, and often use alcohol, sugar, caramel coloring, and monosodium glutamate to approximate a true soy sauce. Read the label.

Soy sour cream, or a soy substitute for sour cream, is easily made by draining soy yogurt. (See the recipe for soy yogurt that follows.) Place the yogurt in a bag made of cheesecloth or gauze, and hang it above the kitchen sink to drain until you have a thick, creamy substance (several hours or overnight). Or, line a colander with a double thickness of cheesecloth, and drain the yogurt in that. A little salt and lemon juice added to this will counteract the beany flavor while bringing out the sourness. Although tofu sour cream (see recipe on page 182) can be used in dips and toppings, soy sour cream made from soy yogurt is more effective when the richness of sour cream is desired.

Soy yogurt is as easily made as dairy yogurt and can be extremely thick, rich, and sweet. The best milk to start with is either homemade or "fresh" refrigerated milk, not a variety in aseptic packaging. Heat a quart of soymilk until it feels warm to your wrist, and mix in 2 to 3 tablespoons of a commercial plain soy yogurt or acidophilus. You may want to mix the commercial yogurt with a small amount of the warm soymilk first to make it easier to mix in. Cover, set it in a warm place, and do not disturb for 3 to 5 hours. It should set nicely. If it does not set, the temperature of the soymilk may have been too high and the culture killed; or you may not have set it in a warm enough place. Some recipes suggest keeping the temperature of the milk at around 110°F. I have never bothered to use a thermometer and have rarely had trouble with yogurt not setting properly. There are really no mysteries to making it.

The Egyptian cook for a family with whom I stayed in Cairo used to pour his yogurt in jars, then wrap them with towels and set them on the kitchen counter, and it worked every time. I've had success wrapping the jars or containers in thick jackets or blankets to enclose the heat. Anywhere with a pilot light, a tub filled with lukewarm water, near a radiator, heater, or fireplace, or a conventional

SOY SOUR CREAM

SOY YOGURT

or microwave oven with a "warm" setting can be used to set the yogurt. Look around and you will find an appropriate place in your house.

If you are going to eat freshly made yogurt, refrigerate it overnight first; it will get thicker and tastier as it chills. If you are using it for sour cream, it can be drained right away. (See the instructions on the previous page.)

Sweeteners have long been a sticking point for those attempting a vegetarian or vegan diet. Some "compassionate" vegans have no qualms about white sugar and use it in everything. I have met countless vegans and vegetarians who claim that when they eat dessert, they only want the "real thing" made with granulated cane sugar. Yet others with a sweet tooth look for desserts made with more healthful sweeteners. I happen to believe that a dessert can be utterly luscious and sweet to the point of deception even if made with alternative sweeteners. The trick is understanding which one to use for each dessert. Maple syrup is a wonderful flavor enhancer for pecan pie. Fruit juice concentrate is preferable for fruit tarts, but does not taste good in chocolate cake. Maple syrup works in cakes, while brown rice syrup alone will yield a heavy, dense texture. Still, some like such results.

SWEETENERS

Whether you use maple syrup, brown rice syrup, FruitSource, fruit juice concentrate, agave, or white sugar is ultimately your own choice. I have tried to leave this as an option for the reader and cook, while providing within each recipe a variety of sweeteners that can be used interchangeably. However, please realize that each sweetener will exert a slightly different flavor profile on the dessert. In recipes where a certain sweetener is crucial, I have indicated just that. Otherwise, I suggest you experiment to find the kind that appeals to you. Fruit juice concentrates, brown rice syrup, agave, and FruitSource are all metabolized by the body more slowly than sugar, resulting in a slower insulin reaction. This may help prevent the "sugar blues."

Fruit juice concentrate—Available in jars in natural food stores, usually a combination of pear, peach, and pineapple juices boiled until syrupy. Great for cakes and cookies (other than chocolate), tofu cheesecakes, and fruit pies.

White grape juice concentrate—Available frozen in supermarkets. Works in almost everything, including chocolate dishes, due to its bland flavor. Produces a light texture in cakes.

SWEETENERS

FruitSource—A patented product sold in liquid and powder form made from brown rice syrup and fruit juice concentrate. (I find the powder does not dissolve as well and quickly becomes hard after the container has been opened.) While its bland flavor makes it a versatile sweetener, I have found that it can produce inconsistent results in baked goods, making heavier, more gooey cakes or other baked products than juice concentrates. Good for puddings, flans, brownies (gooey ones), pies, cobblers, and ice creams.

Maple syrup—Delicious in so many desserts where a subtle maple flavor is desired. Although high in minerals, it is mostly sucrose and is thus not the ideal sweetener for people with diabetes. Can be used in cookies, cakes, candies, flans, puddings, and apple desserts.

Brown rice syrup—Considerably less sweet than other sweeteners, with a delicate caramel-like flavor. Good for puddings, flans, and pie fillings, while trickier to use in cakes, cookies, and other baked items.

Agave—Made from the agave plant (from which tequila is also made), this sweetener apparently is metabolized slowly by the body (making it a good choice for those with diabetes). It is available in light and dark colors, the latter tasting like molasses. Light agave can be used in baked goods, smoothies, and puddings, although in certain baked desserts the color can become darker. Available in natural food stores, it is relatively expensive.

TAHINI

Tahini, or sesame paste or butter, has been a staple in the Middle East and Asia for ages. It is rich and flavorful, and contains a high level of calcium in an easily digestible form. It can be used to make spreads, sauces, dips, baked goods, and desserts, and can act as a binder to replace eggs in many dishes. Several natural food manufacturers produce tahini today, and it varies greatly in flavor and texture. For the recipes in this book, it is best to use a silky, smooth tahini made from lightly toasted hulled white sesame seeds. (Some tahinis are grainier than others.)

Tamari is a soy sauce-like brew made from soybeans only and contains no wheat. It has become popular in the United States recently because it is lower in sodium than soy sauce and has a deep, rich flavor. However, tamari accounts for less than 1% of all soy sauce production in Japan, and most of that is exported to the United States. It is also more expensive than soy sauce. Tamari can be used in place of soy sauce in any of the recipes in this book. It is also a perfect substitute for those on a wheat-free diet.

Tempeh is a cultured soy product that has been the mainstay of the Indonesian diet for centuries. Unlike tofu, which is made from soymilk and thus contains no fiber, tempeh is produced from the entire bean. An edible mold is grown on partially cooked soybeans, forming a dense and easily digestible cake that can be prepared in a variety of ways. Tempeh can be baked, broiled, stewed, marinated, fried, sautéed, and steamed. Crumbled, it is a substitute for ground meat. It is available frozen in natural food stores.

Although it was once thought that all tempeh contained substantial amounts of vitamin B_{12} (a vitamin that is not generally present in a pure vegetarian diet), it has now been found that the sterile manufacturing methods employed in the United States do not yield the bacteria that contains B_{12}. However, tempeh is still an extremely nutritious soy product in an easily digestible form. Tempeh is highly perishable and should be refrigerated or frozen. If the recipe you're using does not indicate that the tempeh should be cooked in some manner for at least 15 minutes, you should steam or simmer it for at least that long before using.

Tofu, which was regarded in America a few years ago as a tasteless, white, soft substance, has become a rather celebrated food as of late. I have encountered so many different types of tofu recently that I feel I should write at least a short exposition on the matter to clear up what I find to be a rather confusing array of white blocks in water.

тоfu

Tofu (soybean curd) is made by adding a coagulant to soymilk, usually calcium sulfate or the more traditional magnesium chloride ("nigari" in Japanese), a mineral extracted from salt. The curds are then separated from the whey and pressed into a block. Various degrees of pressure are applied to produce different degrees of firmness. Japanese tofu, or what is sometimes called "regular tofu," is softer than Chinese tofu, which is often labeled "firm tofu." However, I have often bought a package of each by the same manufacturer and found them to be exactly the same. Other times, I would find that they varied greatly. Unless you find a brand that is consistent, the directions for pressing your own tofu given here should be followed in order to ensure uniformity in cooking each time. If the recipe simply calls for "tofu" and it does not specify "firm," "pressed," or "well-drained," assume that it is the Japanese or regular type. This type is usually found in plastic containers holding about a pound, or it is sometimes sold in bulk in large buckets of water. There is another type that comes vacuum-packed that is much firmer than the regular type. It is similar to pressed Chinese tofu found in Chinese groceries and does not need to be drained or pressed before using in recipes that call for such. This very firm type is excellent for slicing or crumbling and sautéing. Regular tofu is better for blending in sauces, dips, and dessert toppings.

"Silken" tofu is extremely smooth, delicate, and soft. It may be packaged in plastic containers with water or in an aseptic carton that can be kept at room temperature for several months, making it a very convenient food item. Silken tofu is excellent in dishes where a smooth texture is of primary importance.

In Japan almost every neighborhood has a local tofu shop that makes batches of fresh tofu every morning. Tofu sellers also come by on bicycles, blowing their distinctive sounding horn to inform housewives of their approach. But the purity and quality of tofu has fallen greatly in recent years. Originally tofu contained only whole soybeans, water, and nigari. Calcium sulfate has largely replaced nigari now, and fillers and preservatives have been pumped into it. Whereas traditional Japanese tofu was a solid substance with a fresh, beany taste, most tofu today is watery and bland by comparison. Unfortunately, very few Japanese today have tasted truly delicious tofu. Perhaps this accounts for the decline in tofu consumption. Although America seems to carry a wider array of tofu that does not contain the unnecessary extras, a consumer should still read the labels and select as natural a brand as possible.

Freshness is crucial to tofu and can affect the flavor greatly. Tofu should have a clean, fresh smell and flavor; if it has a sharp, biting smell or taste, it has gone bad. Tofu that is to be used raw in recipes like mousses and puddings must be absolutely fresh. If you must use tofu that has a slight smell, boil it for five minutes before using, or better yet, turn it into frozen tofu (see below). This will change the texture from soft and silky to chewy and spongy, however, so frozen tofu is better in a dish like chili or stroganoff and not appropriate for blending or mashing. Unfortunately, tofu in America can sit on the shelf for several days, so check the date on it before buying.

Frozen tofu: Freezing tofu will entirely change the texture to yield a meaty, chewy substance that will soak up marinades and flavorings and perform as a convincing meat substitute in many recipes. Since it defrosts in less than 15 minutes and can be used immediately, it is a good idea to have a stock of it in the freezer at all times.

FROZEN TOFU

The texture and consistency of frozen tofu seems to vary with the type and brand, and you may have to experiment a little to find one that yields the most chewy or "meaty" results. Generally speaking, however, the best frozen tofu is made from firmer fresh tofu, although any type (except silken) can be used. Again, there is a time factor involved; the tofu seems to get more chewy the longer it is frozen. Since this is the case, I recommend freezing it for at least one week, if not longer, before using. (Up to a year is alright.)

To freeze tofu, remove it from its package, wrap in plastic wrap or bag, and place in the freezer. To defrost, unwrap and place in hot or boiling water, changing the water as it cools. This will take anywhere from 5 to 25 minutes, depending on the amount you are defrosting. If you have all day, the tofu can thaw at room temperature; if pressed for time, you can defrost it in a microwave. Before using, squeeze out all the water. The tofu will become considerably lighter and will resemble a natural sponge.

pRessed tofu

Pressed or well-drained tofu: Some recipes call for a very firm tofu. Vacuum-packed brands are usually pressed hard and can be used as is in such recipes. Chinese grocers usually carry small squares of dense tofu that has also been pressed, and these can be used as is. In the absence of these, it is very easy to press or drain your own tofu. Wrap the regular tofu (or even the so-called firm type that is packed in water) in a thick towel, and allow it to drain in the refrigerator overnight. In the morning, the towel will be wet from the moisture of the tofu, and the tofu will be firm and dense. It can now be used.

Recipes in this book calling for this extra-firm pressed or drained tofu will give two quantities, the first for the amount of regular or water-packed firm tofu to start with if you are going to press or drain it yourself. The second quantity will read "pre-pressed." This will indicate the amount of extra-firm vacuum-packed or dense Chinese-style tofu to use as is. (Example: 12 to 14 ounces tofu, pressed, or 8 ounces pre-pressed tofu.)

Gourmet Vegan Recipes
for the
Enlightened Palate

Breakfast

Yield: 12 pancakes

4 ounces silken tofu (regular tofu can be used, but silken produces a fluffier pancake)

2 cups soymilk

3 to 4 tablespoons sweetener of choice (maple syrup is good)

1 teaspoon vanilla

1 tablespoon oil (optional)

2 cups unbleached or whole wheat pastry flour

½ teaspoon salt

1 tablespoon baking powder

Fluffy Pancakes

Eggless, dairyless pancakes are a cinch to make, and every bit as tasty. Kids and adults all love them. As with "regular" pancakes, they can be transformed by the addition of berries, nuts, etc.

Purée the tofu, soymilk, sweetener, vanilla, and optional oil, if using, in a blender until smooth. Pour into a large bowl. Sift the flour with the salt and baking powder. Mix into the liquid mixture all at once with a fork or whisk, using a few light strokes, just enough to combine but leaving it slightly lumpy.

Heat a skillet or griddle until a drop of water on it sizzles. Spray with nonstick spray, or brush on a little oil. Turn the heat down to medium-low, and pour on about ¼ cup batter for each pancake. Cook on one side until the top bubbles. Flip over and cook the other side for about half the time. Consume immediately.

Per serving: Calories 99, Protein 3 g, Fat 1 g, Carbohydrates 19 g

Blueberry Pancakes

Along with the flour, add about 1½ cups fresh or frozen blueberries to the batter.

Banana-Nut Pancakes

Add 1 to 2 sliced bananas and ¾ cup chopped walnuts to the batter.

WHEAT-FREE PANCAKES

Substitute 1 cup each barley flour and oat flour for the wheat flour.

FRENCH TOAST

Yield: 3 to 6 servings

Yes, it is possible to make French toast without eggs! And no one will know the difference.

Purée the soymilk, tofu, flour, arrowroot, vanilla, and cinnamon until smooth. Pour into a shallow dish. Dip the bread on both sides, one slice at a time. Heat a skillet until hot, then brush on oil or spray with nonstick spray. Cook the slices on each side slowly over low heat. Allow the toast to brown completely before flipping and cooking the other side, or it will stick to the pan.

2 cups soymilk
8 ounces regular tofu
½ cup unbleached flour
2 tablespoons arrowroot
2 teaspoons vanilla
½ teaspoon cinnamon
About 12 slices bread: white, whole grain, sourdough, etc. Day-old works great!

Per slice: Calories 237, Protein 11 g, Fat 6 g, Carbohydrates 34 g

Yield: about 15 large scones

1 cup tofu

1 cup oil

*1 cup fruit juice concentrate or
    maple syrup*

½ teaspoon almond extract

½ cup orange juice concentrate

1 teaspoon grated orange zest

*2 pounds whole wheat pastry flour
    or unbleached flour*

2 tablespoons baking powder

Orange Almond Scones

Purée the tofu with the oil and fruit juice concentrate in a blender. Place in a bowl. Mix in the almond extract, orange juice concentrate, and orange zest. Sift together the flour with the baking powder, and mix into the wet ingredients, combining until a stiff dough is produced. Do not knead.

Preheat the oven to 350°F. Scoop out the dough with an ice cream scoop, and place on an oiled baking sheet. Flatten slightly with your hand. Alternately, you may roll the dough out ½ inch thick between two sheets of waxed paper, then cut it with a biscuit cutter. Bake for about 20 minutes, or until the scones have risen slightly and are golden brown.

Per scone: Calories 388, Protein 9 g, Fat 15 g, Carbohydrates 51 g

Cranberry Walnut or Pecan Scones

Make the above dough, but delete the orange zest, almond extract, and orange juice concentrate, and use ½ cup cranberry juice concentrate. Add ½ cup dried cranberries and ½ cup walnut or pecan pieces.

Cheesy Walnut Raisin Blintzes

Yield: 4 to 6 servings

These are nice for a Sunday brunch or a simple dessert. The tofu comes out tasting like ricotta or cottage cheese, and it can be served as is, or with maple syrup or Citrus Brandy Sauce, page 233. If you have frozen crêpes on hand (which you can make ahead of time and freeze), the dish is a breeze to assemble.

Have ready:

4 to 6 large crêpes, page 140

¾ pound firm tofu
3 tablespoons maple syrup
⅓ cup raisins or currants
⅓ cup lightly toasted, chopped walnuts
¼ cup, lightly toasted, slivered almonds (optional)
¼ teaspoon freshly grated nutmeg
A dash or two of cinnamon
Nonhydrogenated margarine for sautéing

Mash the tofu with a fork until it resembles ricotta cheese. Add the sweetener, raisins, nuts, and spices, and mix well. Fill the crêpes as desired (either roll up or fold into quarters), and sauté lightly in margarine over low heat until lightly browned and heated through. Alternately, the crêpes can be heated in a microwave or conventional oven. If you use a conventional oven, cover them with aluminum foil to prevent drying and hardening.

Top with the sauce or syrup of your choice, and serve immediately.

Per serving: Calories 276, Protein 14 g, Fat 12 g, Carbohydrates 31 g

½ cup canola or safflower oil
1 cup fruit juice concentrate
   (pear, peach, and pineapple,
   or white grape concentrate)
   or maple syrup
½ cup soymilk
2 cups unbleached or whole wheat
   flour pastry flour
1 teaspoon salt
1 tablespoon baking powder

Basic Muffin Batter

A five-minute mixture is the base for a variety of delightful muffins.

Combine the oil with the sweetener and milk. Sift the flour with the salt and baking powder. Add to the liquid mixture, and combine with a few quick strokes, using a fork or whisk. Do not overbeat.

Preheat the oven to 400°F. Spoon the batter into 12 oiled muffin tins. Bake for about 20 to 25 minutes, or until lightly browned and a toothpick inserted in the middle comes out clean.

Per muffin: Calories 193, Protein 2 g, Fat 9 g, Carbohydrates 25 g

Blueberry Muffins

Use fruit juice concentrate, not maple syrup. Add 1 teaspoon lemon zest to the liquid mixture. Add 1 cup fresh or frozen blueberries with the flour.

Cranberry Walnut Muffins

Either sweetener can be used. Along with the flour, add 1 cup dried cranberries and ¾ cup walnut or pecan pieces.

Apple Spice Muffins

Yield: 12 muffins

Tender, sweet, and laced with a delicate spice, I enjoy every bite of this muffin. It can be baked in a cake pan with a crumb topping to make a coffee cake, lately out of fashion but still tasty.

Purée the tofu in a blender with the canola oil and fruit juice concentrate. Place in a bowl and combine with the applesauce. Mix in the apple pieces and walnuts.

In a separate bowl, sift together the flour, spices, baking powder, and baking soda. Mix the dry ingredients into the wet ingredients, and combine quickly, being sure not to overmix. A slightly lumpy batter will do just fine.

Preheat the oven to 375°F. Fill 12 muffin tins to the brim, and bake about 20 to 25 minutes, or until a toothpick inserted in the middle comes out clean.

Per muffin: Calories 312, Protein 6 g, Fat 13 g, Carbohydrates 40 g

½ cup mashed tofu
½ cup canola oil
1⅓ cups fruit juice concentrate (pear, peach, and pineapple juices)
1½ cups applesauce
1 cup roughly chopped apple pieces
¾ cup chopped walnuts
3 cups whole wheat pastry flour
1½ teaspoons cinnamon
⅛ teaspoon nutmeg
⅛ teaspoon mace
1 tablespoon baking powder
1 teaspoon baking soda

Yield: 12 to 15 muffins

Filling:

1 cup chopped walnuts

¾ cup raisins

½ cup maple syrup

1 tablespoon cinnamon

2 tablespoons flour

½ cup canola or safflower oil

1 cup maple syrup

½ cup soymilk

2 cups unbleached pastry flour or
   whole wheat flour

1 teaspoon salt

1 tablespoon baking powder

Walnut Surprise Muffins

These add an element of fun, concealing a tasty filling on the inside.

Thoroughly combine all of the ingredients for the filling in a bowl, and set aside.

Mix the oil, maple syrup, and soymilk together in a bowl. Sift the flour with the salt and baking powder, and mix into the liquid mixture quickly with either a fork or whisk. Preheat the oven to 375°F. Spoon the batter about halfway full into 12 oiled muffin tins. Place a rounded tablespoon of the filling mixture in the middle of the batter of each muffin. Fill to the brim with the remaining muffin batter. Bake about 20 to 25 minutes, or until a toothpick inserted in the middle comes out clean.

Per muffin: Calories 307, Protein 3 g, Fat 13 g, Carbohydrates 43 g

Aki's Tofu Eggs

Yield: 3 to 4 servings

Although there are several "tofu scrambler" products on the market, this easy version of scrambled tofu is loved by kids and has a texture similar to eggs. My son, Aki, learned to make it himself at age six and proudly cooks it for his family and friends to this day.

1 tablespoon oil

12 ounces tofu (Japanese style "regular" or firm silken—do not use firm or extra-firm regular tofu, as it will not come out soft and tender)

¼ cup nutritional yeast flakes

2 tablespoons soy sauce

Heat the oil in a pan. Mash the tofu with your hand by squeezing, and add to the pan. Cook for about a minute, stirring with a spoon, until hot. Sprinkle with nutritional yeast and soy sauce, and mix, adding more of either seasoning if desired. Cook for another minute, then serve immediately. Do not overcook, or it can become watery.

Per serving: Calories 143, Protein 11 g, Fat 8 g, Carbohydrates 6 g

Yield: 4 servings

1 tablespoon oil
12 ounces regular tofu (not firm)
2 tablespoons soy sauce, or to taste
¼ cup nutritional yeast flakes

Herbal

½ cup diced zucchini
½ cup red bell peppers
½ cup mushrooms
1 tablespoon chopped fresh thyme
1 tablespoon chopped fresh parsley
1 tablespoon chopped fresh chives

Per serving: Calories 133, Protein 10 g, Fat 7 g, Carbohydrates 7 g

Mushroom

1½ to 2 cups sliced mushrooms
(you can mix 3 to 4 kinds)

Per serving: Calories 168, Protein 12 g, Fat 7 g, Carbohydrates 13 g

Garden Scramble

Your favorite vegetables can be added to the foregoing Aki's Tofu Eggs to make a delightful and satisfying breakfast entrée. Several suggestions are given here for additions and can be varied to suit your palate or the contents of your fridge.

Heat the oil in a pan. Over high heat, add whatever vegetables you are using and sauté, tossing and stirring to cook quickly and brown slightly without becoming watery. (For the piperade style, add the tomatoes only at the very end of this cooking process; herbs should also be added at the end.) When the vegetables are tender, add the tofu to the pan, crumbling with your hand. Stir for a minute, then season with the soy sauce and nutritional yeast. Serve immediately.

Piperade

1 to 2 cloves garlic, minced
½ cup chopped onions
½ cup diced green or
  red bell peppers
½ cup diced fresh tomatoes
¼ cup chopped fresh basil
  or parsley
1 minced jalapeño pepper
(optional)

Per serving: Calories 141, Protein 10 g, Fat 7 g, Carbohydrates 8 g

Mushroom Asparagus

½ cup sliced mushrooms
½ cup chopped red onions
½ cup chopped asparagus

Per serving: Calories 140, Protein 10 g, Fat 7 g, Carbohydrates 8 g

Your Favorite

Any other combination you might desire!

Huevos Florentine

Yield: 1 serving

Be transported south-of-the-border on a leisurely Sunday morning with this one.

Heat the oil in a sauté pan until hot. Add the spinach and sauté briefly until wilted. Keep the heat high and do not overcook, or the spinach will become watery and soggy. Season with salt and pepper to taste. For each serving, place one or two warmed corn tortillas on a plate. Top with the spinach, making sure to drain any liquid in the pan. Spread with Aki's Tofu Egg, then top with the salsa, guacamole, and sour crème. Eat with gusto!

Per serving: Calories 510, Protein 29 g, Fat 21 g, Carbohydrates 48 g

For each serving have prepared:

1 or 2 corn tortillas, briefly warmed or heated in the oven or over an open flame

Approximately ½ to ¾ cup Aki's Tofu Eggs, page 29

¼ cup Roasted Tomato Salsa, below, or your favorite salsa

2 to 3 tablespoons guacamole

2 tablespoons Tofu Sour Crème, page 182

In addition, for each serving have:

1 teaspoon olive oil for sautéing

1 cup baby spinach

Salt and pepper

Roasted Tomato Salsa

Yield: 3½ cups

Not just for Huevos Florentine, but every variety of chips as well.

Roast the tomatoes, red bell pepper, and jalapeño pepper under a broiler until the skins are blackened. Do not peel. Chop all of them finely, blackened skin as well. Combine with the remaining ingredients.

Per ¼ cup: Calories 20, Protein 1 g, Fat 0 g, Carbohydrates 4 g

3 tomatoes

1 small red bell pepper

1 jalapeño pepper

¼ cup chopped cilantro

½ small red onion, minced

1 or 2 cloves garlic, minced

Salt

Yield: about 4 servings

Batter:

1 pound regular tofu, crumbled

¼ cup soymilk

¼ cup flour

¼ cup nutritional yeast flakes

1 teaspoon salt

¼ teaspoon turmeric

Black pepper (optional)

Filling of choice:

sautéed mushrooms and/or onions, briefly sautéed spinach, other sautéed vegetables of choice, diced vegetarian ham or Believable Bacon, page 33, Tofu "Feta" Cheese, page 43, salsa, or any combination thereof

THE ZENMLET

Yes! You can give up eggs and still have an omelet on Sunday morning! Fill these with whatever you please, and enjoy a brunch that won't clog your arteries.

Combine all the batter ingredients in a food processor or blender, and purée until smooth. The mixture should be a pale yellow; it will become more yellow when it is cooked.

Heat a nonstick skillet or omelet pan. Spray with nonstick spray or coat with a little oil. Pour the mixture in the skillet about ⅓ inch thick. (The amount will depend on the size of the pan, so it is better to go with thickness.) Cook over medium heat until the bottom is lightly brown and the top begins to dry. Top one half of the zenmlet with the prepared filling, and flip the other half over. Cook for a couple more minutes, then turn out onto a plate.

Per serving (not including fillings): Calories 141, Protein 12 g, Fat 5 g, Carbohydrates 11 g

Believable "Bacon"

This is the only vegetarian "bacon" I have found to be really satisfying—crispy and chewy, with a smoky flavor. With no cholesterol, it's the perfect complement to any breakfast, or make yourself a great BLT with it. Try the delicious, homey Beans and "Bacon" Casserole on page 167. Double the recipe if you wish— this goes very fast!

Slice the tofu into pieces ⅛ inch thick and about the width of a slice of bacon. Heat the oil in a skillet (preferably non-stick), and cook the tofu slices over a medium-low flame until golden brown and crispy on one side. (This can take up to 15 minutes, depending on the pan used.) Flip and cook the other side until browned. The tofu should be very brown and crispy. Sprinkle with the nutritional yeast, then add the soy sauce and liquid smoke, and stir quickly to coat the tofu slices evenly. Cook for another moment, then serve.

Per serving: Calories 59, Protein 3 g, Fat 5 g, Carbohydrates 1 g

Yield: 2 to 4 servings

8 ounces pre-pressed or firm tofu (see page 18)
1 tablespoon oil plus nonfat cooking spray, or 2 to 3 tablespoons oil
3 tablespoons nutritional yeast flakes
3 tablespoons soy sauce
1 teaspoon liquid smoke

Appetizers

This is where the magic begins. Whether what follows is just a bowl of soup or a complicated multi-course affair, the first course will set the mood for the evening. By taking the time to make and serve an appetizer, you will make the simplest meal seem more elegant, and your guests will reward you well with their appreciation. Because appetizers are something "extra," like dessert, I think of them as very special, and I have a great deal of fun making fancy little tarts, beautifully molded mousses, and other delightful things. I know it will put everybody in the mood and perhaps ease any tension that may be in the air about "vegetarian food." There are many wonderful and unusual creations here, and your guests will delight in new flavors and textures.

Among these recipes you will find dishes that are appropriate for fancy sit-down affairs, as well as pâtés and terrines for entertaining large parties or crowds. You can even make an entire meal from appetizers alone, serving an array of them, and forget the main course entirely. Most of these dishes can be prepared hours or even days in advance, giving you more time to enjoy your guests.

Just remember that an appetizer is something to whet the appetite and thus should not be too large. Be as decorative as possible, arranging and styling the treats as beautifully as you can.

Some of the recipes, such as the quiches or the Mediterranean Stuffed Tomatoes, can be served as a light main course. Others, like the pâtés, are wonderful to have on hand in the refrigerator in case friends drop in or whenever the mood strikes.

Yield: 8 servings

12 ounces regular tofu
   or 8 ounces pressed tofu
½ teaspoon salt
1 cup parsley
2 to 3 tablespoons capers
1 to 2 cloves garlic
¼ cup extra-virgin olive oil
2 tablespoons lemon juice
½ cup walnuts
Salt
8 small or 4 large tomatoes
   (must be very ripe)

Mediterranean Stuffed Tomatoes

Ripe tomatoes stuffed with tofu "cheese," walnuts, and a pungent sauce made from parsley, capers, and garlic evoke images of islands and sun. Serve well chilled on a hot summer evening.

If you are using regular tofu, follow the instructions on page 18 for removing the water. Crumble and place in a nonstick frying pan with the salt. Do not add any oil to the pan. Over very low heat, dry-fry the tofu, stirring almost constantly, until it resembles dry cottage cheese. Do not allow it to burn or brown. This may take 15 minutes. Allow to cool while making the green sauce.

Finely mince the parsley, capers, and garlic, and place in a mortar, "suribachi" (a Japanese mortar with grooves), or blender. If you are using a mortar and pestle or suribachi, grind the ingredients to a rough paste while adding the olive oil, one tablespoon at a time. Add the lemon juice last. If using a blender, add 2 tablespoons of the olive oil, blend for 15 seconds, then add the rest and blend for another 5 or 10 seconds. Do not let it become a homogeneous mass, because some texture is important to this sauce. Mix in the lemon juice by hand.

Chop the walnuts and mix with the tofu and the sauce. Add more salt if necessary.

Cut the tops off the tomatoes. Trim the bottoms slightly so that they stand and do not roll over. Remove the insides of the tomatoes, leaving a wall ⅓ inch thick; the insides can be used for making tomato sauce. Fill with the tofu mixture, and chill 3 to 4 hours before serving. This dish should be made the day you are going to serve it, since the parsley will lose its wonderful bright green color if allowed to stand too long. Serve on a bed of lettuce or other greens.

Per serving: Calories 174, Protein 7 g, Fat: 7 g, Carbohydrates 9 g

Caponata

This is a wonderful medley of eggplants, peppers, and tomatoes, similar to ratatouille but with a sweet and sour touch. It is best served cold or at room temperature and keeps splendidly in the refrigerator for a week or two. Serve as part of a cold plate or a salad on a bed of greens. I like to mound it on leaves of Belgian endive and serve it along with the preceding Mediterranean Stuffed Tomatoes.

Cut the eggplant into ¾-inch cubes, salt lightly, and place in a colander to drain for half an hour. Rinse and squeeze gently or pat dry with paper towels.

Mince the garlic and cut the peppers into rings or large chunks. Heat the olive oil in a large pan or wok, and sauté the onions until they begin to wilt. Add the eggplant and continue to sauté for 5 to 10 minutes, or until relatively soft. Add the tomatoes and peppers, and continue cooking for another 10 minutes. Then add all the remaining ingredients except the pine nuts, salt, and pepper. Cover and cook 15 minutes.

Toast the pine nuts in an oven until golden brown, taking care not to let them burn. Add to the vegetables and allow the entire dish to cool. If possible, wait a day before serving as the flavor improves and mellows. If too sweet, add a dash more vinegar; if not sweet enough, add a touch more sweetener. Season with salt and pepper to taste.

Per serving: Calories 212, Protein 6 g, Fat 8 g, Carbohydrates 21 g

Yield: 6 servings

18 ounces eggplant
   (either American or Japanese)
3 to 4 cloves garlic
2 green bell peppers,
   or 1 green pepper and 1 red or
   yellow pepper
3 tablespoons olive oil
1½ medium onions, sliced
1¼ pounds ripe tomatoes
   (use canned if they are not
   really ripe and juicy)
1 teaspoon salt
3 tablespoons capers
3 tablespoons tomato paste
½ cup chopped parsley
2 teaspoons dried basil,
   or ¼ cup finely chopped fresh
   basil
3½ tablespoons red wine vinegar
1 tablespoon sweetener
½ cup pine nuts
Salt and freshly ground pepper

8 small or 4 large onions

3 tablespoons nonhydrogenated
   margarine or vegetable oil

½ cup raw cashews

1 cup fresh bread crumbs
   (preferably whole wheat;
   white will do, while darker
   breads such as rye and
   pumpernickel are not suitable)

⅓ cup chopped parsley

½ teaspoon rubbed sage

2 to 3 tablespoons soymilk

Salt and pepper

SAVORY STUFFED ONIONS

People always ask what these are made of. It's obvious that the shell is a well-baked onion, but the delectable mixture inside keeps everyone guessing. The preliminary steaming and final baking bring out the sweetness of the onions, harmonizing beautifully with the slightly "meaty" filling. Cutting up all these raw onions may leave you crying, but this dish is worth the tears. Use the smallest onions you can find, preparing one per person, or cut larger ones in half and serve one-half each.

If you are using small onions, cut a slice off the top and bottom of each so they sit up. If you are using large onions, cut each in half horizontally, as for onion rings, then slice a bit off the bottom so that each half sits up. Using a melon scooper or a sharp-edged measuring spoon, scoop out the insides of the onions, leaving a wall ¼ to ⅓ inch thick (2 to 3 layers, depending on their size). Mince the onion pulp and set aside. Steam or microwave the onion shells until they are soft but still retain their shape.

Sauté the minced onions in 2 tablespoons of the margarine. Finely grind the cashews in a blender. Mix the onions, cashews, bread crumbs, parsley, and sage, and moisten with the soymilk. Season with salt and pepper to taste. Stuff the steamed onions with this mixture, then melt the remaining tablespoon of margarine and pour a little on top of each. Bake at 350°F until golden brown, about 15 to 25 minutes, depending on the size of the onions. Serve hot.

Per serving: Calories 170, Protein 5 g, Fat 6 g, Carbohydrates 19 g

Zucchini, Eggplant & Fennel Filling

Yield: 4 to 8 servings

This unusual and tasty filling can go in all sorts of stuffable items. Be creative with the "containers," keeping in mind what else you are serving for the meal. It makes a wonderful filling for baked onions (see recipe for Savory Stuffed Onions, pages 120-21), but it is also nice in tarts, sandwiched between puff pastry layers, or wrapped in crêpes. These would be nice additions to a hot appetizer tray. This recipe makes enough filling for about 12 mushrooms, 8 small onions, 4 to 8 crêpes, 4 to 8 individual tarts, or 20 to 25 canapés. If you select small onions as the shells for this filling, you may use the insides you remove instead of the two onions listed in the ingredients. Refer to the recipe for Savory Stuffed Onions on page 120 for directions on preparing onions for filling.

1 pound eggplant (1 medium)

2 medium zucchini

1 teaspoon salt

2 medium onions

2 tablespoons olive oil

2 cups lightly packed, chopped fennel tops (the feathery part)

5 to 6 tablespoons tomato paste

Salt and pepper

Shells of your choice (such as pre-baked tart shells, puff pastry, crêpes, and giant mushrooms)

Bake the eggplants at 300°F for about 40 minutes until soft and a fork pierces through easily. Allow to cool, then remove the skin and mash the pulp. Grate the zucchini and place in a colander. Sprinkle with the teaspoon of salt, and allow to drain for 20 minutes. Squeeze out the excess liquid.

Chop the onions (or onion pulp if you are stuffing onions). Sauté until tender in the olive oil, then add the zucchini and cook a few more minutes until the zucchini is soft, raising the heat to high if the mixture starts to get watery. Add the eggplant pulp and chopped fennel tops, and sauté another minute or two. Add the tomato paste and season to taste with salt and pepper while continuing to sauté for another 2 to 3 minutes to blend flavors.

Preheat the oven from 350°F to 375°F. Fill whatever shells you are using, and bake until piping hot, about 15 minutes.

Per serving: Calories 110, Protein 3 g, Fat 1 g, Carbohydrates 16 g

4 ripe tomatoes
¼ cup packed chopped fresh basil
½ cup ground almond meal
1 teaspoon chopped garlic
Salt and pepper
1 tablespoon extra-virgin olive oil
¼ cup or more soft bread crumbs

SAVORY TOMATOES ALMONDINE

Easy to make and delicious either hot or at room temperature.

Slice off the tops of the tomatoes, and a little off the bottom as well, so they will stand up. With a small spoon, scoop out the insides of the tomatoes, leaving a wall about ⅓ inch thick. Chop the tomato pulp roughly, and place in a bowl. Combine with the remaining ingredients, adding the bread crumbs at the end so that the mixture holds together but is still moist. Season with salt and pepper to taste.

Preheat the oven to 350°F. Stuff the tomatoes with the mixture, and bake for about 20 minutes, or until the tomato skins burst and the tops are brown. For smaller appetizers, cut the tomatoes in half and stuff.

Per serving: Calories 177, Protein 11 g, Fat 8 g, Carbohydrates 14 g

Stuffed Shiitake Mushrooms

Yield: 4 to 8 servings

I have served this at many parties I have catered, and it is always a favorite. It is definitely something to serve the skeptical nonvegetarian guest. The frozen tofu takes on the texture of meat, and the ground walnuts add richness. These can be made a day or two in advance and baked before serving time, or even baked several hours in advance and reheated or served at room temperature. If you can get shiso leaves from a Japanese grocery store, place them under the mushrooms; they not only look pretty but can be eaten—a delicious experience!

Defrost the tofu as described on page 18, squeeze dry, and crumble. Sauté the onion and garlic in the olive oil until tender. Add the finely crumbled tofu, and sauté another 5 minutes. Add the chopped tomato and the rosemary, and continue cooking for about 10 minutes until the flavors meld and the mixture is fairly dry. Add the ground walnuts, miso, tomato paste, salt and pepper to taste, and an additional few drops of olive oil if the mixture seems dry.

Cut off the stems from the shiitake mushrooms, and fill with the mixture, pressing the filling firmly with the inside of a spoon to form a smooth mound. Bake at 350°F for 15 to 20 minutes until browned. Place on a shiso leaf, and serve either hot or at room temperature.

Per serving: Calories 183, Protein 9 g, Fat 9 g, Carbohydrates 7 g

12 to 14 ounces tofu, frozen (see pages 17-18)

1 medium onion, chopped

1 large clove garlic

2 tablespoons olive oil

1 tomato, chopped

½ teaspoon rosemary

⅓ cup ground walnuts

2 teaspoons miso

2 tablespoons tomato paste

Salt and pepper

8 to 10 large shiitake mushrooms, either fresh, or dried and soaked

8 to 10 shiso leaves (optional)

Yield: 1 to 1½ cups

*1 pound tofu, well-pressed (follow
the directions on page 18)*

1 cup miso
½ cup white wine
¼ cup (or more) mirin

Cheesecloth (optional)

Tofu "Cheese"

*Tofu transforms into a smooth, spreadable, cheese-like substance when "pickled" in a mixture of miso, wine, and mirin. Miso alone will do the trick but will produce a very salty cheese. Tofu cheese has many uses, the most delightful being my mock "boursin," the French herb and garlic cheese. It is also used in making an eggless version of aïoli, the sticky, garlicky, wonderful French mayonnaise that can be added to soups or serve as a dip or sauce. It can be mixed into white sauces and dressings to lend a cheesy flavor or soaked in olive oil to become "feta" cheese. It will not, however, melt like mozzarella on a pizza.
It is crucial to use a mild miso. Use a light-colored "sweet kohji" miso if available. The quantity of wine and mirin will vary slightly with the saltiness of the miso, so it is hard to give exact quantities in this recipe. When you find a miso that seems to work well for this, stick with it so you can always be sure of the proportion of miso to wine and mirin. It is not absolutely vital to use an exact ratio, and there is quite a bit of leeway that will produce "cheese."*

Mix the miso, wine, and mirin to produce a slightly sweet but salty flavor. The consistency should be like a very thick salad dressing or light mayonnaise.

Slice the tofu ½ inch thick lengthwise. Wrap each piece in cheesecloth. Using cheesecloth is not crucial, but it helps hold the tofu together. You may simply layer the tofu in the container, making sure that each slice is submerged in the miso mixture.

Place in a container with the miso so that each slice is covered on all sides with the mixture. Cover and refrigerate for 1 week. After that time, remove the tofu from the miso, take off the cheesecloth, and check the consistency. It should be like a soft cream cheese, and it may have taken on a light, yellowish-brown hue. If it does not spread smoothly like cream cheese, you may have added too much wine and will have to put it back in the miso mixture for another day or two. If you use only miso and no wine or mirin, this process will take only 24 to 36 hours to produce "cheese," although the resulting product may be saltier. Use as suggested in many of the recipes in this book, or as desired in other recipes. This keeps in the refrigerator for 1 to 2 weeks.

Per 2 tablespoons: Calories 99, Protein 7 g, Fat 4 g, Carbohydrates 9 g

Tofu "Feta" Cheese

As close to the real thing as it gets.

The tofu "cheese" for this recipe doesn't need to marinate for a full week if you'd rather use it sooner; about 5 days would do. Break the marinated "cheese" into ½-inch pieces, place in a container, and add the salt. Fill with enough olive oil to cover the pieces. Cover the container and marinate the tofu mixture for 12 to 24 hours. Drain to use in salads or pasta recipes. The olive oil can be reused as long as it smells fresh.

Per 2 tablespoons: Calories 114, Protein 7 g, Fat 6 g, Carbohydrates 9 g

Yield: 1 cup

1 cup Tofu "Cheese," pages 42-43
1 to 2 teaspoons salt
Olive oil

1 recipe Tofu "Cheese,"
    pages 42-43
½ teaspoon dried marjoram
½ teaspoon dried thyme
2 to 3 teaspoons lemon juice
2 to 4 cloves garlic, finely minced
½ to ¾ cup unsalted
    nonhydrogenated margarine
⅓ cup minced fresh chervil
    (fresh tarragon or dill may
    be substituted—flavor will
    differ, however)
⅔ cup finely minced parsley
1 to 1½ cups lightly toasted,
    chopped walnuts or pecans,
    (optional—for cheese ball only)

Tofu "Boursin" or Herb-Garlic Cheese

I make no claims for this being low in fat or calories, but it is dairy-free and absolutely wonderful. This tastes so much like real cheese that I fooled a group of unsuspecting French friends with it.

Combine the tofu, dried herbs, lemon juice, garlic, and margarine in a food processor or blender, and whiz until very smooth and homogenized. The amount of margarine will vary slightly each time with the moisture content of the tofu. Add enough to make it smooth. Finally, add the fresh herbs and blend for another moment. (Be careful not to overblend, or it will turn green.)

Transfer to a bowl and refrigerate several hours or overnight until firm enough to mold. In warm weather you may have to freeze it for 30 minutes or so before being able to mold the mixture into a ball. Roll it in the chopped nuts, and serve with thin slices of bread or crackers, or just pack it in a bowl and serve as is.

This can also be used for Hot Herb Cheese Puffs on page 45.

Per tablespoon: Calories 69, Protein 3 g, Fat 6 g, Carbohydrates 6 g

Hot Herb Cheese Puffs

Use the Tofu "Boursin" to make these delicious little canapés. Piping hot from the oven, they're the perfect thing to serve with an aperitif or cocktail. Since they can be assembled in a matter of seconds if you have the "cheese" on hand, you can always treat your guests to a gourmet treat when they surprise you by showing up unexpectedly.

Trim the crust off the bread slices, and cut the trimmed slices into circles with a cookie cutter, preferably 1½ inches in diameter. Melt the margarine in a skillet, and sauté the bread circles on one side until they are just a light golden brown. These are now called "croûtes."

With a teaspoon, pile about 2 teaspoons of the cheese onto the uncooked side of the croûtes, pressing lightly with the concave side of the spoon to make smooth little mounds. Preheat the oven to 375°F. Place on a cookie sheet, and bake for 8 to 10 minutes until golden brown. Serve immediately.

Per serving: Calories 55, Protein 2 g, Fat 1 g, Carbohydrates 7 g

Yield: 25 servings

¼-inch to ⅓-inch thick slices of whole wheat or white bread
Several tablespoons nonhydrogenated margarine
Round cookie cutter (other shapes can also be used)
½ recipe Tofu "Boursin," page 44

Tofu Cream Cheese Spread with Herbs

This is a simple and easy-to-make spread with herbs for bread, crackers, and tasty cucumber sandwiches.

Yield: about 1 cup

12 to 14 ounces tofu,
    well pressed (follow the
    directions on page 18)
3 tablespoons safflower oil
1 teaspoon salt
1 teaspoon dried thyme
½ teaspoon dried basil
¼ teaspoon dried marjoram
2 tablespoons minced fresh chives
¼ cup minced fresh parsley
2 teaspoons lemon juice (optional)

Blend the tofu, oil, salt, and dried herbs in a food processor until perfectly creamy. Fold in the fresh chives and parsley. Add lemon juice for a tangy flavor, if desired. Refrigerate for several hours or overnight to allow the flavors to mingle and develop. This spread keeps for several days in a covered container in the refrigerator.

Per 2 tablespoons: Calories 83, Protein 4 g, Fat 7 g, Carbohydrates 2 g

Easy Tofu Aïoli Spread

Instead of butter, this is the spread we served with bread at the restaurant. It is rich and creamy and full of flavor. Guests were always asking to buy some to take home. Not only can it be used as a spread for bread at dinnertime, it can be used in place of mayonnaise to make savory sandwiches and will even cook up like a soft, melted cheese in lasagnes. The longer you purée this, the tastier it seems to get.

Yield: about 2½ cups

1 pound tofu
3 to 6 cloves garlic (or more)
¼ to ⅓ cup mild miso (start
    with the lesser amount, and
    increase as desired)
½ cup extra-virgin olive oil

Combine all the ingredients in a food processor, and purée until absolutely smooth, about 10 minutes. This is delicious slightly warm out of the processor, or it can be served chilled. The spread will keep for 3 to 4 days in the refrigerator in a tightly closed container.

Per tablespoon: Calories 37, Protein 1 g, Fat 3 g, Carbohydrates 1 g

Mousses, Pâtés & Terrines

Here is a selection of some of the most impressive looking delicacies you will encounter. Garnished properly, they may even look too beautiful to eat. Most are fairly simple to make and require few seasonings, allowing the sweetness and flavor of the vegetables to come through. Although the mousses can be made in a large mold, they will look nicer in individual ones. If you do not own fancy mousse molds, use custard or espresso cups, cupcake tins, or a square baking dish and cut them into small squares. The terrines and pâtés can be made in small bread pans or ring molds, then sliced. The mousses and terrines set with agar can be easily removed from their molds by inserting a thin knife or toothpick between the mousse and the mold, then knocking on the mold lightly.

Most of the baked terrines and pâtés will keep for a week or longer if refrigerated; some even improve in taste if left to sit for a couple of days. The ones made with agar should be eaten within a day or two.

2 carrots, sliced ¼ inch thick

2 tablespoons raw cashews

¼ medium onion, sliced

1¼ cups vegetable stock

1 teaspoon sweetener

½ to ⅓ cup rich soymilk or soy
  cream

1½ tablespoons white wine

3 tablespoons frozen green peas

3 to 4 mushrooms, quartered

10 to 12 ginkgo nuts, shelled
  (optional)

Salt and white pepper

½ bar, ½ teaspoon powdered, or
  2 tablespoons flaked agar

½ recipe Cashew Crème Sauce,
  page 82 (optional)

CARROT & CASHEW MOUSSE

*This delicate mousse, slightly sweet from the carrots and
cashews, will delight both adults and children, even if they swear
they hate carrots. This is best made the day before serving.
A note on ginkgo nuts: They are available shelled, cooked,
and canned in Asian food stores. Use them right out of the can
without cooking. If only unshelled ones are available,
dry-roast them in a pan for 5 or 6 minutes, then crack them
to remove the golden nutmeat inside.*

Place the carrots, cashews, onion, stock, and sweetener in a
small covered saucepan. Bring to a boil, then reduce the
heat and simmer until the carrots and cashews are very
soft. Strain, reserving the stock for later.

Purée the carrot mixture in a blender or food processor
with the soymilk and wine. Steam or cook the peas, mushrooms, and ginko nuts in a small amount of water until tender. Season lightly with salt and pepper to taste.

Measure the reserved stock. If you have more than a ½ cup
left, boil down rapidly over high heat until it has been
reduced to ½ cup. Prepare the agar as described on pages 2
and 3. If you are using bar agar, shred and dissolve in the
½ cup of stock, keeping covered while simmering.
Otherwise, add powdered or flake agar directly to the
stock. Add it to the carrot mixture in the blender, and blend
for 20 to 30 seconds. Mix in the green peas, mushrooms,
and ginkgo nuts by hand. Immediately pour into molds.
Chill overnight in the refrigerator, and unmold at serving
time. Pour Cashew Crème Sauce around it, if desired.

Per mousse: Calories 51, Protein 2 g, Fat 2 g, Carbohydrates 7 g

Spinach & Basil Mousse

Yield: 8 to 10 servings

Another wonderful combination that goes perfectly with a little Cashew Mayonnaise, page 82. Make it at the height of summer when fresh basil abounds in either your garden or the supermarket.

Sauté the onion and garlic in the oil until soft. Add the spinach and continue cooking until the spinach is fairly tender but still a deep green. Place the spinach mixture, tofu, lemon juice and zest, and the basil in a food processor or blender, and blend until very smooth. Remove and pour into a bowl. Rinse out the blender or food processor, and purée the cashews and water until creamy and thick. Add the the spinach-tofu mixture and the wine, and season with salt and pepper to taste.

Dissolve the agar in the stock as described on page 2. Before turning off the heat, dissolve the arrowroot or kuzu in a small amount of water (about 2 or 3 tablespoons), and add it to the simmering agar, stirring constantly until thickened. Blend this immediately into the tofu-spinach-cashew mixture, and pour into individual molds or ramekins. Chill completely. After several hours you will be able to unmold these delicate mousses and decorate them prettily with Cashew Mayonnaise, page 82.

Note: Molds for mousses need not be oiled, although oiling does ease removal. It also leaves an oily film on the surface which I prefer not to have.

1 medium onion, chopped

1 clove garlic, minced

2 tablespoons canola or
   extra-virgin olive oil

1 pound fresh spinach, washed
   and roughly chopped

8 ounces pressed tofu

1 to 3 tablespoons lemon juice

Grated zest of ½ small lemon

8 ounces fresh basil

½ cup raw cashews

¾ cup water

2 tablespoons white wine

Salt and white pepper

1 bar, 1 teaspoon powdered, or
   4 tablespoons flaked agar

⅔ cup vegetable stock

2 tablespoons arrowroot,
   or 1 tablespoon kuzu

Per serving: Calories 125, Protein 6 g, Fat 3 g, Carbohydrates 8 g

1⅔ cups baked eggplant pulp
    (1 very large or 2 medium
    eggplants)
1 large onion, finely chopped
1 tablespoon oil
1⅔ cups roasted almonds
    and walnuts, mixed and
    ground finely
Approximately ⅓ cup mild miso
⅓ cup plus 1 tablespoon tahini
    or sesame butter
12 ounces tofu, pressed (follow
    the directions on page 18)
1 tablespoon grated raw ginger
½ teaspoon allspice
Freshly ground black pepper

Eggplant & Tofu Pâté

Unsuspecting Japanese friends praised me for this "delicious liver pâté" and were surprised when I told them that it contained no meat. This is a soft, spreadable pâté, great on bread and crackers. It is also tasty thinly sliced and sautéed until browned for sandwiches.

Bake the eggplants whole at 350°F until a fork pierces easily through. (The length of time will vary with the size of the eggplants.) Cut in half and scoop out the pulp, measuring 1⅔ cups. Discard the skins. Beat the pulp with a fork or beater until creamed.

Sauté the onion in the oil until tender. Mix all the ingredients and adjust the seasonings as necessary. The amount of miso will depend on its saltiness; increase or decrease as necessary.

Line a loaf pan with brown paper that has been saturated with oil. If you are using an earthenware terrine mold with a lid, simply oil the mold. Fill with the pâté mixture, and fold the oiled brown paper loosely over the top. Cover with a lid that has a steam vent, or use a double layer of aluminum foil with several holes in it for steam to escape. Bake in a 350°F oven for 2 hours with a pan of hot water underneath, then remove the water and continue baking for an additional 30 minutes. Do not attempt to remove the pâté from the pan while it is warm. Let it cool completely, then refrigerate for 36 to 48 hours before serving. Keeps refrigerated for up to 2 weeks.

Per serving: Calories 140, Protein 6 g, Fat 8 g, Carbohydrates 8 g

Mushroom Pâté

Yield: 1 loaf (8 to 12 servings)

Simple to make, but ever so delicious! Serve as an appetizer with bread or crackers, or slice and eat with a fork.

Grind the walnuts in a food processor. Chop the mushrooms up roughly, then process all of the ingredients in the food processor until fairly smooth. Adjust the seasonings as necessary.

Preheat the oven to 350°F. Line a loaf pan with parchment or wax paper, and pack in the mixture. Cover the top with more parchment, then a layer of aluminum foil. Set in a pan with ½ inch of water around it. Bake for about 1¼ hours, until it has risen and is lightly browned. Allow to cool completely before removing and serving. This keeps refrigerated for several days.

Per serving: Calories 98, Protein 3 g, Fat 2 g, Carbohydrates 14 g

8 ounces ground walnuts (about 2 cups)
8 ounces mushrooms
8 ounces fresh shiitake mushrooms
4 ounces bread crumbs
3 tablespoons brandy
2 to 3 tablespoons light miso
½ bunch parsley, chopped
½ teaspoon dried thyme
½ teaspoon dried rosemary
½ teaspoon dried savory
Freshly ground pepper

Consommé:

3½ cups vegetable stock

3 tablespoons Madeira

6 to 8 fennel seeds

⅛ teaspoon dried tarragon

1 teaspoon tomato paste

Salt or soy sauce

¾ bar, ¾ teaspoon powdered,
    or 3 tablespoons flaked agar

Vegetables:

½ onion, quartered and
    separated into leaves

1 cup cut asparagus (about 6 to 8
    stalks, depending on thickness)

4 carrot sticks the length of your
    mold or bread pan

½ to 1 sweet red bell pepper, cut
    into strips ¼ inch wide

1 cup broccoli florets

1 cup or more small mushrooms

1 pack enoki (white straw)
    mushrooms (optional)

VEGETABLE ASPIC TERRINE

*This is absolutely beautiful to look at and very delicately flavored.
Seasoned vegetable jewels are held together by a clear jellied
consommé which rests on a bedding of bright green pea
or asparagus mousse. Impress your mother-in-law with this one.*

Combine all the ingredients for the consommé, except the
agar, in a large saucepan with a tight-fitting lid. The vegetables will be cooked in this, and both the consommé and
vegetables will benefit from the joint simmering. Bring the
consommé to a gentle boil, and cook the vegetables in it, a
few pieces at a time, until they are tender but still crisp.
Remove the vegetables as they cook, and drain well in a
colander placed over a bowl to catch the drippings. Strain
and measure the broth. If you have more than 2 cups, boil
it down rapidly to 2 cups. Check the flavor; you might have
to adjust the seasonings with a little additional salt, soy
sauce, Madeira, or tomato paste.

Prepare the agar as instructed on page 2, and dissolve it in
the 2 cups of consommé. Immediately pour ⅓ inch into a
1-quart bread pan or terrine mold, and set it over a tray of
ice or in the freezer for a few minutes until it begins to jell
slightly. Start layering the cooked vegetables, making sure
to leave a ½-inch space on both sides or the terrine will
crumble when cut. Broccoli flowers look pretty down the
middle, surrounded by carrot sticks and asparagus. Pour a
little more hot consommé into the mold, being careful not

Vegetable Aspic Terrine

to disrupt the layer of vegetables inside, and allow it to jell slightly before layering in more vegetables. Repeat this process of layering vegetables, pouring in consommé, and allowing it to partially set until all the consommé is used up. (You will probably have some vegetables left over.) This takes time, since the consommé must thicken slightly before the vegetables can be put in and held in place. Don't allow it to harden completely during the process. A few minutes in the freezer each time more consommé has been poured in is all that is necessary to get it to the proper soft-jell consistency.

You will have plenty of time while the consommé is jelling to make the green pea or asparagus mousse. Cook the peas or asparagus and the onion in the stock with the sweetener and salt until tender. Drain, reserving the liquid. Purée the vegetables with the soymilk or soy cream, then dissolve the agar in the remaining stock. (You should have at least ¼ cup or more.) Add it to the puréed vegetables, and blend for 10 seconds. Pour this very carefully on top of the consommé and vegetable mold when the previous layers have jelled slightly. Chill in the refrigerator several hours or overnight, and carefully invert onto a plate. Slice and serve.

Per serving: Calories 51, Protein 3 g, Fat 0 g, Carbohydrates 9 g

Pea or Asparagus Base:

½ cup fresh or frozen green peas,
*   or 1 cup chopped asparagus*
*   (6 to 8 spears)*
¼ small onion
Stock to cover the vegetables
½ teaspoon sweetener
Salt
½ cup soymilk or soy cream
½ bar, ½ teaspoon powdered, or
*   2 tablespoons flaked agar*

Sushi Crêpes, page 62

1⅓ pounds carrots, trimmed,
    peeled, and sliced
1 medium onion, sliced
bouillon??
1 scant teaspoon salt
¾ cup white wine
⅓ cup raw cashews
2 cups vegetable stock
½ pound tofu
⅓ cup arrowroot
Leeks for braising (optional)
¾ cup Tangy or Sweet White Wine
    Sauce, pages 72-73 (optional)

CREAMY CARROT FLAN

This delicately delicious dish was highly popular at our restaurant. You will need individual timbale or flan molds in which to bake these.

Combine the carrots, onion, bouillon, salt, wine, cashews, and stock in a saucepan, and cover. Bring to a boil, lower the heat to a simmer, and cook until the carrots are absolutely tender. Pour the contents into a blender, and purée briefly.

Preheat the oven to 350°F. Add the tofu and arrowroot to the blender mixture. Purée again until absolutely smooth. Spray the molds well with nonstick spray, and pour the mixture almost to the top. Bake for about 30 minutes. It will rise slightly and look firm on top while remaining tender inside. Invert onto a plate and serve as is, or on a bed of braised leeks and topped with white wine sauce.

Per serving: Calories 173, Protein 5 g, Fat 5 g, Carbohydrates 21 g

Savory Pastries

Tiny Tarts, Quiches & Other Delights

Although a little extra time and effort are required to make individual tarts and pastries, you will find that they are also a great deal more fun to eat and look at. A decorative platter loaded with tasty looking savory tidbits will tempt everyone.

If you are short on time and patience, most of the following can be baked in a large pie pan and cut into slices, but they will lose some of their visual appeal.

Tarts can be filled with a variety of savory items, and aside from the specific recipes in this section, you will find other mixtures throughout the book that could fill a tart or two. Either the zucchini and fennel filling, (page 39), or mushrooms or spinach creamed with the white wine, soubise, or béchamel sauces (pages 68-73) would be delicious. Use your imagination to create different combinations of sauces, vegetables, and legumes to fill pastry shells.

Assembling pastries goes rapidly if the pie crust and fillings have been made in advance. Fill and bake them twenty minutes before serving. Most of the crusts and fillings can be made days ahead of time and refrigerated or frozen, so you can even make enough for two occasions and freeze a batch.

Fancy miniature tart shells can be purchased inexpensively at most cookware shops. You can also use muffin tins or custard cups, although they are considerably deeper than tart tins. Quiches can be baked in a large pan and cut, but softer fillings, like creamed mushrooms, do better if baked in individual shells.

Unless specified, the following savory pastries can be made with any of the pie crusts on pages 207-08.

Smoky Marinated Tofu, page 142
1 clove garlic per canapé
Several tablespoons olive oil
Thin slices of whole wheat or
    white bread (A closely
    textured bread works best.)
Nonhydrogenated margarine,
    corn oil, or olive oil
One mushroom per canapé if very
    small, or ½ per canapé if large

Smoked Tofu, Mushroom & Garlic Canapés

*This was a hit at a large party we held. The combination of flavors
is superb, and the little treasures are easy to assemble.
Expect each person to down several of these.*

Have the tofu marinating from the day before, if possible.
It will be cooked just before assembly.

Place the bulbs of garlic in aluminum foil, and sprinkle
with olive oil. Close up the foil and bake in a 350°F oven
until tender, about 20 to 30 minutes. Set aside until assembly time.

Prepare croûtes by cutting out bread circles from the thin
slices of bread with a 1½-inch circular cookie cutter. Melt
the margarine, corn oil, or olive oil in a skillet, and sauté the
bread circles over low heat on one side until golden brown.

Rinse and prepare the mushrooms. If large, cut in half; otherwise, leave whole. Heat a few tablespoons of oil or margarine in a skillet, and sauté the mushrooms over high heat
until tender and browned. Do not cook on low heat, or
juices will flow out of the mushrooms and they will not
brown properly. Season with salt.

While the mushrooms are cooking, sauté the marinated
tofu as directed on page 142. When browned, cut into
squares the approximate size of the croûtes (bread circles).

Preheat the oven to 400°F. To assemble the canapés, separate the garlic into cloves, and squeeze out the tender meat
inside onto the croûtes (one clove per croûte). Spread with

a knife. Top with a slice of tofu and garnish with a mushroom.

Place on a cookie sheet, and bake at for 3 to 4 minutes. Serve while hot.

Per canapé: Calories 45, Protein 2 g, Fat 2 g, Carbohydrates 3 g

Provençale Spinach Tarts

Another very tasty and quick recipe.

Line tart shells with pie crust rolled out ⅛ inch thick. Prick all over with a fork. Prebake for 3 to 4 minutes at 400°F.

Thoroughly wash, dry, and roughly chop the spinach. Sauté the onions and garlic in the olive oil, then add the spinach and cook at a high temperature until soft and most of the water has evaporated. Add the chopped tomato and cook another 3 or 4 minutes. Season with salt and pepper to taste. Add the toasted pine nuts, fill the prebaked tart shells, and top with soy cheese, if desired. Bake for 10 minutes at 375°F. Serve immediately.

Per medium tart: Calories 174, Protein 3 g, Fat 9 g, Carbohydrates 15 g

Yield: anywhere from 6 to 16 tarts

*Dough for 1 whole wheat pie crust
   of your choice
   (see pages 207-08)*
*About 4 cups roughly chopped
   spinach*
1 onion, minced
2 to 3 cloves garlic, minced
3 tablespoons olive oil
*1 ripe but firm tomato, finely
   chopped*
Salt and pepper
¼ cup lightly toasted pine nuts
½ cup grated soy cheese (optional)

Yield: 32 pieces

1 medium onion, finely chopped

*3 to 8 tablespoons melted
   nonhydrogenated margarine
   or olive oil*

*About 4 cups roughly chopped
   spinach*

1 bunch dill, chopped

Salt and pepper

*8 ounces tofu, firm or pressed
   (see page 18)*

*2 tablespoons nonhydrogenated
   margarine or safflower or
   canola oil*

4 tablespoons flour

1 cup hot soymilk

¼ teaspoon nutmeg

*8 leaves filo (puff pastry may be
   substituted for the filo leaves)*

Spinach Napoleons

Sauté the onion in 1 tablespoon of the melted margarine or olive oil until tender. Add the spinach to the onion, and sauté until wilted. Keep sautéing until most of the juices have evaporated. Add the chopped dill and sauté another 2 to 3 minutes. Season with salt and pepper to taste. Crumble the tofu and dry-fry in a skillet over very low heat for 10 to 15 minutes, stirring constantly until it resembles dry curds.

Make a thick white sauce by melting the 2 tablespoons of margarine in a small saucepan and whisking in the flour, cooking for 2 to 3 minutes until thickened. Add the hot soymilk all at once, stirring constantly, and cook for 2 to 3 minutes. Season with the nutmeg and more salt and pepper to taste. Combine the sauce with the tofu.

Oil an 8-inch square pan, and preheat the oven to 350°F. Rapidly put 1 filo leaf down in the pan, brush with some of the melted margarine or olive oil, and fold the overhanging edges of the leaf back in over itself. Lay down another leaf and repeat the process, using a total of 4 leaves. Spread the tofu mixture evenly over the leaves, and then spread the spinach mixture down over the tofu. Repeat the brushing and folding process with the other 4 leaves of filo. Bake for 25 to 30 minutes until nicely brown. Cut into 1-inch by 2-inch squares, and serve.

Per piece: Calories 50, Protein 2 g, Fat 4 g, Carbohydrates 3 g

Basic Quiche

Here is a basic tofu quiche recipe with several variations. Although they contain no eggs, cream, milk, or cheese, I think they are every bit as delicious as their dairy counterparts. A little turmeric will add the golden egg color.

Cream the tofu, soymilk, oil, and turmeric in a blender or food processor until absolutely smooth. Sauté the onions in oil until soft, then combine with the tofu mixture in a bowl. Season to taste with salt, pepper, and nutmeg. At this point, add various ingredients as suggested in the variations on pages 60-61, or use as is to fill shells.

Roll out the crust ⅛ inch thick and line a 9-inch pie pan or individual tart shells. Prebake the shells in a 400°F oven, 3 to 4 minutes for small tartlets, 10 to 12 minutes for a 9-inch pan. Fill with the above mixture, and bake in a 350°F oven (15 minutes for individual shells or 45 minutes for a large quiche) until the top is firm and puffed up. Serve "quichettes" immediately, but wait 15 minutes before cutting a large quiche. These may also be served at room temperature.

Per hors d'ouevre serving: Calories 123, Protein 5 g, Fat 8 g, Carbohydrates 9 g

Yield: 8 to 16 servings as an appetizer or hors d'ouevre

14 to 16 ounces tofu
½ cup soymilk or soy cream
2 tablespoons oil (corn oil will give a more buttery flavor)
¼ to ½ teaspoon turmeric
2 medium onions, minced
Enough oil or nonhydrogenated margarine for sautéing
Salt and pepper
¼ to ½ teaspoon nutmeg, freshly grated if possible
Dough for 1 whole wheat pie crust of your choice (see pages 207-08)

Curried Carrot Quiche

Yield: 8 to 16 servings as an appetizer or hors d'ouevre

3 medium carrots
4 tablespoons raw cashews
Vegetable stock
1 teaspoon curry powder
2 tablespoons white wine
1 recipe Basic Quiche, page 59
Almond slices

Cook the carrots and cashews in enough stock to cover. When cool, purée with the curry powder and wine, and add to the basic quiche recipe. Top with almond slices and bake as directed in that recipe. Leeks can be substituted for onions.

Per serving: Calories 133, Protein 5 g, Fat 8 g, Carbohydrates 11 g

Mushroom Quiche

Yield: 8 to 16 servings as an appetizer or hors d'ouevre

1 recipe Basic Quiche, page 59
1 pound mushrooms, sliced, or a mixture of mushrooms
2 to 3 tablespoons Madeira or sherry (optional)

This can be made very interesting by the addition of several types of mushrooms: champignons (the type most often found in your grocery store), shiitake, oyster, or any variety of mild mushroom now available in produce sections. Much of the flavor will come from the champignons, so they should make up half the blend.

Add the mushrooms to the onions in the basic quiche recipe once the onions are soft, and continue sautéing until the mushrooms are also soft. Add Madeira or sherry, if desired, and cook 3 to 4 minutes to burn off the alcohol. Add to the quiche filling, and bake as directed.

Quiche Lorraine

Add Believable "Bacon," page 33, to the quiche filling above.

Per serving: Calories 133, Protein 5 g, Fat 8 g, Carbohydrates 10 g

Greek Olive & Basil Quiche

Yield: 8 to 16 servings as an appetizer or hors d'ouevre

This one is a real winner. You must, however, use good-quality oil-cured or kalamata olives from Greece or Italy. Watery canned American olives just will not do.

Make the basic quiche recipe without the nutmeg (page 59), and fill as directed. Top each quiche with fresh basil leaves and pitted oil-cured or kalamata olive halves. Be decorative and throw on some pine nuts, if desired. Cherry tomatoes cut in half will also add a nice touch. Bake as for the basic quiche recipe.

Per serving: Calories 138, Protein 5 g, Fat 8 g, Carbohydrates 9 g

1 recipe Basic Quiche, page 59
Fresh basil leaves
Pitted kalamata or oil-cured olives, halved
Pine nuts (optional)
½ cherry tomato per serving (optional)

Spinach & Dill Quiche

Yield: 8 to 16 servings as an appetizer or hors d'ouevre

Add the dill and spinach to the basic quiche recipe (page 59). Fill shells and top with pine nuts or sliced mushrooms. Bake as directed in the quiche recipe.

Per serving: Calories 129, Protein 5 g, Fat 8 g, Carbohydrates 10 g

1 recipe Basic Quiche, page 59
3 tablespoons chopped fresh dill
1 bunch spinach, steamed, drained well, and chopped, or 10 ounces frozen chopped spinach, well drained
Pine nuts or sliced mushrooms (optional)

See photo facing page 53 and on the front cover.

Dipping sauce:

⅓ cup soy sauce

⅓ cup rice vinegar

2 to 3 tablespoons mirin

½ teaspoon chili sesame oil

3 tablespoons chopped fresh cilantro

8 crêpes, page 140

1 to 2 avocados

1 cucumber

1 to 2 carrots

1 red bell pepper (optional)

3 sheets nori (optional)

Several leaves red leaf or buttercrunch lettuce (optional)

Sushi Crêpes

Quick, simple, imaginative, and tasty are qualities that many cooks seek in an appetizer. This dish hits the mark on all these points.

Combine all the dipping sauce ingredients in a small bowl, and set aside. Cut the vegetables into thin sticks about 2 inches long.

If desired, place a half-sheet of nori on each crêpe. Towards one end, lay a strip of vegetables. Roll tightly, then cut each crêpe into 3 or 4 pieces. Place on a platter. Serve with dipping sauce.

Per appetizer: Calories 49, Protein 1 g, Fat 1 g, Carbohydrates 6 g

Green Onion Pancakes with Pineapple Salsa

Yield: 6 pancakes

These pancakes were whipped up by John Murray, a good friend and wonderful chef who worked at Now and Zen Bistro for several years. Great with beer as a starter for a summer meal!

Combine the tofu, soymilk, and salt in a blender, and process until smooth. Transfer to a bowl. Sift the flour with the baking powder. Quickly whisk the flour into the tofu mixture. Mix in the nutritional yeast flakes, green onions, and garlic. Heat a griddle over medium heat, and coat or brush with oil. Use about ¼ cup mixture per pancake, and cook them on one side, flipping over after bubbles have formed on top. Cook on the other side until golden brown. Top with Pineapple Salsa (below) and Tofu Sour Crème, if desired, and serve immediately.

Per pancake: Calories 262, Protein 11 g, Fat 5 g, Carbohydrates 45 g

Pancakes:

8 ounces tofu

3 cups soymilk

2 teaspoons salt

2½ cups unbleached flour

1 tablespoon baking powder

1 tablespoon nutritional yeast flakes

2 bunches green onions, chopped

⅓ cup chopped garlic

Oil for coating griddle
Tofu Sour Crème, page 182 (optional)

Pineapple Salsa

Yield: 2 cups

Combine all ingredients. This can be made ahead several hours in advance.

Per ⅓ cup serving: Calories 64, Protein 2 g, Fat 3 g, Carbohydrates 8 g

1 cup roughly chopped fresh or frozen pineapple

1 cup diced fresh tomato

¼ cup chopped green onions

¼ cup pine nuts, toasted lightly

2 tablespoons fruit juice concentrate

½ teaspoon salt

Yield: 6 to 8 servings

5 cups water

1 teaspoon salt

1 cup coarse cornmeal*

2 tablespoons extra-virgin olive oil

3 to 4 cloves garlic, minced

1½ tablespoons ume paste

¼ to ⅓ cup nutritional yeast flakes

15 to 20 shiso leaves, slivered

* Be sure to use a coarse grind specifically milled for use in making polenta, often labeled "polenta" on the package.

Ume-Shiso Polenta

Bring the water to a boil. Stir in the salt and cornmeal in a stream, whisking constantly. Turn the heat to low, and simmer for 30 to 40 minutes until thick and cornmeal granules are tender. If necessary, add up to 1 cup additional water if it has thickened in less than 25 minutes; most likely the granules could still be firm. Stir in the olive oil, garlic, ume paste, and nutritional yeast. Cook another minute, then add the shiso leaves. Mix thoroughly, then pour into an oiled pan or mold. Allow to cool and solidify. To reheat, unmold or cut into squares or triangles, and bake for 10 to 15 minutes at 350°F, depending on thickness; alternately, it can be grilled. Serve with Roasted Red Bell Pepper Sauce, page 86.

Per serving: Calories 122, Protein 4 g, Fat 4 g, Carbohydrates 17 g

Curried Mushroom Filo Triangles with Mango Chutney

Heat 2 tablespoons of the oil in a sauté pan, and cook the onions in it over low heat until tender and sweet. Add the curry powder and cook for a minute. Add the mushrooms and cook over medium-high heat until brown. If they are exuding water, the heat is too low—turn it up. There should be no liquid in the pan. Mix in the cashew sour crème, and season to taste with salt and pepper.

Brush three sheets of filo with oil, or spray with nonstick spray, stacking them on top of each other. Cut into five horizontal strips. (Each will have three layers.) Place 2 tablespoons of filling on the end of each strip, and fold over one corner to the opposite side to form a triangle. Continue folding tightly to form a nice, tight triangle. Brush the exterior with additional oil, or spray with nonstick spray. Preheat the oven to 350°F. Place the triangles on a cookie sheet, and bake them for about 25 minutes, or until puffy and golden brown. Top with mango chutney and serve.

Per triangle: Calories 120, Protein 2 g, Fat 7 g, Carbohydrates 12 g

Yield: 24 triangles

½ cup oil (less if using nonstick cooking spray for filo)
1 onion, chopped
2 teaspoons or more curry powder
1 pound mushrooms, sliced (can be a mixture of button or crimini, shiitake, oysters, chanterelles, etc.)
1 cup Rich Cashew Sour Crème, page 83
Salt and pepper
12 ounces filo sheets (defrosted if frozen)

Mango Chutney

Place all the ingredients except the cilantro in a heavy-bottomed pot, cover partially, and simmer for 20 minutes. It will thicken slightly as the fruit juice caramelizes. Mix in the chopped cilantro. Adjust the salt as necessary.

Per serving: Calories 50, Protein 0 g, Fat 0 g, Carbohydrates 12 g

Yield: 1 pint

3 medium mangos, peeled, seeded, and chopped
½ cup fruit juice concentrate
¼ cup white wine vinegar
½ teaspoon salt or to taste
1 jalapeño pepper, minced
¼ cup chopped fresh cilantro

Sauces

Sauces have transformational powers. Yesterday's leftovers will come alive enrobed in a nice sauce, and even a simple vegetable or a few potatoes will somehow seem more worthy of reverence. Licking up every last drop of Madeira Mushroom or Rich Brown Sauce, your guests will ask you where in France you were trained as a chef.

Sauces are thickened in a variety of ways. Traditional white sauces are thickened with a roux (flour and butter), while fancier ones are often made by the reduction method (cooking down), which results in a richer and deeper flavor. Some require a long simmering, while others can be made in just minutes. You will find all sorts of sauces here and learn that even the more complicated-looking ones become easy once the method for making them is acquired.

Many of these freeze nicely, so go ahead and make a large batch. Then when you have some dish that doesn't pack enough punch by itself, you can take out one of your sauces from the freezer to reheat and pour on.

Yield: about 2 cups

3 tablespoons nonhydrogenated
    margarine or vegetable oil
4 tablespoons flour (unbleached
    white or whole wheat pastry
    flour with the bran sifted out)
2 cups hot soymilk or almond milk
¼ medium onion, separated
    into leaves
4 cloves
6 to 8 peppercorns or white pepper
Several dashes freshly grated
    nutmeg
1 teaspoon maple syrup, if you
    are using an unblended
    soymilk (see pages 10-11)
Salt

Béchamel or White Sauce

This is your traditional white sauce made with soymilk or almond milk instead of dairy milk. The trick to producing a smooth sauce without lumps is to heat the milk before adding it to the roux (flour and butter). Then it all blends very smoothly with just a few turns of the whisk. And yes, soymilk makes perfectly good béchamel with no "beany" taste if a few tricks are observed. Your guests will never know the difference. For a sauce with more character, try the soubise sauce on page 70 or one of the following variations.

Melt the margarine or heat the oil in a heavy-bottomed pan or the top of a double boiler. Add the flour, and cook for 2 or 3 minutes over low heat. Add the hot milk, stirring with a whisk. It will thicken quickly. Add the onion, cloves, peppercorns, nutmeg, maple syrup, if necessary, and salt to taste. Cover and continue to cook for 10 to 15 minutes. Stir frequently with a wooden spoon to prevent it from scorching. Strain through a sieve. Use immediately or pour a coating of milk on top to prevent a skin from forming—mix the milk in when you reheat the sauce.

Per ¼ cup: Calories 75, Protein 3 g, Fat 5 g, Carbohydrates 5 g

Quick White Sauce

Follow the recipe above, but delete the onion, cloves, and peppercorns. Cook only until thickened. Season with salt, pepper, and nutmeg.

Paprika Sauce

Add a tablespoon of a good Hungarian paprika to the sauce, whisking until smooth.

Nutty Almond Sauce

Ground roasted almonds are added to the basic béchamel to make a rich and flavorful sauce that is excellent over grains, vegetables, and Wild Rice Crêpes (page 116), as well as in casseroles and gratins.

Follow the instructions for making the béchamel sauce on page 68, and if using margarine, allow it to brown a little first before adding the flour. (Don't let it burn.) Strain. Roast the almonds to a golden brown, then pulverize them in a blender or nut grinder. Add the almonds to the strained sauce, and cook for 4 to 5 minutes. A teaspoon of soy sauce may be added if desired. If you prefer a smoother sauce you can purée it all, but I like it best with a very fine crunch.

Per ¼ cup: Calories 106, Protein 4 g, Fat 5 g, Carbohydrates 5 g

Yield: about 2½ cups

3 tablespoons nonhydrogenated margarine or vegetable oil
4 tablespoons flour (unbleached white or whole wheat pastry flour with the bran sifted out)
2½ cups hot soymilk or almond milk
½ cup almonds
¼ medium onion, separated into leaves
4 cloves
6 to 8 peppercorns or white pepper
Several dashes freshly grated nutmeg
1 teaspoon maple syrup, if you are using an unblended soymilk (see pages 10-11)
1 teaspoon soy sauce (optional)
Salt

Yield: 3 cups

1¼ pounds onions, sliced
4 tablespoons oil or
   nonhydrogenated margarine
1 teaspoon salt
4 tablespoons flour (unbleached
   white or whole wheat pastry
   flour with the bran sifted out)
2½ to 3 cups hot soymilk
Salt, white pepper, and nutmeg

Soubise Sauce

A traditional béchamel with the addition of onions. Good in casseroles, gratins, with pasta or crêpes, or with brown rice.

Sauté the onions in the oil or margarine and salt in a covered pan over low heat for 30 to 40 minutes, stirring occasionally. Do not let them brown. Add the flour and cook for 1 minute, stirring constantly. Add the hot soymilk and whisk continuously until smooth and thick. Partially cover and continue cooking for another 15 minutes over low heat, stirring occasionally. Be careful not to scorch the sauce. Purée in a blender or food processor, and season with nutmeg, pepper, and more salt if necessary.

Per ¼ cup: Calories 87, Protein 3 g, Fat 6 g, Carbohydrates 7 g

Yield: 4½ cups

1¾ pounds onions, sliced
4 tablespoons oil or
   nonhydrogenated margarine
1 teaspoon salt
5 tablespoons flour
1 cup hot, flavorful vegetable stock
1 cup dry white wine
2 to 2½ cups hot soymilk
Salt, pepper, and nutmeg

Soubise Sauce Suprême

Wine and stock are used to replace part of the soymilk to make it lighter and yet give it more character. Use as you would the soubise sauce above.

Sauté the onions in the oil or margarine with the salt in a covered saucepan for 20 minutes until very soft. Add the flour, cook a minute, then add the hot stock and wine, stirring constantly. Simmer gently for 10 minutes, then add the soymilk and continue simmering for 20 more minutes. Purée, diluting with more soymilk if it seems too thick. Season with salt, pepper, and nutmeg to taste.

Per ¼ cup: Calories 65, Protein 2 g, Fat 3 g, Carbohydrates 9 g

Tofu "Mornay" Sauce

Tofu "cheese" adds a subtle, cheesy flavor to white sauce.

Make the béchamel sauce. After straining, whisk in the crumbled "cheese." Reheat and serve.

Per ¼ cup: Calories 104, Protein 4 g, Fat 5 g, Carbohydrates 9 g

Yield: about 2¼ cups

1 recipe Béchamel Sauce,
    page 68
⅓ to ½ cup Tofu "Cheese,"
    pages 42-43

Teriyaki Sauce & Marinade

Dip steamed vegetables in this, or marinate tofu, tempeh, or vegetables before grilling or sautéing.

Combine the soy sauce, mirin, water, and sweetener in a small saucepan, and bring to a gentle boil. Simmer for 1 minute. Place the sesame seeds in a small skillet, and dry-roast until they give off a nutty aroma and crackle slightly. ***Do not burn or allow to darken.*** Add to the sauce along with the sesame oil.

Only a small amount of this sauce is needed for dipping. You may dilute it with more water if you want to pour it over vegetables or rice.

Per tablespoon: Calories 40, Protein 1 g, Fat 0.5 g, Carbohydrates 8 g

Yield: 1⅓ cups

Scant ⅔ cup soy sauce
⅓ cup mirin
⅓ cup water
4 to 5 tablespoons sweetener
    of choice
4 tablespoons hulled sesame seeds
1 teaspoon toasted sesame oil

1 medium onion, sliced

A handful of mushrooms or
   mushroom stems, sliced

½ stalk celery, sliced

1 bay leaf

¼ teaspoon dried thyme

Several sprigs parsley

1 cup flavorful vegetable stock

2¾ cups dry white wine

10 peppercorns

Salt

1 cup soy cream or almond milk

1 teaspoon arrowroot to thicken
   (optional)

Tangy White Wine Sauce

A slightly tangy sauce that is wonderful over crêpes, surrounding bouchées filled with creamed mushrooms, over asparagus, delicately flavored warm terrines, and other elegant concoctions. This is not your typical white sauce that can be cooked up in ten minutes; it takes over an hour of simmering. However, there is little work involved, and the results are fabulous. For those who prefer a slightly sweeter sauce, try the sweet white wine sauce on page 73.

Place all the ingredients except the soy cream or almond milk and arrowroot in a covered pot. Simmer for 1 hour or more until it is reduced to one-fourth or less of its original volume. Add the soy cream or almond milk, and simmer gently for 5 minutes. Strain, pressing the juices out of the vegetables. This makes less than 2 cups of sauce, but the recipe can easily be doubled. It is also a much thinner sauce than béchamel, but a little arrowroot dissolved in water can be added at the end if you prefer it a little thicker.

Per ¼ cup: Calories 61, Protein 3 g, Fat 1 g, Carbohydrates 17 g

Sweet White Wine Sauce

Yield: scant 2 cups

Slightly sweeter than the preceding recipe.

Make as for the tangy white wine sauce on page 72. Cashew milk can be used in place of almond milk since it adds a sweetness of its own. Once again, this can be thickened at the end with a little arrowroot, if desired.

Per ¼ cup: Calories 38, Protein 2 g, Fat 1 g, Carbohydrates 11 g

1 medium onion, sliced
A handful of mushrooms
   or mushroom stems, sliced
½ stalk celery, sliced
1 apple, chopped
1 bay leaf
¼ teaspoon dried thyme
Several sprigs parsley
2¾ cups flavorful vegetable stock
1 cup dry white wine
10 peppercorns
Salt
1 cup soy cream, almond milk,
   or cashew milk
1 teaspoon arrowroot to thicken
   (optional)

Yield: 2 cups

1 small onion, minced
1 stalk celery, minced
3 tablespoons oil or
    nonhydrogenated margarine
4 tablespoons flour
1¾ cups hot stock
⅔ cup red wine
1 small apple, chopped
1 tablespoon mirin
1 to 2 tablespoons soy sauce
1 tablespoon miso
1 to 2 tablespoons tomato paste
Salt
⅓ cup or more rich soymilk
    or soy cream
Pepper

Red Wine Cream Sauce

Try this over crêpes, loaves, casseroles, or grains.

Sauté the onions and celery in the oil or margarine until soft. Add the flour, cook 2 minutes, then add the hot stock and wine, stirring constantly. Add the chopped apple, cover, and simmer over low heat for 30 minutes. Strain out the vegetables. Add the mirin, soy sauce, miso, tomato paste, and salt to taste, and simmer for another 10 minutes. Add the soymilk and pepper to taste, and heat thoroughly.

Per ¼ cup: Calories 112, Protein 2 g, Fat 6 g, Carbohydrates 11 g

Yield: about 2¼ cups

1 recipe Béchamel or White
    Sauce, page 68
⅓ to ½ pound mushrooms
1 to 2 tablespoons sherry or
    white wine (optional)

Quick Mushroom Sauce

Make the basic béchamel sauce. While it is simmering, sauté the mushrooms in a separate pan. After straining the sauce, add the mushrooms and cook for another 5 to 6 minutes. A tablespoon or two of sherry or white wine can be added along with the mushrooms, if desired.

Per ¼ cup: Calories 71, Protein 3 g, Fat 5 g, Carbohydrates 5 g

Shiitake Béarnaise Sauce

Yield: 8 servings

A rich sauce that is excellent with seitan or tofu "steaks," grilled portobello mushrooms, or roasted potatoes.

¾ cup dried shiitake mushrooms

3 cups water

½ cup white wine

½ cup white wine vinegar

¼ cup shallots, minced

1 tablespoon dried tarragon

4 ounces tofu

¼ cup oil

Salt and pepper

Soak the shiitake mushrooms in the water for several hours or overnight until fully reconstituted. Remove the shiitake and cut off the stems; set aside. Pour the water used for soaking into a saucepan, making sure not to pour off the sediment at the bottom. Discard the last 2 or 3 tablespoons of soaking liquid, as it generally contains sediment. Bring the liquid to a boil over high heat, and continue to simmer until it is reduced to 1 cup.

Simultaneously, put the white wine, white wine vinegar, shallots, and tarragon into a small saucepan, and bring to a boil. Turn down the heat slightly and continue a gentle boil until this has been reduced to about ¼ cup. Pour into a blender.

To the blender add the reduced stock, reconstituted and trimmed shiitake, and tofu. Purée until smooth, turning off the blender and scraping the sides occasionally. Pour in the oil in a thin, steady stream, and season with salt and pepper to taste.

This sauce should be served warm but not hot. Pour the sauce into a tureen or small metal or glass bowl, and keep it warm in a hot water bath (hot water in a pot).

Per serving: Calories 97, Protein 2 g, Fat 7 g, Carbohydrates 4 g

3 cups hot gluten stock from making gluten (see recipe on page 161)

1 pound mushrooms (use ½ pound brown mushrooms, if available)

4 ounces fresh or reconstituted shiitake mushrooms

4 ounces fresh shimeji or oyster mushrooms

4 tablespoons nonhydrogenated margarine or vegetable oil

⅓ cup finely minced onions or shallots

3 tablespoons flour (unbleached white or whole wheat pastry flour with the bran sifted out)

⅓ to ½ cup Madeira, or more to taste

Salt and pepper

MADEIRA MUSHROOM SAUCE

Utterly, incredibly delicious—the kind of sauce that makes life seem worth living! The secret is using stock from stewing gluten (see below). Using anything else will give a less than out-of-this-world result. This is the perfect sauce for crêpes and other wonderful things.

For the hot gluten stock, follow the directions for making stove-top gluten on page 161, and use onions, celery, and 12 to 15 dried shiitakes, with salt being the only seasoning (no soy sauce, tomatoes, etc.). Drain off the resulting stock, and set aside.

Slice the mushrooms and shiitake, and separate the shimeji or oyster mushrooms into individual mushrooms or small clumps. Sauté all the mushrooms and the onions or shallots in the margarine or oil in a covered saucepan for 10 minutes. Add the flour and cook for 2 minutes, stirring constantly. While whisking, add the hot gluten stock and Madeira, and cook until slightly thickened. Cover and simmer over low heat for 20 minutes. Uncover, turn the heat to high, and boil rapidly to reduce by one-third, stirring occasionally. Season with salt and pepper, adding more Madeira, if necessary, for flavor.

Per ¼ cup: Calories 55, Protein 1 g, Fat 3 g, Carbohydrates 4 g

Mushroom Aurora Sauce

Yield: about 2½ cups

My late mother enjoyed this mild but creamy, tasty sauce over her tofu burgers. It is also good over fettuccine and crêpes.

Slice the mushrooms and shiitake thickly, and separate the oyster mushrooms into small clumps. Sauté the onions and garlic in the margarine or oil in a covered saucepan until tender, then add the mushrooms. Cover and cook for 5 minutes to release their juices. Add the flour, cook for 2 minutes while stirring, then add the stock and wine, stirring constantly. Simmer gently for a minute. Add the tomatoes, bay leaf, basil, salt, and pepper to taste. Cover and simmer 30 to 40 minutes until the tomatoes have broken down and the sauce has been reduced by at least one-third. Add the soymilk and gently simmer for another minute.

Per ¼ cup: Calories 85, Protein 2 g, Fat 5 g, Carbohydrates 7 g

12 ounces mixed mushrooms (such as button, oyster, and shiitake)

½ medium onion, minced

2 cloves garlic, minced

4 tablespoons nonhydrogenated margarine or vegetable oil

5 tablespoons flour

1 cup hot vegetable stock (or the soaking water from reconstituting the shiitake if dried ones are used)

½ cup white wine

2 ripe tomatoes, chopped

1 bay leaf

½ teaspoon dried basil

Salt and pepper

½ cup soymilk or soy cream

Yield: about 3 cups

1½ to 2 cups finely diced onions

1 cup diced celery

1 cup diced carrots

1 tablespoon oil or
   nonhydrogenated margarine

3 very ripe tomatoes, chopped

1 cup or more red wine

½ bulb garlic, sliced
   (half a bulb, not a clove)

6 dried shiitake mushrooms

½ cup sliced mushrooms

2 tablespoons soy sauce

1 to 2 tablespoons miso
   (mild or medium)

½ teaspoon dried rosemary

½ teaspoon dried thyme

3½ to 4 cups vegetable stock

For the roux:

4 tablespoons oil or
   nonhydrogenated margarine

6 tablespoons flour

RICH BROWN SAUCE

Friends have often compared this to a demi-glace sauce as they lick every drop off their plates. This is definitely not anything like the lumpy, brown, floury substance called "gravy"; it is rich, with complex over- and undertones. It is excellent with French moussaka, pages 146-47, wild rice crêpes, page 116, and tofu or tempeh burgers. Any leftover brown sauce can be added to stir-fry vegetables with a little soy sauce for a rich, Oriental flavor. It also freezes beautifully, so make twice the amount and freeze half for later.

In a large covered pot, sauté the onions, celery, and carrots in 1 tablespoon oil or margarine until relatively tender. Add the tomatoes, wine, garlic, shiitake, mushrooms, soy sauce, miso, and herbs, and bring to a boil. Add the stock. When it has reached a second boil, cover, lower the heat, and simmer for 1 hour or longer. Taste and adjust the seasonings, adding more stock or water if the flavor seems too strong or boiling down rapidly to concentrate if the flavor seems weak. Set a colander over a bowl, and pour it through to strain the vegetables. Press as much juice out of the vegetables as possible, then discard them.

To make the roux, heat or melt the 4 tablespoons of oil or margarine and add the flour. Cook for 2 minutes, stirring with a wooden spoon. While whisking, add the hot liquid and cook over low heat until thickened.

Per ¼ cup: Calories 95, Protein 2 g, Fat 5 g, Carbohydrates 12 g

Brown Sauce Suprême

An extra portion of vegetables and cooking time results in a superior sauce.

Make two times the recipe for brown sauce, page 78, except do not thicken with roux (oil or margarine and flour) at the end. Sauté the additional onions, carrots, and celery in the oil or margarine. Add the flour, stir, and cook for 2 to 3 minutes. Add the strained, hot brown sauce liquid. Lower the heat, cover, and simmer for an additional 1 to 1½ hours. Strain out the vegetables. Although the whole process takes 2½ to 3 hours of simmering, the results are simply grand.

Per ¼ cup: Calories 73, Protein 1 g, Fat 2 g, Carbohydrates 8 g

Yield: about 6 cups

2 recipes Rich Brown Sauce,
  page 78, without roux
½ cup diced onions
½ cup diced carrots
½ cup diced celery
2 tablespoons oil
6 tablespoons flour

Yield: about 2½ cups.

1 medium onion, minced
1 clove garlic, minced
3 tablespoons oil or
    nonhydrogenated margarine
3 tablespoons flour
2 cups hot vegetable stock
1 cup tomato juice
¼ cup soy sauce
1 to 2 tablespoons mild miso
2 tablespoons mirin
1 tablespoon red wine vinegar
¼ cup or more Madeira

Quick Brown Sauce

A time-saving brown sauce that is fine for many homestyle dishes.

Sauté the onions and garlic in the oil or margarine until soft. Add the flour, cook a minute or two, then add the hot stock, stirring constantly. Add all the remaining ingredients except the Madeira, and cook rapidly over high heat to reduce by one-third to one-half. Add the Madeira, cook a few more minutes, and if desired, add a swirl of margarine in the end to enrich.

Per ¼ cup: Calories 76, Protein 1 g, Fat 4 g, Carbohydrates 8 g

Easy Mushroom Brown Sauce

Yield: about 2 cups

Here is a tasty sauce that can be whipped up in ten minutes, although you will have to soak the shiitake an hour or so beforehand. This is thickened with arrowroot or kuzu rather than flour and has a glazed appearance. Serve it over tofu burgers (page 145), grains, or vegetables.

4 to 5 dried shiitake mushrooms
1 cup warm water

2 tablespoons oil or
   nonhydrogenated margarine
4 ounces mushrooms, sliced
2 tablespoons sherry, sake, or wine
1 clove garlic, minced
½ cup tomato juice
1 tablespoon soy sauce
1 tablespoon mirin
1 to 3 teaspoons nutritional
   yeast flakes
½ tablespoon miso
1½ tablespoons arrowroot,
   or 2 teaspoons kuzu

Soak the shiitake in the warm water for about an hour. If you are pressed for time, soak in boiling water for 20 to 30 minutes. Drain the mushrooms and save the soaking liquid. Squeeze the mushrooms dry and slice thinly. Melt the oil or margarine in a small covered saucepan, and sauté the mushrooms and shiitake for 4 to 5 minutes until they are partly reduced in size and have begun to exude their juices. Add the sherry or sake, turn the heat up high, and add the garlic, shiitake soaking liquid, and tomato juice. Boil rapidly for a minute, then add the soy sauce and mirin, and continue boiling for another 2 to 3 minutes. Turn the heat down low, and add the nutritional yeast and miso. Dissolve the arrowroot or kuzu in a small amount of water. While stirring the sauce constantly, add the arrowroot or kuzu mixture, and cook the sauce until it has thickened and become transparent.

Per ¼ cup: Calories 58, Protein 1 g, Fat 4 g, Carbohydrates 5 g

½ cup raw cashews
3 tablespoons lemon juice
¼ cup water
½ cup safflower oil
Pinch of salt

Cashew Mayonnaise & Crème Sauce

Cashews form the base of a lovely, tangy mayonnaise that can accompany vegetable mousses, cold asparagus, canapés, and salads. Diluted with a bit of water, it works as a creamy sauce to surround some of the cold mousses on pages 48-49.

Place the cashews, lemon juice, and water in a blender, and whip until very creamy. Add the oil a little at a time, scraping down the sides of the blender whenever necessary, until the mixture becomes very thick and creamy like mayonnaise. Add the salt, blend a moment longer, and refrigerate until needed.

Per tablespoon: Calories 87, Protein 1 g, Fat 7 g, Carbohydrates 2 g

Cashew Crème Sauce

Dilute a desired amount of mayonnaise with water, adding a little at a time, to reach a heavy cream consistency. Add an extra pinch of salt or lemon juice to taste.

Rich Cashew Sour Crème

This basic mock sour crème forms the base for many recipes, including the stroganoff (page 164), Deep Sea Crêpes (page 117), and Curried Mushroom Filo Triangles (page 65). You can cook and bake with it; try adding it to a variety of soups and sauces for richness, texture, and flavor. It also makes a zesty topping for crêpes, pancakes, baked potatoes, and vegetables.

Purée the cashews and water in a blender at high speed until creamy. Add the tofu, lemon juice, and salt, and purée until smooth. Then add the oil in a steady stream until thickened.

Per tablespoon: Calories 32, Protein 1 g, Fat 3 g, Carbohydrates 1 g

Yield: 3 cups

1 cup raw cashews
1 cup water
8 ounces firm tofu
3 tablespoons lemon juice
½ teaspoon salt
¼ cup or more canola oil

Coconut Crème Fraiche

Serve with Curried Sweet Potato Cakes, page 184, or with other curry dishes, as a dip or salad dressing, or with fruit.

Purée the cashews and water in a blender to form a thick cream. Add the tofu, lemon juice, and salt, and purée until smooth. Thin with the coconut milk as desired.

Per ¼ cup: Calories 90, Protein 3 g, Fat 7 g, Carbohydrates 4 g

Yield: 1⅔ cups

⅓ cup raw cashew pieces
⅔ cup water
One-half 12.3-ounce box firm silken tofu
3 tablespoons lemon juice
½ to 1 teaspoon salt
½ cup or more coconut milk

Dijon Mustard Sauce

Yield: ½ to ¾ cup

3 tablespoons boiling water
3 tablespoons Dijon-style mustard
⅓ to ½ cup extra-virgin olive oil
Lemon juice, salt, and pepper

An excellent cold sauce for cold artichokes, asparagus, avocado, and broccoli. Only a small amount is needed.

In a small bowl, beat the boiling water into the mustard a little at a time. Then beat in the olive oil drop by drop so that the entire mixture emulsifies and becomes a thick sauce. Add lemon juice, a half teaspoon at a time, and season with salt and pepper to taste.

Per tablespoon: Calories 80, Protein 0 g, Fat 9 g, Carbohydrates 0 g

Pesto Sauce

Yield: 2 cups

2 cups packed fresh basil leaves
2 to 4 cloves garlic
½ cup plus 2 tablespoons
   pine nuts
1 cup extra-virgin olive oil
2 tablespoons light miso

Pesto has become extremely popular in recent years, and understandably, since it is such a highly versatile sauce. It is a natural over pasta, but it can also be added to soup, tomato sauce, or pizza, extended with vinegar as a salad dressing, or simply spread on bread. At the height of summer, I like to take advantage of the fresh basil that abounds in stores and make a large batch. It keeps for several weeks refrigerated or can be frozen for longer periods. Although a true Italian may frown upon you, by all means go ahead and use a blender!

Combine all the ingredients in a blender or food processor. Blend until a thick green sauce is produced, but take care to leave some texture. Store refrigerated in a jar with a coating of olive oil on top to keep the sauce from discoloring.

Per tablespoon: Calories 75, Protein .5 g, Fat 8 g, Carbohydrates .5 g

Paella, page 125

Fresh Marinara

Yield: 2½ to 3 cups

Unlike the puréed and long-stewed counterpart, this tomato sauce is made from fresh tomatoes and cooks up in less than half an hour to produce a light, fresh taste. The addition of mushrooms is optional, but they do provide a nice contrast in texture. Serve with vermicelli, linguini, tortellini, or crêpes.

1 large onion, finely chopped

2 cloves garlic, minced

2 tablespoons olive oil

2 pounds fresh, ripe tomatoes, chopped (approximately 3 very large or 5 to 6 regular)

4 tablespoons red wine

1 teaspoon dried or 3 tablespoons chopped fresh basil

½ teaspoon dried rosemary

Salt and pepper

½ pound mushrooms, sliced (optional)

1 tablespoon olive oil (optional)

Salt (optional)

In a large, covered skillet, sauté the onion and garlic in the olive oil until soft. Add the tomatoes and red wine, cover, and cook for 5 minutes. Add the basil and rosemary, cover again, and continue cooking for 20 minutes, stirring occasionally. Season with salt and pepper to taste.

If you want to add mushrooms, sauté them in the olive oil over high heat until lightly browned. Salt lightly, add the sauce, and simmer an additional 5 minutes.

Per ¼ cup: Calories 47, Protein 1 g, Fat 3 g, Carbohydrates 4 g

Clockwise from top left: Shiitake Consommé, page 93, Chilled Curried Carrot & Fruit Soup, page 110, Cold Cream of Watercress & Apple Soup, page 105

Roasted Red Bell Pepper Sauce

Yield: 1 cup

2 red bell peppers
3 cloves garlic
3 to 4 tablespoons olive oil
Salt

Grill, broil, or roast peppers until blackened. Place in a paper bag, and allow to "weep" for 30 minutes. Peel the charbroiled skins off. Cut the peppers in half, remove the seeds and veins, and purée the pepper halves in a blender along with the garlic and olive oil until a sauce consistency is achieved. Season with salt to taste. Serve with polenta, pasta, or roasted asparagus, or as a dip for vegetables or bread.

Per tablespoon: Calories 28, Protein 0 g, Fat 2 g, Carbohydrates 0 g

Grilled Tomato Concassé

Yield: 6 cups

6 tomatoes
1 tablespoon olive oil
3 to 4 cloves garlic
1 tablespoon sweetener of choice
Salt and pepper

A saucy pasta topping with incomparable flavor.

Grill the tomatoes over the open flame of a gas burner or under a broiler, turning every few minutes, until the skins are blackened and the juices are beginning to ooze. Heat the olive oil in a sauté pan, and add the tomatoes, blackened skin and all. Chop or mash roughly with a spoon in the pan. Add the garlic and sweetener, and simmer for about 10 minutes. Season with salt and pepper to taste.

Per cup: Calories 55, Protein 1 g, Fat 2 g, Carbohydrates 8 g

Tofu Aïoli

Yield: (⅔ cup) 4 to 8 servings

Here's a rich, assertive sauce for garlic lovers only. Serve as a dipping sauce for steamed vegetables, potatoes, and cubes of French bread. A bold red wine can accompany this.

½ to 1 recipe Tofu "Cheese,"
   page 42-43
2 to 6 cloves garlic, minced
   or pressed
3 to 6 ounces extra-virgin olive oil

Place the garlic and "tofu cheese" in a blender, and whiz until smooth, adding the olive oil a little at a time. Or simply place the tofu in a bowl, and cream thoroughly. Add the garlic, then whisk in the olive oil a little at a time until smooth and thick. This keeps for only a day or two.

Per serving: Calories 232, Protein 7 g, Fat 5 g, Carbohydrates 19 g

Instant Seitan Gravy

Yield: 2½ cups

The perfect complement for my UnTurkeys.

4 tablespoons oil
6 tablespoons flour
2 cups hot vegetable stock
2 to 3 tablespoons soy sauce
3 tablespoons nutritional yeast
   flakes (optional)
3 tablespoons white or red wine
½ cup diced seitan

Heat the oil in a saucepan. Add the flour and cook, stirring constantly, for 2 minutes. Pour in the hot vegetable stock at once, whisking until smooth. (If the stock is not hot, it will be difficult to whisk in without producing lumps.) Add the soy sauce, nutritional yeast, wine, and seitan tidbits. Allow to simmer briefly until thickened, then serve.

Per tablespoon: Calories 23, Protein 1 g, Fat 1 g, Carbohydrates 1 g

Soups

Soups need no introduction; everybody loves them. Here you will find some new versions of traditional favorites, such as French onion soup and gazpacho, as well as some new and different ones, such as the Chilled Curried Carrot and Fruit Soup on page 110. All of them are sure to please.

A word about stocks: If you save your vegetable scraps and make a batch of stock every two or three weeks, you will always have some on hand for a pot of soup. If, however, making a stock from scratch seems too laborious, then go ahead and opt for a good quality packaged broth or bouillon, making sure that it is all-natural and contains no MSG. Natural food stores now carry a wide variety, and you will surely find one that you like. Some are sodium-free, allowing you to control the saltiness of the soup. Also, match your stock with your soup. A tomato-based stock would be too strong for the delicate and sweet Chilled Carrot and Orange Soup on page 109, although perfect for the Pesto Vegetable Soup on page 97. Follow the guidelines for making basic vegetable stock on pages 90-91, or shop around until you find a packaged stock that you like.

Basic Vegetable Stock

Fruits and vegetables suitable
for any type stock:

Apples, to add a slight sweetness

Carrots, tops and all, sliced

Celery, tops and all, sliced

Cucumbers, peel if skin is bitter

Garlic—you can add a whole head
as the long simmering leaves
only a mellow aroma

Leeks, sliced (bottoms too)

Lettuce, an old head or wilted outer
leaves

Mushrooms, whole or just stems

Onions, sliced (also skins of any
color)

Parsley, stems and all

Parsnips, sliced

Potatoes and potato peels

Scallions (bottoms too)

The scraps of vegetables accumulating in your refrigerator will make a good vegetable stock. Save carrot tops, potato skins, scallion ends, and other bits and pieces, and supplement them with a couple of sliced onions, carrots, and celery to fill a big soup pot for your own homemade stock. The following guidelines will help you in making and seasoning stocks for a variety of soups. Onions, carrots, and celery are fairly essential to producing any stock. Use all or a combination of the vegetables and seasonings suggested here, filling a soup pot with them. Seasonings are optional—you can make a stock from just vegetables and water if desired.

Add water to cover the vegetables. Cover with a tight-fitting lid and bring to a boil. Lower the heat and simmer gently for 1 to 2 hours, adding a little more water if necessary. Strain the stock and discard the vegetables. Taste and adjust the seasonings as desired. If it tastes weak, boil it down rapidly to concentrate it.

The stock can be used immediately or stored in the refrigerator or freezer for later use. If kept in the refrigerator, it should be brought to a boil at least once a week.

This recipe is for a nonfat vegetable stock. For a richer flavor, sauté the onions, celery, and carrots in 2 to 4 tablespoons of vegetable oil until tender, then add the other vegetables, seasonings, and water, and proceed with the recipe as previously given.

For stronger flavored or "Italian"-type soups (minestrone, lentil, basil-vegetable, tomato, etc.): In addition to the aforementioned vegetables and seasonings, tomatoes, fresh basil, rosemary, lots of garlic, and extra soy sauce may be added if desired.

Avoid vegetables from the cabbage family, such as broccoli, cabbage, or cauliflower, since they are too strong unless used in making a broccoli or cabbage soup. However, mild vegetables and varieties from the squash family (zucchini, pumpkin, etc.) may be added to the ones suggested here.

Seasonings to be added as desired:

Herbs and spices of choice— Remember to keep in mind the soup you will make with it. Otherwise, stay basic by using bay leaves, thyme, and parsley.

Miso—add a small amount, 1 to 2 tablespoons—for a richer flavor

Nutritional yeast—several tablespoons will add a deep, hearty flavor

Salt and pepper

Soy sauce—depending on soup, add anywhere from 2 teaspoons to several tablespoons; adds a "meatier" flavor

Wine or sherry—for a gourmet touch

Chicken-Free Stock

2 tablespoons oil

2 large onions, sliced

2 medium carrots,
  sliced ¼ inch thick

1 large parsnip, diced

2 stalks celery, sliced

2 bay leaves

½ teaspoon celery seeds

1 large cucumber, peeled
  and diced (Japanese cucumbers
  do not need to be peeled)

2 quarts water

This excellent stock is rich with a natural sweetness.
It is a fine replacement for chicken stock.

Heat the oil in a large pot. Sauté the onions, carrots, parsnip, and celery, covered, for 10 minutes. Add the remaining vegetables and water, cover, and bring to a boil. Lower the heat and simmer gently for 1½ hours. Strain, pressing the juices out of the vegetables. If the flavor seems weak, boil rapidly, uncovered, to reduce by 10 to 20 percent.

Per cup: Calories 165, Protein 4 g, Fat 5 g, Carbohydrates 28 g

Shiitake Consommé

The meaty depth of the shiitake and their broth is nicely rounded out by the sweetness of red bell peppers. This is a good soup to serve at the start of a rich meal. It can be made up to two hours ahead of serving, but is best if served as soon as possible.

Soak the shiitake in the water for 3 to 4 hours. Drain and reserve the soaking water for stock. Cut off the stems with a sharp knife, and slice very thinly. Combine the shiitake stock, sliced shiitake, sliced mushrooms, red wine, soy sauce, and consommé or bouillon cubes in a pot, cover, and simmer for 30 minutes. Add the red peppers and continue to simmer for another 15 minutes. Season with freshly ground black pepper, and add the parsley just before serving.

Per serving: Calories 52, Protein 3 g, Fat 0 g, Carbohydrates 14 g

Yield: 6 to 8 servings

See photo facing page 85.

15 to 20 dried shiitake mushrooms
8 cups water

8 ounces mushrooms, sliced
1½ cups red wine
3 tablespoons soy sauce
2 vegetable consommé or
   bouillon cubes
2 medium red bell peppers,
   sliced into thin rings
Plenty of freshly grated black
   pepper
⅓ cup finely chopped parsley

Yield: 4 to 6 servings

4 large bulbs garlic

*10 to 12 dried shiitake mushrooms,
    reconstituted*

*1 pound button mushrooms,
    sliced thinly, or ⅔ pound
    button mushrooms and
    ⅓ pound shimeji oyster
    mushrooms*

3 tablespoons olive oil

*8 cups vegetable stock (part or
    all may be shiitake stock)*

3 to 4 pinches saffron

3 to 4 tablespoons soy sauce

¾ cup red wine

*An extra 6 to 8 cloves garlic,
    finely minced*

Salt and pepper

Minced parsley, for garnish

CLEAR GARLIC SOUP WITH MUSHROOMS & SAFFRON

*A highly unusual and delicious soup. Do not be put off by the idea of
using four to five entire bulbs of garlic for this soup, because
simmering leaves only a mellow flavor. Of course, garlic lovers can
always increase the quantity of garlic added at the end.*

Separate the 4 bulbs of garlic into cloves, and dunk in boiling water for 30 seconds. The skins should slip off easily. Discard the skins and simmer the cloves of garlic in the stock for 10 to 15 minutes until very tender. Strain and discard the garlic.

Slice the shiitake thinly and sauté in a covered pan with the mushrooms and shimeji oyster mushrooms (if you are using them) in the olive oil for 5 minutes. Add the garlic, stock, saffron, soy sauce, red wine, and the minced garlic, and simmer for 15 to 20 minutes. Adjust the flavorings, adding more garlic, saffron, or soy sauce as desired. Season with salt and pepper to taste, and garnish each bowl of soup with a sprinkling of parsley.

Per serving: Calories 140, Protein 3 g, Fat 8 g, Carbohydrates 9 g

French Onion Soup

The sweetness of onions really comes through in this rich and hearty soup. It is excellent by itself, but feel free to serve it "au gratin" with a slice of thick French bread and cheese (soy, of course). The secret to excellent onion soup lies in the slow cooking and browning of the onions, so take your time with this soup.

Heat the oil and margarine in a large Dutch oven or soup pot with a heavy bottom. Add the onions, cover, and cook slowly over low heat for 20 minutes, stirring frequently. Add the sweetener and salt, uncover, and continue to cook for another 30 minutes until the onions are sweet and nicely browned. This browning process is very important. Add the stock and wine, and simmer, partially covered, for 30 minutes. Add the soy sauce and brandy, and continue simmering for another 15 minutes. Add salt, pepper, a little more soy sauce, and brandy to taste, if necessary, being sure to simmer for several minutes after adding. Serve with a sprinkling of parsley to garnish or "au gratin"—topped with a "croûte" (round slices of French bread baked in a slow oven until dry) and a thick slab of soy cheese, and placed under the broiler until the cheese melts.

1 tablespoon oil plus 1 tablespoon
    nonhydrogenated margarine, or
    2 tablespoons oil
3 pounds onions, sliced
1 teaspoon sweetener
1 teaspoon salt
1½ to 2 quarts vegetable stock
½ cup white or red wine
3 tablespoons soy sauce
3 tablespoons brandy or cognac
Salt and pepper
Parsley, for garnish
Stale or lightly toasted slices of
    French bread and soy cheese
    (optional)

Per serving: Calories 241, Protein 7 g, Fat 5 g, Carbohydrates 39 g

Yield: 2 to 3 servings

2 tablespoons extra-virgin olive oil

4 to 5 cloves garlic, finely minced

1½ pounds very ripe tomatoes,
    chopped

2 cups hot vegetable stock

⅓ cup fresh basil,
    or 2 teaspoons dried basil and
    several sprigs fresh parsley

Salt and pepper

3 to 4 slices French bread,
    ½ inch thick

Fresh Tomato & Bread Soup

Use ripe (even overly ripe) red tomatoes for this delightful repast that is sure to capture the flavors of summer's bounty. Made in just minutes, it is the perfect soup for a romantic dinner for two with pasta and a chilled white wine. For a larger crowd, double the recipe.

Heat the olive oil in a pot, and sauté the garlic over low heat for 3 to 4 minutes. Add the tomatoes, turn the heat up to high, and bring to a boil. Reduce the heat and simmer for 5 minutes. Add the stock and basil (plus parsley if dried basil is used), and continue simmering uncovered for about 10 minutes, until the tomatoes are tender but still fresh tasting. (Do not overcook.) Season with salt and pepper to taste. Tear the bread into large chunks, and stir into the soup. Cover and allow to sit for at least 5 minutes before serving.

Per serving: Calories 247, Protein 6 g, Fat 11 g, Carbohydrates 30 g

Pesto Vegetable Soup

Flavorful pesto sauce makes a lively brew out of a pot of fresh summer vegetables. Best if freshly picked vegetables from your garden are used, but perfectly satisfying using whatever you can find in the produce section, along with some frozen peas and beans.

Place the onions, carrot, mushrooms, tomatoes, and potatoes in a large pot, and add the stock. Cover and bring to a boil, then lower the heat and simmer gently for about 15 minutes. Add the broccoli, green beans, peas, zucchini, and small white beans, and continue cooking until the vegetables are soft. Add the soy sauce and pesto, and turn off the heat. Grate plenty of fresh pepper on top, and check the flavoring. You may want to add more pesto. Serve with a crusty bread to soak up the tasty broth.

Per serving: Calories 227, Protein 9 g, Fat 9 g, Carbohydrates 30 g

Yield: a big pot of soup, about 10 or 12 servings

2 medium onions, chopped
1 carrot, sliced or diced
¾ pound mushrooms, quartered
1½ pounds ripe red tomatoes, chopped
1 pound waxy new or red potatoes, diced
2 quarts vegetable stock
1 large stalk broccoli, cut into small florets, stalk peeled and sliced
1 cup diced string beans
1 cup fresh or frozen peas
1 large or 2 small zucchini, sliced ¼ inch thick
1 cup cooked small white beans
1 tablespoon soy sauce
½ cup or more Pesto Sauce, page 84
Lots of freshly grated pepper

Note: Other vegetables that are good to use are cauliflower, eggplants, leeks, bell peppers, snow peas, etc. Use whatever you have or can get.

Yield: 6 to 8 servings

2 cups dried shiitake mushrooms

1 large onion, minced

2 tablespoons oil

1 to 2 cups mushroom or
  vegetable stock

¾ cup white wine

1 teaspoon salt

1 tablespoon fresh chervil,
  chopped, or ½ teaspoon dried

1 tablespoon fresh thyme

1 tablespoon fresh tarragon,
  chopped, or ½ teaspoon dried

1 tablespoon fresh savory,
  chopped, or ½ teaspoon dried

⅓ cup minced fresh parsley

1 cup almond milk (commercial
  or homemade)

Salt and freshly ground pepper

Herbal Shiitake Bisque

*Fragrant and delicate, this delicious soup is
a wonderful start to any meal.*

Soak the shiitake in 5 cups of water for several hours or overnight. Remove the shiitake from the soaking liquid, reserving the liquid for the soup. With a sharp knife, cut off the stems. (The stems can be discarded or frozen for use in other recipes.) Slice the shiitake caps as thinly as possible. Heat the oil in a heavy-bottomed pot, and sauté the onion, covered, until translucent and tender. Add the sliced shiitake, soaking liquid, stock, white wine, and salt, and bring to a simmer. If you are using dried herbs, add them now, and simmer gently for 20 minutes. If using fresh herbs, add them after the 20 minutes of simmering, along with the minced parsley and almond milk. Simmer gently for another 5 minutes. Adjust the seasonings and add salt and pepper to taste.

Per serving: Calories 153, Protein 3 g, Fat 10 g, Carbohydrates 11 g

Roasted Red Bell Pepper Bisque

Yield: 6 servings

Elegant and delicious.

Roast the red peppers until blackened and soft by either grilling, placing directly over a gas burner, placing under a broiler, or baking at 450°F. Place the peppers in a brown paper bag, and allow to steam in their own heat for 20 minutes. Remove from the bag and peel the blackened skin. Cut in half, remove the tops, and clean out the seeds and veins. Set aside.

Sauté the onion in the oil in a covered, heavy-bottomed pot until tender. Add the celery and carrot, and continue to sauté for 5 minutes. Add the stock, wine, garlic, fruit juice concentrate, and the roasted pepper halves. Cover and simmer for 20 minutes. Purée in a blender until absolutely smooth, and return to the pot. Add the soymilk and reheat briefly. Season with salt and pepper to taste. If desired, swirl in cashew crème or top with tofu sour crème.

4 red bell peppers
1 onion, diced
1 tablespoon oil
1 stalk celery, sliced
1 carrot, sliced
4 cups vegetable stock
⅓ cup white wine
1 clove garlic
*1 tablespoon fruit juice
    concentrate (optional)*
½ to 1 cup soymilk
Salt and pepper
*Cashew Sour Crème, page 83, or
    Tofu Sour Crème, page 182, as
    garnish*

Per serving: Calories 66, Protein 1 g, Fat 2 g, Carbohydrates 6 g

Yield: 6 to 8 servings

2 cups chopped onions

1 tablespoon oil

6 to 8 ears sweet white
    corn, husked

3 cups vegetable stock

¾ cup white wine

1 to 2 cups soymilk

1 teaspoon dried or 1 tablespoon
    fresh thyme (optional)

Salt and pepper

Fresh Corn Chowder

Children and adults both love this lovely chowder which captures the essence of summer. It is seasoned ever so lightly to allow the sweetness of the fresh corn to come through. Do not try to substitute frozen corn; it will just not do the trick.

In a 4-quart pot, sauté the onions in the oil, covered, until very tender. With a sharp knife, hold each cob of corn upright on a cutting board and cut off the kernels. Add the kernels, stock, and wine to the pot, and bring to a boil. Reduce the heat, cover partly, and simmer gently for 10 minutes, or until relatively tender. Pour the soup into a blender, not filling the container more than halfway, and purée briefly, leaving some texture to the corn. Repeat with the rest of the soup. Return to the pot, add the soymilk and thyme, and season with salt and pepper to taste. Gently reheat until hot, but do not allow to boil.

Per serving: Calories 188, Protein 5 g, Fat 2 g, Carbohydrates 31 g

Yukon Gold Potato & Broccoli Chowder

Sauté the onion in the oil, covered, until tender. Add the potatoes, stock, and wine, and simmer until almost tender. Add the broccoli and lemon zest, and cook for 10 or 15 minutes until tender. Purée in a blender to a chunky consistency. Return to the pot, and thin down with soymilk. Season with salt and pepper to taste, and reheat gently. Do not boil.

Per serving: Calories 246, Protein 5 g, Fat 2 g, Carbohydrates 48 g

Yield: 4 to 6 servings

1 large onion, diced
1 tablespoon oil
2 pounds Yukon gold
    potatoes, peeled and cubed
1½ quarts stock
½ cup white wine
1 bunch broccoli tops, chopped
    roughly (about 4 or 5 cups)
Grated zest of ½ lemon
1 to 1½ cups soymilk
Salt and white pepper

Zesty Cauliflower & Fennel Soup

The mildness of cauliflower is given a bit of zip with the addition of fennel to produce a luscious soup.

Heat the oil in a heavy-bottomed pot. Sauté the onion in the oil, covered, until translucent. Add the celery and sauté an additional 5 minutes. Add the cauliflower, fennel, fennel seeds, stock, lemon zest and salt, and simmer for 20 minutes or until all the vegetables are very tender. Purée in batches in a blender until smooth. Return to the pot, add the soymilk, increasing the amount if necessary, and reheat gently. Adjust the seasoning with salt and pepper to taste.

Per serving: Calories 52, Protein 2 g, Fat 2 g, Carbohydrates 5 g

Yield: 6 to 8 servings

1 tablespoon oil
1 onion, sliced
2 stalks celery, sliced
1 head cauliflower, cut into
    1-inch pieces
1 bulb fennel (optional), sliced
1 tablespoon fennel seeds
3 to 4 cups stock (4 cups if fennel
    bulb is used)
Grated zest of 1 lemon
1 cup soymilk
Salt and pepper

2 tablespoons olive oil

1½ onions, sliced

1 stalk celery, sliced

2 pounds potatoes, peeled
    and cubed

3 cloves garlic, peeled and
    crushed or chopped

4 cups vegetable stock

½ cup white wine

⅓ cup sun-dried tomato bits,
    reconstituted in hot water
    to cover, then drained

1 cup packed basil leaves,
    julienned or minced

1 cup soymilk

Salt and pepper

MEDITERRANEAN POTATO SOUP

*This creamy potato soup is given a sun-drenched twist with the
addition of dried tomatoes, garlic, and fresh basil.*

Heat the oil in a heavy-bottomed pot. Add the onion and
celery, and sauté, covered, until translucent. Add the potatoes, garlic, stock, and wine. Cover partially and simmer
for 20 minutes, or until the potatoes are tender. Purée in
batches in a blender until smooth. Return to the pot and
add the sun-dried tomato bits, basil, and soymilk. Reheat
gently and season with salt and pepper to taste.

Per serving: Calories 195, Protein 4 g, Fat 5 g, Carbohydrates 31 g

Chestnut Soup with Apple Garnish

Yield: 4 to 6 servings

*A warm and wintery soup for Thanksgiving or Christmas.
Canned or bottled chestnuts can be substituted for
fresh chestnuts and are easier to use.*

In a large covered pot, sauté the chestnuts, onion, and carrot in 2 tablespoons of the margarine or oil for 5 to 6 minutes. Add the stock and simmer for about 20 minutes until the vegetables are soft. Purée in a blender or food processor until smooth. Add the soymilk or soy cream, and season with salt and pepper to taste. Add the brandy. Reheat gently but do not allow to boil.

Chop the apple into small pieces, and sauté over relatively high heat in the remaining tablespoon of margarine. Sprinkle with nutmeg and spoon some of the mixture on top of each serving.

*12 ounces chestnut meat (from
    1½ pounds fresh chestnuts,
    shelled and cooked)*
1 large onion, sliced
1 medium carrot, sliced
*3 tablespoons nonhydrogenated
    margarine or vegetable oil*
3 to 3½ cups vegetable stock
1½ cups soymilk or soy cream
Salt and pepper
1 to 2 tablespoons brandy
1 apple
Freshly grated nutmeg

Per serving: Calories 255, Protein 6 g, Fat 8 g, Carbohydrates 39 g

2 onions, chopped

2 cloves garlic, crushed

1 tablespoon oil or
    nonhydrogenated margarine

2 cups red wine

1½ pounds mushrooms, sliced

4½ cups soymilk

3 tablespoons powdered broth
    or 3 or 4 cubes bouillon

½ teaspoon dried tarragon

Salt and pepper

CREAMY MUSHROOM & RED WINE SOUP

Rich, deep, and delicious.

Sauté the onions and garlic in the oil, covered, until soft. Add 1¾ cups of the red wine and simmer, uncovered, for 5 to 7 minutes. Add the mushrooms, soymilk, broth, and tarragon, and simmer, partially covered, for 30 minutes. Purée in a food processor, leaving some texture. Return to the pot and season with salt and pepper to taste, and the remaining ¼ cup of wine, reheating gently.

Per serving: Calories 189, Protein 10 g, Fat 5 g, Carbohydrates 17 g

Cold Cream of Watercress & Apple Soup

This is one of my favorite soups. My good friend, Jamelia Saied, an excellent chef and an inspiration to all, first made this soup for me one wonderful Christmas Eve at her home. I immediately went back to my kitchen and tried to figure out the recipe. Here is my vegan version.

Sauté the onions and celery in the margarine in a large pot over low heat for 5 minutes. Add the potatoes and stock, cover, and simmer gently until the vegetables are soft. Add the thinly sliced apple, and continue cooking for another 3 or 4 minutes. Add the watercress and cook only another minute or two until the watercress wilts. Remove from the heat and purée in a blender or food processor until completely green and creamy—this may take a few minutes. Chill thoroughly. Add the soymilk or soy cream, and chill for another half hour.

Before serving, grate the apple and add it to the soup. Garnish with watercress sprigs and thin slices of apple if you like.

Per serving: Calories 152, Protein 6 g, Fat 7 g, Carbohydrates 19 g

Yield: 6 to 8 servings

See photo facing page 85.

2 medium onions, sliced

2 stalks celery, thinly sliced

3 tablespoons nonhydrogenated margarine

4 small potatoes, scrubbed well, peeled, if desired, and diced

6 cups vegetable stock (Chicken-Free Stock, page 92, works well for this)

¼ apple, thinly sliced

2 cups packed watercress

2 cups rich soymilk or soy cream

1 large or 2 small crisp, sweet apples, grated

2 cups diced cucumbers
(preferably Japanese or
European seedless variety)
⅓ cup chopped onions
¾ cup diced potatoes
2 cups vegetable stock
½ cup soymilk
½ cup soy yogurt or soy sour
cream, page 12
Salt and pepper

Cucumber Vichyssoise

*A refreshing vichyssoise with the addition
of cucumbers. Serve it on a hot day.*

Peel the cucumbers if their skins are bitter or waxed. Place the vegetables and stock in a covered pot, and cook until soft, about 10 or 15 minutes. Purée in a blender or food processor. Add the soymilk and soy yogurt or soy sour cream, season with salt and pepper to taste, and refrigerate until thoroughly chilled. Garnish with a few slivers of cucumber.

Per serving: Calories 65, Protein 5 g, Fat 2 g, Carbohydrates 9 g

Quick Avocado & Cucumber Soup

Yield: 4 servings

This delicate soup can be whipped up in minutes.
If you don't have time to chill it, add ice cubes!

Sauté the onion in the oil, covered, until soft. Combine the onion in a blender with all the other ingredients except the soymilk or soy cream, and whip until smooth and creamy. Mix in the soymilk or soy cream, and season with salt and pepper to taste. Chill thoroughly before serving, if possible. If all the ingredients are cold, the soup should chill in a couple of hours. Do not let it stand overnight, as the avocado will cause the soup to change color. To help prevent discoloration, place plastic wrap directly on top of the soup.

Per serving: Calories 204, Protein 5 g, Fat 8 g, Carbohydrates 13 g

1 small onion, chopped
1 tablespoon oil or
    nonhydrogenated margarine
1½ ripe avocados, pitted and diced
1 large cucumber, peeled and diced
2 tablespoons white wine
3 tablespoons orange juice
2 tablespoons lemon juice
1 cup chilled vegetable stock
1 cup soymilk or soy cream
Salt and pepper

Yield: 4 to 6 servings

4 *very ripe tomatoes, diced*

1 *Japanese cucumber with peel
    intact, diced, or ½ salad
    cucumber, diced (peeled if
    skin is bitter or waxed)*

½ *green, red, or yellow bell
    pepper, diced*

½ *medium onion, diced*

1 *to 2 cloves garlic*

1 *cup vegetable stock*

1 *to 3 tablespoons red wine vinegar*

1 *to 2 tablespoons extra-virgin
    olive oil (optional)*

2 *tablespoons red wine (optional)*

Salt and pepper

*Optional toppings: finely chopped
    tomatoes, onions, red or green
    peppers, cucumbers, capers, and
    croutons*

GAZPACHO

*Here is my version of the famous Spanish soup that is so good during
summertime when vegetables are at their sweetest.*

Blend all the ingredients in a food processor or blender to
the desired consistency. Some people like it absolutely
smooth, while others like to leave some texture. Chill thoroughly and pass the various toppings around at serving
time, if desired.

Per serving: Calories 74, Protein 2 g, Fat 4 g, Carbohydrates 9 g

Chilled Carrot & Orange Soup

Yield: 6 to 8 servings

I was once asked to prepare a dinner where every dish served had to contain carrots as the main ingredient. Here is the unusual and refreshing soup I created for that hot summer day.

Sauté the onions and carrots in the oil or margarine for about 10 minutes in a covered saucepan, stirring frequently. Add the stock, diced potato, and orange zest. Cover and simmer gently until the vegetables are soft. Add the wine and continue cooking for 5 more minutes to take the edge off the wine. Allow to cool. Purée until smooth, then add the soymilk or soy cream. Add the freshly squeezed orange juice a little at a time, checking the flavor all the while. It should taste pleasantly sweet, but not like juice. Season with salt and pepper to taste, and chill for several hours before serving.

Per serving: Calories 104, Protein 3 g, Fat 5 g, Carbohydrates 13 g

1 medium onion, sliced

1 pound carrots, sliced

2 tablespoons oil or nonhydrogenated margarine

3½ cups vegetable stock

1 small potato, peeled or scrubbed well, and diced

3 strips orange zest, ½ inch wide and 2 inches long

¼ cup white wine

1 cup soymilk or soy cream (more if necessary)

Juice of ½ orange (or less)

Salt and white pepper

See photo facing page 85.

Yield: 4 to 6 servings

1 medium onion, sliced

1 tablespoon nonhydrogenated
    margarine or vegetable oil

6 ounces potatoes (approximately
    1 medium), preferably new or
    waxy-type, peeled and diced

1 cup vegetable stock

12 ounces carrot juice, freshly
    squeezed or commercial

8 ounces unsweetened tropical
    fruit juice (preferably
    containing pineapple, orange,
    and banana juice)

1 teaspoon curry powder (or
    more, depending on strength)

Salt

1 cup rich soymilk

Chilled Curried Carrot & Fruit Soup

*A delectable soup that is slightly spicy and sweet at the same time.
Simple to make because it uses carrot and fruit juices, it is quite
unique and will surely stimulate appetites.*

Sauté the onion in the margarine or oil in a covered
saucepan until soft. Add the potatoes, stock, juices, curry
powder, and salt to taste. Bring to a boil, cover, and simmer
gently for 20 minutes, or until the vegetables are very soft.
Allow to cool a bit before puréeing. Place in a blender or
food processor, and purée until very smooth. Chill thoroughly, then add the soymilk and chill for another hour or
so before serving. Adjust seasonings as necessary, adding
more salt or curry. If desired, swirl some soy cream or
cashew cream in each portion as garnish.

Per serving: Calories 138, Protein 5 g, Fat 3 g, Carbohydrates 23 g

Chilled Spiced Autumn Soup

Yield: 4 to 6 servings

A new twist on pumpkin soup, as good on a summer's eve as in the autumn.

Sauté the onion, celery, and garlic in the oil until soft. Add the stock, squash, yam, nutmeg, and ginger. Cover and cook until very soft. Purée until smooth in a food processor or blender. Add the soymilk, season to taste with salt and pepper, and chill overnight or for several hours before serving.

Per serving: Calories 518, Protein 13 g, Fat 9 g, Carbohydrates 102 g

1 large onion, sliced

1 stalk celery, sliced

2 cloves garlic, crushed

1 tablespoon oil

1½ quarts Chicken-Free Stock, page 92

1½ pounds banana squash, kabocha (Japanese pumpkin), acorn squash, or pumpkin, peeled and cut into slices or chunks

1 pound yams, peeled and sliced or diced

½ teaspoon nutmeg

4 to 6 slivers fresh ginger (½ inch x 1 inch x ⅛ inch)

½ cup soymilk or cashew milk

Salt and pepper

Quick & Tasty
Tofu Cream Soups

Almost any vegetables can be creamed with tofu to make tasty, low-calorie soups that contain no added fat, flour, or other thickening agent. I love these soups because they are not only easy to make but don't taste like diet food! Here are several versions, all of which can be served hot or cold. Try other vegetables as well, and create your own soups.

Cream of Pumpkin Soup

Yield: 4 servings

You might want to try using Japanese pumpkin (kabocha). The meat is richer and sweeter than that from American pumpkins.

Peel the pumpkin or kabocha, chop into 1-inch chunks, and cook with the onion in the stock until tender, about 15 minutes. Purée the tofu and soymilk in a blender until perfectly creamy. Transfer to another dish. Without washing the blender, pour in the soup mixture and purée until smooth. Pour this back into the pot, and mix in the tofu purée. Chill thoroughly if you are going to serve it cold; otherwise, heat gently, but do not allow it to boil, or it will curdle. Season to taste with salt, pepper, and nutmeg.

Per serving: Calories 128, Protein 8 g, Fat 3 g, Carbohydrates 19 g

1 pound pumpkin, banana squash, or kabocha
½ medium onion, sliced
2½ cups vegetable stock
8 ounces tofu
½ cup soymilk
2 tablespoons white wine
Salt, pepper, and nutmeg

12 ounces frozen corn
½ medium onion, sliced
2½ cups vegetable stock
8 ounces tofu
½ cup soymilk
2 tablespoons white wine
Salt and pepper

CREAM of CORN SOUP

Follow the cream of pumpkin soup recipe on page 113, using the ingredients listed here and substituting the corn for the pumpkin.

Per serving: Calories 134, Protein 8 g, Fat 3 g, Carbohydrates 21 g

Yield: 4 servings

8 ounces frozen or fresh peas
½ medium onion, sliced
2½ cups vegetable stock
8 ounces tofu
½ cup soymilk
2 tablespoons white wine
1 teaspoon sweetener
Salt and pepper

CREAM of GREEN PEA SOUP

Follow the cream of pumpkin soup recipe on page 113, using the ingredients listed here. For this soup the amount of tofu and soymilk may be decreased if desired. This soup is especially good chilled.

Per serving: Calories 120, Protein 8 g, Fat 3 g, Carbohydrates 15 g

Entrees

These recipes range from the very simple to the highly elaborate. All of them are extremely good; some make good choices for family dining and others will be perfect for entertaining. Gone are the heavy, beany vegetarian creations of yore and "gourmet" efforts relying heavily on cheese and eggs. The following recipes are delicious, not simply as vegetarian food, but as food in itself.

As the weather begins to cool in the fall, serve the wonderful chestnut cabbage rolls with red wine sauce or make some tofu fettuccine and serve it with tofu bourguignon. For that really special dinner, try French moussaka with rich brown sauce. For a simple winter repast, try the herbed soybean casserole with some homemade whole grain bread. Whatever the mood and occasion, you will find a recipe here to suit it.

8 to 12 crêpes, page 140

¾ cup wild rice
2¾ cups vegetable stock
¼ medium onion, finely minced

2 stalks celery, thinly sliced
2 tablespoons canola oil
¾ medium onion,
  roughly chopped
¼ pound mushrooms,
  thickly sliced
5 to 6 shiitake mushrooms,
  fresh or reconstituted
  (pages 9-10), cut into
  quarters or eighths
½ cup oyster mushrooms,
  separated into small clumps,
  or other mushrooms
  (chanterelles or morels)
1 large tomato, chopped
½ teaspoon rubbed sage
1 tablespoon soy sauce
Salt and pepper

Wild Rice Crêpes

Thank goodness wild rice is really not a rice at all, but a type of grass. If it were rice, I would have had to smuggle it into Japan all those years I lived there in order to enjoy it in luscious dishes such as these crêpes. Serve with Nutty Almond Sauce, page 69, Madeira Mushroom Sauce, page 76, or Rich Brown Sauce, page 78, for a gourmet entrée.

Prepare the crêpes as described on page 140 (or according to your favorite recipe). If you have a supply stored in your freezer, take them out to defrost.

Place the wild rice with the stock and the finely minced onion in a saucepan with a tightly fitting lid. Turn the heat up to high. After it comes to a boil, turn the heat to low, and cook for about an hour, or until all the liquid is gone and the rice is tender.

While the rice is cooking, sauté the sliced celery in the oil until relatively tender. Add the roughly chopped onion, mushrooms, shiitake, and oyster mushrooms, and continue sautéing until the vegetables are relatively soft. Add the cooked rice, the chopped tomato, sage, soy sauce, salt, and pepper, and continue to cook for another 10 or 15 minutes. Fill the crêpes with the mixture, roll up, and heat for 10 minutes in a 350°F oven before serving. Serve with Nutty Almond Sauce, page 69, Rich Brown Sauce, page 78, or Madeira Mushroom Sauce, page 76.

Per serving: Calories 542, Protein 18 g, Fat 18 g, Carbohydrates 78 g

Tri-Colored Pepper & Quinoa Charlotte, page 130

Deep Sea Crêpes

Oyster mushrooms, chanterelles, and wakame (a sea vegetable) are combined with a cashew sour crème to produce the textures and flavors of seafood, sans the scallops, shrimp, and other living critters. Serve with white wine sauce or béchamel sauce.

Sauté the shallots and garlic in the oil until tender. Add the mushrooms and sauté over high heat for several minutes. Deglaze the pan by adding the white wine and scraping the bottom with a spatula. Finely chop the wakame and add to the pan, along with the herbs and sour crème. Combine over low heat for a minute, then season to taste with salt and pepper. The filling can be set aside until later or used right away.

Place several tablespoons of this filling along the bottom of each crêpe, and roll up tightly. Place on a baking tray or cookie sheet, and bake at 350°F for about 5 to 10 minutes to warm thoroughly. Serve with either of the white wine sauces or béchamel sauce.

Per serving: Calories 272, Protein 7 g, Fat 10 g, Carbohydrates 34 g

Yield: 6 servings

¼ cup minced shallots

1 tablespoon minced garlic

2 tablespoons oil

½ pound chanterelle mushrooms

½ pound oyster mushrooms

2 tablespoons white wine

approximately 1 tablespoon dried wakame, reconstituted in water (to make ¼ cup)

3 tablespoons minced fresh tarragon

3 tablespoons minced fresh chervil

½ cup Rich Cashew Sour Crème, page 83

Salt and pepper

12 crêpes, page 140

Tangy or Sweet White Wine Sauce, pages 72-73, or Béchamel Sauce, page 68

Portobello & Polenta Lasagne, pages 136-37

Have ready:

8 crêpes, page 140

Lemon Pepper Sauce

1½ cups vegetable stock

1 cup white wine

1 cup carrot juice

1 tablespoon whole black
   peppercorns

½ teaspoon fennel seeds

2 mushrooms, sliced

1 medium onion, sliced

Zest of two lemons

½ cup or more rich,
   unflavored soymilk

1 tablespoon cornstarch

Approximately 2 tablespoons water

1 tablespoon oil

1 tablespoon chopped garlic

8 ounces asparagus, trimmed and
   cut into 2-inch lengths or left
   mostly whole, as desired

8 ounces oyster mushrooms

2 to 3 tablespoons white wine

Salt and pepper

Asparagus & Oyster Mushroom Crêpes with Lemon Pepper Sauce

Very light and simple, yet elegant; great if you happen to have some leftover crêpes on hand and want to make something rewarding without much effort. The lemon pepper sauce is creamy and light, a nice balance of flavors with hints of sweet, tangy, savory, and peppery. Also fat free!

Prepare the lemon pepper sauce by placing the vegetable stock, white wine, carrot juice, peppercorns, fennel seeds, mushrooms, and onion slices in a saucepan, cover, and simmer over medium-high heat about 1 hour until reduced by two-thirds. Add the lemon zest and simmer for another 10 minutes. Strain the mixture through a strainer or colander over a bowl to catch the juices, pressing the juices out of the vegetables with the back of a wooden spoon. Discard the vegetables.

Pour the juice back into the pan, add the soymilk, and warm over low heat. Dissolve the cornstarch in the water, and drizzle it in, stirring constantly, until the sauce is lightly thickened.

To make the crêpe filling, heat the oil in a large skillet. Add the garlic and allow it to sizzle until it turns white. Over high heat, add the asparagus and mushrooms, tossing and stirring, until the mushrooms have browned. Add the wine to deglaze the pan by scraping up any browned vegetable bits into the liquid. Season to taste with salt and pepper, and roll in the crêpes. Serve with the sauce

Per serving: Calories 284, Protein 8 g, Fat 6 g, Carbohydrates 36 g

Orange Coconut Curry with Grilled Vegetables

This is an elegant curry, fragrant, slightly sweet, and light. The sauce is very simple and can be prepared ahead of time, and the vegetables can be either roasted in the oven or grilled. Excellent with fluffy couscous (with a few currants thrown in) or basmati rice.

Heat the oil in a sauté pan. Add the seeds and sauté for a minute until they pop. Add the onion and sauté over low heat until translucent. Add the curry powder and continue to sauté for another minute. Add the orange juice and coconut milk, and simmer for another 5 minutes if you plan to serve immediately. Do not overcook; the fragrance will be lost. If you are setting the sauce aside for a day or so, do not simmer; turn off the heat. Season with salt to taste. At serving time, arrange grilled or roasted vegetables on a plate, and pour the sauce over them.

Per serving: Calories 316, Protein 4 g, Fat 21 g, Carbohydrates 23 g

Yield: 4 to 5 servings

1 tablespoon oil
1 teaspoon coriander seeds
1 teaspoon fennel seeds
1 teaspoon mustard seeds
1 onion, finely chopped
2 tablespoons curry powder
½ cup frozen orange juice concentrate
1 can coconut milk
Salt
About 4 to 5 cups sliced vegetables such as asparagus, red or yellow bell peppers, zucchini, sweet potatoes, mushrooms, fennel, green beans, etc., grilled or roasted in the oven (see Roasted Vegetables, page 183)

6 large onions

2 tablespoons nonhydrogenated
  margarine
1 cup ground cashews
1¾ cups cooked long grain brown
  rice, or brown basmati rice
  (for a slightly nuttier flavor)
½ cup chopped parsley
1¼ teaspoon rubbed dried sage
Salt and pepper

½ cup white wine
½ cup vegetable stock

½ cup rich soymilk or soy cream,
  or almond milk (optional)
Tangy White Wine Sauce, page 72
  (optional)

SAVORY ONIONS WITH CASHEW-RICE STUFFING

These can be made a day or two ahead and baked an hour or so before serving. If you have the time, make the tangy white wine sauce to serve with it. A simpler sauce can be made by adding some soymilk or cream to the basting liquid, as explained below.

You can save yourself the tears when dealing with onions if you refrigerate them at least overnight or soak them in cold water for 30 minutes after you peel them. Cut a slice off the top and bottom of each onion. The onions should then sit upright without rolling over. With a tablespoon or a melon ball scooper, remove the insides of the onions from the top, leaving a wall ⅓ inch thick all around. Chop this pulp finely and set it aside.

Place the onion shells in a stovetop steamer or covered dish in a microwave, and cook until a fork pierces through the sides easily but the onions still retain their shape. They should not become mushy. Allow to cool before handling.

Melt the margarine in a large skillet, add the chopped onion, and toss together. Cover the skillet and sauté the onion until tender, stirring occasionally. Mix with the ground cashews, brown rice, parsley, sage, and salt and pepper to taste. If the mixture seems dry, a little soy or almond milk can be added, but the sautéed onions should provide enough moisture, especially if they were covered while being cooked.

Preheat the oven to 425°F. Stuff the cooked and cooled onions with the rice and cashew mixture. Place the onions in a shallow casserole or gratin dish, and pour the stock and white wine around them. Cover loosely with aluminum foil, and bake for 20 minutes. Then turn down the oven to 375°F, and continue baking for another 40 minutes.

Remove the aluminum foil during the last 20 minutes to allow the tops to brown. If you find that the onions are not browning during that period, pour the liquid from the baking dish into a saucepan, and continue baking the onions dry.

For the sauce, either make and serve Tangy White Wine Sauce, page 72, or add the soymilk or almond milk to the remaining cooking liquid, and simmer for a few minutes in a saucepan to let flavors mingle and thicken slightly.

Per serving: Calories 324, Protein 10 g, Fat 15 g, Carbohydrates 41 g

Vol-au-Vent with Three Mushrooms

You can use any three types of wild mushrooms for this dish.

Sauté the shallots and red pepper in the margarine or oil until tender. Add the mushrooms to the shallots, and sauté until the mushrooms are tender. Add the flour to the sautéed vegetables, and cook for 2 to 3 minutes. Combine 2 cups of the white wine sauce with the mushrooms and shallots, and cook until thick. Add the chopped parsley and cook for another minute. Immediately pour the creamed mixture into 4 to 6 hot pastry or vol-au-vent shells. Serve on individual plates with the additional wine sauce poured around.

Per serving: Calories 380, Protein 12 g, Fat 12 g, Carbohydrates 62 g

Yield: 4 to 6 servings

4 shallots, minced
½ red bell pepper, chopped
2 tablespoons nonhydrogenated margarine or vegetable oil
20 ounces any combination of 3 varieties of mushrooms (fresh shiitake, oyster, button, morels, chanterelles etc.,) sliced or torn, depending on the variety used
6 tablespoons flour
3 to 4 cups Tangy White Wine Sauce, page 72
½ cup chopped parsley
4 to 6 commercial puff pastry or vol-au-vent shells

*1¼ pounds whole chestnuts,
    or one 14-ounce can or bottle
    shelled chestnuts*

*1 medium cabbage (savoy, if
    possible)*
1 tablespoon oil
1 medium onion, finely chopped
1 cup cooked brown rice

Chestnut-Filled Cabbage Rolls
with Red Wine Sauce

*In Japan chestnuts come into season in the fall, and for a brief month
the markets are filled with them. Although I have always found
cooking and peeling chestnuts to be a chore, I always manage to make
these cabbage rolls at least once or twice during chestnut season—they
are delicious enough to be worth the trouble. The rich but fat-free red
wine sauce is cooked along with the cabbage rolls, so aside from the
task of removing chestnuts from their shells (a job which is greatly
expedited by following the instructions below), it is a relatively simple
dish to make. I have tried using dried chestnuts in this dish without
good results. Canned or bottled chestnuts, if they have been packed in
water and not sugar syrup, can be substituted for the fresh ones
successfully and will make preparing the dish a breeze. The filling can
be made several days in advance and refrigerated or frozen. Final
assembly and cooking should begin two hours before serving.*

If using fresh, whole chestnuts, boil them for 20 to 30 minutes, and allow to cool enough to handle before removing
them from their shells. I find the whole job goes much
faster if the flat side of the chestnut is simply sliced off with
a small, sharp knife, then the meat scooped out with a
small spoon. The chestnuts do not have to come out whole,
as they will be chopped up anyway. Remove any inner
brown skin that comes out, since it can be bitter. Chop the
chestnuts roughly.

If you are using canned or bottled chestnuts, simply drain,
rinse, and chop up roughly. (Some brands are already
chopped.)

Core the cabbage with a sharp knife, then remove the outer
12 to 16 leaves. Shred the rest of the cabbage, and steam or
microwave the outer leaves until tender, but not overly

soft—they should be pliable, not mushy. Heat the oil in a pan, and sauté the onion and shredded cabbage until soft and reduced in volume. Place in a bowl with the chopped chestnuts and brown rice.

Make a thick white sauce by melting the margarine in a small saucepan, adding the flour, and cooking a minute. Then add the hot soymilk, stirring with a whisk. Cook over low heat, stirring constantly, until very thick. Flavor to taste with salt and pepper. Add this to the cabbage and chestnuts, along with the dill seeds, allspice, and nutmeg. Mix well, adjusting the seasonings as desired. (The flavor of the dill will be released during the cooking.)

To stuff the cabbage leaves, take one leaf at a time and place it in front of you with the outside of the leaf facing up. With a small, sharp knife, slice off the hard rib that forms a bump. Turn the leaf over and place about ⅓ cup of the mixture at the bottom of the leaf over the rib. Fold the right and left sides over, then roll up tightly. Secure with a toothpick or piece of thread if the rolls won't fit absolutely snug in the pan.

Place the rolls loose side down in a deep frying pan or Dutch oven. Mix the ingredients for the red wine sauce, and pour it over the rolls. Top with a tight-fitting lid, and cook over low heat for 45 to 50 minutes, or until the sauce has been reduced to a thick glaze.

Per serving: Calories 258, Protein 5 g, Fat 6 g, Carbohydrates 46 g

2 tablespoons nonhydrogenated
   margarine or vegetable oil
4 tablespoons flour
1 cup hot soymilk
Salt and pepper
½ teaspoon whole dill seeds
½ teaspoon ground allspice
¼ teaspoon nutmeg

Red Wine Sauce:

1½ cups vegetable stock
1 cup red wine
2 tablespoons soy sauce
4 tablespoons mirin
4 tablespoons tomato paste
2 bay leaves

1 medium onion, chopped

1 large clove garlic, minced

2 tablespoons olive oil

1½ cups cooked soybeans
(firm but tender)

1 medium potato, preferably
waxy, cut into ½-inch cubes

⅓ pound mushrooms,
thickly sliced

1½ cups red wine

1 tablespoon miso

1 tablespoon tomato paste

1 teaspoon salt

1 teaspoon dried marjoram

1 teaspoon dried rosemary

½ teaspoon ground sage

½ cup minced parsley

Bread crumbs for topping
(optional)

Herbed Soybean Casserole or Stew

This rich and delicious concoction will warm you through and through on a cold winter night. The quantity of liquid given here will produce a luscious casserole, but a few extra cups of stock, red wine, and seasonings can be thrown in to extend it and produce a hearty stew that is quite fine to serve an after-theater crowd. If you opt for the stew rather than the casserole, you may cook it on top of the stove instead of the oven. With a salad and some crusty bread, it is a meal in itself.

Preheat the oven to 350°F. Sauté the onions and garlic in the oil until tender, then mix with the remaining ingredients, and place in a casserole dish. Cover and bake for 1 hour. If desired, remove the cover for the last 10 minutes of baking, and top with bread crumbs. The liquid will have reduced to a nicely flavored sauce, and the potatoes and soybeans will be very tender.

Per serving: Calories 278, Protein 11 g, Fat 7 g, Carbohydrates 27 g

Soybean Stew

Sauté the onions and garlic in a large Dutch oven until tender. Add the remaining ingredients, plus an extra ½ cup of red wine and about 3 cups of vegetable stock. Cover and simmer for 45 minutes to 1 hour. Adjust the seasonings as necessary, adding more miso, tomato paste, etc.

Paella

Yield: 6 to 8 large servings

See photo facing page 84.

This happens to be one of my favorite dishes. Having turned vegetarian at a young age, I must admit to never having tasted the real thing. However, some Spanish visitors of the restaurant told me that this vegetarian rendition was reminiscent of some of the best they'd had. I happen to adore the flavor of saffron and use it liberally, although you may decrease (or increase) to taste.

Heat the olive oil in a large sauté pan. (Cast-iron works great and boosts the iron content!) Cook the onions in the oil until tender, stirring often. Add the rice and saffron, and cook until slightly nutty. Add the remaining ingredients except the vegetables, stir well, and bring to a simmer. After 5 minutes, add the vegetables and taste the broth, adding more salt if necessary. Cover loosely and continue cooking for another 15 minutes or so, stirring every few minutes, until the rice is tender but suspended in a delicious red glaze. Serve immediately with a big salad.

Per serving: Calories 249, Protein 4 g, Fat 8 g, Carbohydrates 33 g

¼ cup extra-virgin olive oil
2 onions, sliced
2 cups medium or short grain rice
2 to 3 very large pinches of saffron
6 cloves garlic, minced
2⅔ cups vegetable stock
2 cups crushed tomatoes, canned,
*   or very ripe fresh diced tomatoes*
1⅓ cups red wine
2 teaspoons dried basil
Approximately 4 cups sliced
*   vegetables of choice, such as red*
*   bell peppers, mushrooms,*
*   zucchini, snap peas, shiitake*
*   mushrooms, eggplant, lobster*
*   mushrooms, yellow summer*
*   squash, and asparagus.*
*   (Cabbage family veggies, such*
*   as cabbage, broccoli, and bok*
*   choy, are not good in this.)*
Salt and pepper, to taste

1 cup wild rice

1 cup brown basmati rice

4 cups vegetable stock

1 teaspoon sea salt

1 winter squash of choice (6 to 8
    pounds): sugar pie pumpkin,
    kabocha pumpkin, gold nugget,
    etc., or two 3- to 4-pound
    pumpkins

2 tablespoons olive oil

3 stalks celery, sliced

1 large onion, minced

6 ounces sliced fresh shiitake
    mushrooms

¾ cup whole almonds

⅓ cup marsala or Madeira

½ cup chopped fresh parsley

1 tablespoon rubbed sage

1 teaspoon dried thyme

1 teaspoon dried rosemary

1 teaspoon dried marjoram

Salt and pepper

The Great Holiday Pumpkin

Several years ago, I received a call from a local television station asking if I could demonstrate a recipe for a vegetarian Thanksgiving entrée on television the next day. As with many of the TV appearances I had made to date, it was to be but a five-minute segment. I set to work immediately coming up with the dish below to present, testing it on a group of eager diners that night to make sure that it would receive approval from the "tasters" on the show. It met with everyone's approval that night and yielded a surprised, "That's delicious!" from the newscaster the next day. Naturally, the dish I created did indeed take more than five minutes to prepare, but it is relatively simple to make. If made in steps, as I did for the show, it can actually be assembled in five minutes, and you can put on your own show for your guests.

In a 2-quart pot with a tight-fitting lid, combine the wild and basmati rice with the vegetable stock and salt, and bring to a boil. Reduce the heat to low, and cook for 45 minutes, or until the rice is tender.

Meanwhile, preheat the oven to 350°F. With a sharp knife, carve or cut out the top of the pumpkin. Scrape out all the seeds and threads. Replace the top and place the pumpkin in a baking dish with 1 inch of water. Prebake for 20 to 25 minutes, depending on the size of the pumpkin, or until slightly, but not thoroughly, tender. Most of the water should have evaporated. If not, pour off the water and set the pumpkin aside. (This can be done one day ahead.)

Heat a sauté pan, then add the oil and heat another moment. Sauté the celery and onion for about 5 minutes, or until crispy-tender. Add the shiitake mushroom slices, and cook for a brief moment. Toast the almonds on a small pan in the oven for about 10 minutes until slightly browned, and then chop roughly.

In a large bowl, combine the rice, vegetables, almonds, marsala and herbs. Season to taste with salt and pepper. (This filling can be made one to two days ahead if desired.) Stuff the pumpkin, replace the lid, and return to the oven to bake for another 20 to 25 minutes, or until the pumpkin is completely tender. To serve, scoop out some of the filling with the flesh of the pumpkin, and top with Holiday Gravy (below).

Per serving: Calories 414, Protein 9 g, Fat 12 g, Carbohydrates 61 g

Holiday Gravy for Pumpkin

Yield: 3⅓ cups (4 to 6 servings)

Heat the oil in a saucepan. Add the flour and cook over low heat for about 2 minutes, stirring constantly with a wooden spoon. While whipping quickly with a whisk, pour in the hot stock all at once. It will thicken quickly. Add the wine, soy sauce, miso, and nutritional yeast, and simmer gently for an additional 5 to 6 minutes.

For a fat-free version, delete the oil and combine all the ingredients in a blender until smooth. Heat in a saucepan, stirring constantly, until thickened.

5 tablespoons canola or olive oil
½ cup unbleached flour
2 cups hot vegetable, vegetarian chicken, or mushroom stock
½ cup dry white wine
2 tablespoons soy sauce
2 tablespoons light or medium miso
3 tablespoons nutritional yeast flakes

Per serving: Calories 152, Protein 3 g, Fat 10 g, Carbohydrates 10 g

Two 12-ounce blocks atsuage
   (the deep fried tofu available
   in Asian groceries and
   some supermarkets,
   also sold as tofu "cutlets")

Marinade for tofu:

3½ tablespoons cider or rice
   vinegar
1 teaspoon tomato paste
2 tablespoons sake or sherry
   (optional)
2 tablespoons mirin
1 tablespoon soy sauce
Salt and pepper

Vegetables:

1 large onion, cut into eighths
   and separated into leaves
1 tablespoon oil
1 small carrot, cut into sticks
   or slices
4 to 8 shiitake mushrooms,
   fresh or reconstituted,
   cut into halves or quarters
1 green bell pepper, cut into
   1-inch squares
1 cup pineapple chunks

SWEET & SOUR TOFU

Here is a vegetarian version of sweet and sour pork. Deep-fried tofu cutlets (called "atsuage" in Japanese) are first marinated, then baked until chewy before being combined with vegetables and a sauce sweetened primarily with apple juice.

If you are unable to buy atsuage ready-made, you can deep-fry pressed or firm blocks of tofu at 375°F for 3 to 5 minutes until golden brown. Drain well.

Cut the deep-fried tofu into 1-inch chunks. Mix the ingredients for the marinade, and marinate the tofu in it for 2 hours, basting or turning the pieces over occasionally. Bake on an oiled cookie sheet for 30 to 35 minutes in a 350°F oven, or until brown and chewy.

Sauté the onion in the oil until tender but still crisp. Add the carrots, shiitake, and green pepper, and sauté 3 to 4 minutes. Add the pineapple along with all the ingredients for the sweet and sour sauce, except the kuzu or arrowroot. Simmer gently for 10 minutes to allow the flavors to mingle. Add the baked tofu. Dissolve the arrowroot or kuzu in a small amount of water, and add slowly in a steady stream. Stir constantly until the sauce is thick and has a glazed appearance. If too thin, add more kuzu or arrowroot.

Serve with brown rice. If desired, a little chopped cilantro may be sprinkled on top.

Per serving: Calories 354, Protein 13 g, Fat 9 g, Carbohydrates 60 g

Sweet and Sour Sauce:

2¼ cups apple juice

3 tablespoons tomato paste

½ cup rice or cider vinegar*

3½ tablespoons soy sauce

3 tablespoons sweetener

1 to 2 tablespoons mirin

1 to 2 teaspoons or more miso (optional—it will add some depth to the flavor)

1 tablespoon kuzu, or 2 to 3 tablespoons arrowroot or cornstarch

*Rice vinegar is milder and sweeter than cider vinegar. If you use cider vinegar, reduce the amount slightly.

Yield: 6 to 10 servings

See photo facing page 116 and on
the front cover.

1 cup quinoa

2 cups vegetable stock

2 tablespoons white wine

1/3 cup currants

1 tablespoon oil

1/4 cup pine nuts

2 red, 2 green, and 2 yellow
    bell peppers

Tri-Colored Pepper &
Quinoa Charlotte

*Although easy to make, this light dish is so colorful and elegant that
your guests will marvel at your prowess in the kitchen. Quinoa is a
welcome change to the usual grains and is extremely light. The
peppers can be roasted the day before to make assembly go quickly.*

Place the quinoa, stock, wine, currants, and oil in a 2-quart
pot, and bring to a boil. Reduce heat to low, cover, and cook
for about 30 minutes, or until the quinoa is light, fluffy, and
tender. Toast the pine nuts lightly in a frying pan over low
heat. (No oil is needed; just stir every minute or so until
lightly browned.) Add the toasted nuts to the quinoa, and
stir to combine everything.

While the quinoa is cooking (which you can do up to one
day ahead), prepare the peppers for roasting. They may be
grilled over an open flame until blackened, or placed in a
400°F oven for about 20 to 30 minutes until somewhat
blackened. Place in a paper bag to allow them to "weep,"
and set aside until cool enough to handle. When they are

cool, remove the blackened skin and seeds, and discard. Cut the peppers into strips ½ inch wide.

Preheat the oven to 350°F. To assemble the individual charlottes, you will use a muffin tin or a similar small mold. Cut out small rounds of parchment or waxed paper, and place at the bottom of each muffin insert. Oil the sides and parchment well. Place the peppers in each insert, strip by strip, next to each other and up the sides of the muffin cups so the entire bottom and sides are covered. Place 2 tablespoons of the "chevre" on the bottom, then pack in the quinoa mixture lightly. Bake for 10 minutes. Flip over at once onto a cookie sheet; the individual charlottes should come right out. Carefully place each individual charlotte on a plate, and surround with tomato concassé. Serve immediately.

Per serving: Calories 302, Protein 13 g, Fat 8 g, Carbohydrates 37 g

1 cup Tofu "Chevre," page 172
Salt and pepper
1 recipe Grilled Tomato Concassé,
  page 86

Yield: 4 to 6 servings

8 ounces tofu
1 tablespoon oil (optional)
½ teaspoon salt
2 cups high-gluten flour,
    unbleached white, whole
    wheat, or a combination
    (Semolina can also be used.)

Homemade Tofu Pasta

Tofu substitutes wonderfully for eggs in this great cholesterol-free homemade pasta. Be sure to use a flour with a high gluten content to get a pasta that will hold up. It is much simpler than it may seem to make your own pasta, and the rewards are great.

Cream the tofu in a blender or food processor, and add the oil and salt. If you are using a food processor, the flour can be added directly to the work bowl and processed until mixed. Otherwise, remove the tofu after creaming, and mix it with the flour in a separate bowl. Since a pliable dough is desired, start with 1½ cups of flour and add the remaining ½ cup a little at a time to produce an earlobe consistency that is soft but not sticky. Knead the dough for about 10 minutes until stretchy and very smooth. Allow to rest for 5 minutes before rolling it out.

Flour the rolling surface and roll out the dough ¹⁄₁₆ inch thick (or twice that if you like thicker pasta). Allow it to dry for 15 minutes before cutting it into the desired shape and length. With a sharp knife, cut the dough into lasagne, fettuccine, linguine, spaghetti, or whatever you like. If you have a pasta machine, follow the manufacturer's directions for cutting.

Freshly made pasta cooks in 2 to 3 minutes, depending on the size and length. After bringing a pot of salted water to boil, add the pasta and cook al dente. Drain and serve immediately with the sauce of your choice, as it will cool quickly, softening as it does.

If you are not going to cook the pasta right away, leave it on the surface where it was cut, covered loosely with plastic wrap, or sprinkle with flour and pile neatly on a plate so that the noodles do not stick together.

An Asian way to serve homemade pasta is to cook it al dente, drain it, and toss the strands lightly with a little bit of oil, using your fingers to be sure the pasta strands separate. Keep covered until dinner time. Coil the strands in a nonstick frying pan, cover, and warm over low heat. Flip over when lightly browned on the bottom, and continue cooking until heated through. Transfer to a platter and top with sauce.

Per serving: Calories 245, Protein 27 g, Fat 3 g, Carbohydrates 28 g

Summer Florentine Pasta with Balsamic Vinaigrette

Yield: 2 servings

Slightly unusual, this pasta dish features a sauce of warm balsamic vinaigrette. Best made for two people, it is quickly rendered.

Heat a large skillet. Pour in the olive oil, heat a moment, then add the pine nuts. Toss for a minute until golden brown, then add the sun-dried tomatoes and spinach. Toss or stir for a few seconds. Pour in the balsamic vinaigrette, toss, and then add the feta. Toss or stir again. Pour over the hot linguine, and serve immediately. The whole process should take no more than 1½ to 2 minutes.

Per serving: Calories 607, Protein 16 g, Fat 40 g, Carbohydrates 54 g

1 teaspoon olive oil

3 tablespoons pine nuts

5 to 6 reconstituted sun-dried tomatoes, halved

1½ to 2 cups loosely packed baby spinach (a large handful)

⅓ cup Balsamic Vinaigrette, page 177

3 to 4 chunks Tofu "Cheese," page 42-43

2 cups hot cooked linguine

Filling:

⅓ cup sun-dried tomatoes, soaked
    in 1 cup hot water

¾ cup lightly packed basil leaves

8 ounces Tofu "Cheese,"
    pages 42-43

1 pound tofu

2 tablespoons lemon juice

1 teaspoon salt

⅓ cup pine nuts, toasted

1 recipe Tofu Pasta, rolled out
    into sheets, pages 132-33,
    fresh store-bought pasta
    sheets (eggless),
    or large pasta shells or rigatoni

Grilled Tomato Concassé, page 86,
    Fresh Marinara, page 85, or
    your favorite marinara sauce

Stuffed Pasta with "Ricotta" & Sun-Dried Tomatoes

This dish is another good reason for making tofu cheese! With a supply of tofu cheese on hand, creations such as this take but a few minutes. You can enjoy the trouble of making your own pasta (pages 132-33), buy some fresh pasta sheets, or just use large pasta shells. If you have a ravioli mold or pasta maker, the chore of forming ravioli can be quite easy. Otherwise, you can make them by hand and ease the process by making giant ravioli. (You won't have to fill as many!).

Drain the dried tomatoes and chop roughly. Sliver the basil by stacking, rolling, and slicing the leaves thinly with a sharp knife. Combine with all of the filling ingredients, and set aside.

If you are using dried pasta shells or rigatoni, simply cook them in boiling water until al dente, then pour into a colander, and run cold water over them until cool. Preheat the oven to 350°F. Stuff each shell or rigatoni with the mixture. Place in a lightly oiled baking pan, cover with half of the grilled tomato concassé or marinara, and bake for about 15 minutes. Serve on individual plates, and top with additional marinara.

To make ravioli, roll out fresh pasta into ⅛-inch thick sheets, and cut into 2-inch squares. Place about a tablespoon of filling in the center of each square. Fold one corner over the filling to meet the opposite corner, and form a triangle. Using the tines of a fork, press the edges together. Do not overfill or the filling will ooze out. Dust the ravioli lightly with flour so they do not stick together before cooking. Add 1 tablespoon salt to 4 quarts of water, and bring to a gentle boil. Boil the ravioli gently until they float and look pillowy. Test one for doneness. Do not overcook.

Per serving: Calories 352, Protein 41 g, Fat 11 g, Carbohydrates 20 g

French Onion Pie

Yield: 6 to 8 servings

Over four pounds of onions go into this luscious pie, between layers of flaky filo pastry. The onions get a slow cooking, so their sweetness is brought out with no special seasoning or embellishment. Serve with a salad, some crusty bread, and a buttery Chardonnay.

2 tablespoons oil
4½ pounds onions, sliced
1 teaspoon sweetener of choice
Salt and pepper

1 pound firm tofu
1 teaspoon salt
1 tablespoon soy sauce

6 to 8 ounces commercial filo
   dough (check the freezer
   section of your supermarket)
½ to ¾ cup oil

Heat the oil in a large skillet, and sauté the onions in it, covered, for 30 minutes over low heat, stirring occasionally. Add the 1 teaspoon of sweetener, uncover, and continue cooking for another 20 to 30 minutes. The onions should become brown and very sweet. Season with salt and pepper to taste. You may not be able to add all the onions to the skillet at once; adding them in increments as they cook down during the first 10 minutes is fine. If there is more than a couple of tablespoons of liquid from the onions in the pan, turn the heat up to high and cook a few minutes, uncovered, to evaporate it. This step can be completed several hours or the day before the pie is assembled and baked.

Crumble the tofu and place it in a dry skillet with the salt. Over very low heat, dry-fry the tofu about 15 minutes, stirring almost constantly, until it resembles a dry curd cheese. Add the soy sauce and cook a moment until it is absorbed.

Preheat the oven to 350°F. Assemble the pie for baking. In an oiled pie plate, lay down single layers of filo pastry in a circular fashion, overlapping and brushing oil over each leaf. Keep layering and brushing oil until half the filo has been used up. Put the tofu in the bottom, and place the onions on top. Cover the pie with the remaining filo in a similar fashion, and fold the overhanging edges over so as to enclose the pie. Bake for 35 to 40 minutes until nicely browned. Wait 5 to 10 minutes before cutting and serving.

Per serving: Calories 441, Protein 14 g, Fat 24 g, Carbohydrates 50 g

Yield: 8 to 10 servings

See photo facing page 117

2 quarts water

1½ teaspoons salt

2 cups coarse cornmeal*

1 cup chopped fresh basil

¾ cup sun-dried tomato bits

½ cup nutritional yeast flakes

3 tablespoons chopped garlic

1 pound sliced portobello
  mushrooms

3 tablespoons extra-virgin olive oil

Salt and pepper

8 ounces baby spinach

4 tomatoes

1 cup Tofu "Feta," page 43, or Tofu
  "Cheese," page 42

1 recipe Roasted Red Bell Pepper
  Sauce, page 86

** Be sure to use a coarse grind
  specifically milled for use in
  making polenta, often labeled
  "polenta" on the package.*

Portobello & Polenta Lasagne

*This tasty variation on the old lasagne theme is a popular dish
from our restaurant. To simplify the recipe, you may omit the
feta and roasted red bell pepper sauce and make a double batch
of the grilled tomato sauce with which to top it.*

Bring the water to a boil in a heavy-bottomed 4-quart pot.
Add the salt, then stir in the cornmeal gradually, whisking
to incorporate so that it does not lump up. Turn the heat to
a low simmer, and stir every few minutes. Cook for 20 to 30
minutes until the grains are tender and the concoction is
thick. Add the basil, dried tomato bits, nutritional yeast,
and 2 tablespoons of the chopped garlic. Simmer another
minute, then pour immediately into a large, oiled cookie
sheet. Allow to cool completely; refrigerating will speed up
this process. When the polenta is cool enough to handle, it
should be fairly firm. Cut into three equal pieces, horizontally.

While the polenta is cooling, prepare the vegetables. Toss
the sliced portobello mushrooms with 2 tablespoons of the
olive oil, and salt and pepper to taste. Spread out onto
another cookie sheet, and bake for about 15 minutes, or
until browned and sizzling. The mushrooms should be
quite succulent and intense in flavor. Toss the spinach with

the remaining tablespoon of olive oil, and season to taste with salt and pepper.

To make a grilled tomato sauce, roast the tomatoes over an open burner or under the broiler until blackened. Chop, blackened skin and all, then place in a sauté pan with the remaining tablespoon of garlic, and salt and pepper to taste. If the tomatoes are not especially sweet, a teaspoon or two of a sweetener can be added. Simmer for 5 to 10 minutes.

Preheat the oven to 375°F. To assemble the lasagne, remove two of the polenta pieces so that only one remains. Center that piece in the sheet pan. Layer on top of it the portobello slices and "feta" pieces. Place on top another layer of the polenta. Top the second layer with the spinach and the grilled tomato sauce. Top with the final layer of polenta. Bake for 30 minutes.

To serve, cut into individual portions and top with Roasted Red Bell Pepper Sauce, page 86.

Per serving: Calories 337, Protein 13 g, Fat 14 g, Carbohydrates 44 g

Yield: 6 to 8 servings

See photo facing page 149.

For the Gâteau, have ready:

7 crêpes, page 140
1 recipe Fresh Marinara, page 85

Filling 1:

2 large eggplants (1½ pounds)
Olive oil, for brushing eggplants
½ cup ground walnuts
2 cloves garlic, minced
Salt

Gâteau de Crêpes

Literally a "cake of crêpes," this epicurean delight looks like a colorful Provençal painting; thin pancakes alternate with green, brown, and red and white fillings, and the whole concoction is frosted with a chunky tomato sauce. In both flavor and appearance, this will definitely be the pièce de resistance of any menu. For the crêpes themselves I give a recipe without eggs for vegans. When pressed for time, you could even use store-bought flour tortillas.
The crêpes can be made days, even weeks, ahead and frozen, and the fillings and sauce made the day before, leaving only the simple assembly and baking for the day you are to serve it. This organization makes the recipe far less complicated and time-consuming than it may first appear. You may have a good half-dozen or more crêpes left over, so wrap and freeze them for later use in something like Wild Rice Crêpes with Nutty Almond Sauce, page 116.

Prepare the crêpe mix as directed on page 140.

To cook the crêpes, the choice of skillet is important. Use either a well-seasoned omelette or crêpe pan, or a nonstick skillet with an 8-inch bottom. Place it over a low flame, and brush it lightly with oil; you will only need to oil it once for the whole batch. Let it heat for a few moments, then ***take the pan off the heat***, pour in about 3 or 4 tablespoons of batter, and tilt the pan all around so that the batter coats the bottom of the pan lightly. If the batter does not adhere to the pan to coat it, the pan is not hot enough; if it solidifies before you are able to coat the entire pan, the pan is too hot. Allow it to cool. If you have extra batter, pour it back into the bowl before returning the pan to the stove. Put the pan back on the burner, and cook for a minute or two over medium heat until the top looks lightly dry in appearance. Flip it out onto a plate, and set aside. (Crêpes do not have to be cooked on both sides.) Repeat the procedure until all the batter is used up, stacking the crêpes on a plate or tea towel. They can be used immediately or wrapped well and refrigerated or frozen.

For the first filling, preheat the oven to 350°F. Cut the eggplants in half lengthwise, and make several gashes with a sharp knife into the flesh of the cut side. Brush the surfaces lightly with olive oil, and bake for about 30 to 40 minutes until very soft. When cool enough to handle, scoop out the flesh with a spoon, and chop well. Mix with the walnuts and garlic, and salt to taste. Set aside.

For the second filling, sprinkle the grated zucchini with the teaspoon of salt, and set in a colander to drain for 15 minutes. Then squeeze the zucchini to rid it of most of its juice. (This juice can be saved for use in soup stock.) Chop the spinach roughly.

Heat the olive oil in a large skillet, and sauté the zucchini with the garlic for 3 to 4 minutes over medium heat. Add the spinach and cook until wilted and the vegetables are tender-crisp. There should be very little liquid in the pan. Set aside.

For the third filling, cut the peppers in half, and remove the tops and seeds. Broil the outsides of the peppers until charred, then peel the skins off. Dice the peppers into small pieces. Mash the tofu very well (an electric mixer can be used), and mix with the peppers and lemon juice. Add salt and plenty of black pepper to taste.

Preheat the oven to 350°F. To assemble the gâteau, lightly oil a round baking dish or ovenproof platter a little larger than the crêpes. Place one crêpe in the dish, and spread ½ of the first filling on it. Place another crêpe on top, and spread ½ of the second filling on it. Sprinkle on half of the

Filling 2:

1½ pounds grated zucchini

1 teaspoon salt

1 bunch spinach, washed, well drained, and trimmed

1 tablespoon olive oil

1 to 2 cloves garlic

Filling 3:

1 pound red bell peppers (3 to 4 medium)

½ pound firm tofu

2 tablespoons lemon juice

Salt and freshly ground pepper

4 ounces soy mozzarella or garlic-herb soy cheese (optional)

optional soy cheese, if desired. Top with another crêpe and spread ½ of the third filling. Repeat the procedure once more, topping it with a nice looking crêpe—torn ones can be used for the lower layers. Spread ½ cup of the fresh marinara on top, and bake for 1 hour.

Allow the gâteau to cool for 10 minutes before cutting. With a sharp knife, cut in wedges like a pie, and serve with additional marinara.

This is also very tasty served cold the next day.

Per serving: Calories 413, Protein 15 g, Fat 21 g, Carbohydrates 42 g

Yield: 12 to 16 crêpes

2¾ cups water

2 ounces tofu

1 tablespoon oil

1 cup whole wheat pastry flour
  plus 1 cup unbleached flour,
  or 2 cups unbleached flour

1 teaspoon salt

2 teaspoons baking powder

1 to 2 tablespoons nutritional
  yeast flakes (optional)

CRÊPES

If you want to make sweet crêpes for a dessert, try the variation of this recipe on page 207.

Blend the water and tofu in a blender, then add the remaining ingredients, and blend for 60 seconds. Allow the mixture to rest for 1 to 2 hours so the crêpes will hold together better when cooked. Prepare according to the directions on page 138.

Per crêpe: Calories 69, Protein 2 g, Fat 2 g, Carbohydrates 12 g

Marinated Tofu

This dish is quite succulent and tasty. It can be sautéed or baked, or baked first, then sautéed for those who like their tofu chewy.

Mix the ingredients for the marinade, and place in a large, shallow baking dish or container. Slice the tofu at least ¼ to ⅓ inch thick, and marinate for at least 8 hours. (In hot weather, don't let it sit out for longer than 24 hours.) You may marinate it as long as you like in the refrigerator—3 or 4 days will result in a deep, rich flavor, but shorter periods will still give you a delicious dish.

Sauté the marinated tofu in 1 tablespoon olive oil on both sides until browned. Add several tablespoons of the remaining marinade, and sizzle for a moment. Serve immediately. Or you may first bake the slices on an oiled cookie sheet at 350°F for 30 minutes. Serve as is with a little marinade, or sauté quickly and serve with the extra marinade. Baked tofu is quite chewy, while simply sautéing it will render a tender, succulent tofu.

Per serving: Calories 154, Protein 12 g, Fat 11 g, Carbohydrates 4 g

Yield: 6 servings

Marinade:

1 cup red wine

½ cup soy sauce

2 tablespoons red wine or balsamic vinegar

¼ cup plus 1 tablespoon olive oil

3 to 4 cloves garlic, pressed or finely minced

3 tablespoons tomato paste

1 teaspoon rosemary

Freshly ground pepper

1½ pounds firm tofu

Yield: 6 servings

1 cup red wine

⅓ cup tomato paste

2 tablespoons red wine vinegar

2 tablespoons olive oil

2 tablespoons toasted sesame oil

3 tablespoons sweetener

1 tablespoon molasses (optional)

½ cup soy sauce

*3 to 4 cloves garlic, pressed
    or minced, or 1 teaspoon
    garlic powder*

*½ teaspoon cayenne pepper
    (optional)*

2 tablespoons liquid smoke

1½ pounds firm tofu

Smoky Marinated Tofu

*This works well alone as a snack or dressed up in the
Smoked Tofu, Mushroom & Garlic Canapés on page 56.*

Mix, marinate, and prepare as in the Marinated Tofu recipe
on the previous page.

Per serving: Calories 154, Protein 12 g, Fat 11 g, Carbohydrates 4 g

Mediterranean Eggplant & Tofu Gratin

Yield: 4 servings

Great for those occasions when only something hearty, "meaty," and Italian-tasting with garlic and herbal overtones will satisfy. Serve with French bread and a big salad. This makes wonderful leftovers.

If you have time, it's a good idea to salt the eggplant to remove the bitter flavor and keep it from absorbing too much oil. Slice the eggplant into ⅜-inch thick rounds, sprinkle liberally with salt, and place in a colander to drain for 20 to 30 minutes. Scrape the surface with a knife, or rinse quickly and pat dry with paper towels. Leave a little salt clinging to the eggplant, as it enhances the flavor. Heat 2 tablespoons of the olive oil in a skillet, and sauté the eggplant slices on both sides until golden brown and tender. Set aside.

Wipe out the skillet. Mix the soy sauce, peanut butter, tomato paste, water, and cayenne pepper together in a bowl. Crumble or shred the tofu so it resembles large breadcrumbs, and mix it with the soy-peanut butter marinade, squeezing with your hands so that the tofu absorbs it all. Heat 2 more tablespoons of the olive oil in the same skillet, and sauté the tofu until well-browned, stirring constantly.

Preheat the oven to 375°F. Slice the tomatoes ⅜ inch thick. In a 10-inch shallow gratin or casserole dish, layer half the sautéed eggplant. Spread the browned tofu over it, then layer half the tomatoes. Sprinkle on half the minced garlic, a little salt, and ½ teaspoon of rosemary. Add the remaining eggplant, then the rest of the tomatoes. Sprinkle with more garlic, rosemary, and a little salt, if desired. Fresh basil leaves can also be added. Bake for 45 to 50 minutes.

Per serving: Calories 512, Protein 21 g, Fat 27 g, Carbohydrates 50 g

1⅓ pounds eggplant
   (approximately 1 medium)
4 tablespoons olive oil

2 tablespoons soy sauce
2 tablespoons peanut butter
2 tablespoons tomato paste
3 to 4 tablespoons water
2 to 3 dashes cayenne pepper
1 pound frozen tofu, thawed and
   squeezed dry (see pages 17-18)
2 tablespoons olive oil

1⅓ pounds ripe tomatoes
   (approximately 3½ medium)
3 to 6 cloves garlic, or more,
   minced or pressed
1 teaspoon dried rosemary
Salt
Fresh basil, to decorate (optional)

Yield: 6 servings

1 large onion, chopped

2 stalks celery, chopped

One 15-ounce can garbanzo
   beans (chick-peas), drained
   and mashed well

½ cup ground walnuts

⅓ cup wheat germ

1 pound frozen tofu, defrosted,
   squeezed dry, and crumbled in a
   food processor (see pages 17-18)

2 tablespoons tomato paste

2 tablespoons miso

1 to 2 tablespoons soy sauce

½ teaspoon allspice

1 teaspoon dried thyme

½ teaspoon dried chervil

1 teaspoon freshly ground oregano

Pepper

3 to 4 tablespoons tahini mixed
   with a little water to make a
   thick paste

Topping:

⅓ cup ketchup

2 tablespoons soy sauce

Jeff's Favorite Neat Loaf

Here's a quite convincing substitute for meat loaf; it's a great
homestyle dish for skeptics of tofu and other natural goodies.
Serve with ketchup mixed with soy sauce, or a tasty gravy.

Preheat the oven to 350°F. Sauté the onions and celery in a little oil or water until tender. Combine all the ingredients and pat into an oiled loaf pan.

Combine the ingredients for the topping, and spoon on top of the loaf. Bake for 1 hour. Turn off the heat and allow to sit in the oven for an additional 20 to 30 minutes, or at room temperature for 15 minutes, before unmolding and slicing. This last step is important so that the loaf will hold together well.

Serve with additional topping mix, the fat-free gravy on page 168, or the instant gravy on page 87.

Per serving: Calories 499, Protein 27 g, Fat 18 g, Carbohydrates 63 g

Tofu Burgers Suprême

This is what convinced my younger brother that vegetarian food could be delicious. Because frozen tofu is used, these burgers are nice and chewy. Try them with a sauce, such as the easy brown mushroom sauce, page 81, or leftover rich brown sauce, page 78. They taste great in a bun or pita with all the fixin's too!

In a covered pan, sauté the onions, mushrooms, and celery in a tablespoon of the oil until tender. The vegetables can also be microwaved until tender, using no oil.

Shred the defrosted tofu into little bits, and mix with the vegetables, garlic, soy sauce, miso, and tomato paste. Thin the tahini with the water to produce a smooth, thick white sauce that will bind the mixture. Add it to the tofu and vegetable mixture, mix well, and add the bread crumbs and parsley. The mixture should be moist but not too wet and firm enough to form into patties. Cook in a lightly oiled pan over low heat until browned on both sides. Don't cover while cooking or some of the chewiness will be lost.

Per burger: Calories 272, Protein 15 g, Fat 14 g, Carbohydrates 24 g

Yield: 4 large burgers

½ cup finely chopped onion
⅓ cup chopped mushrooms
⅓ cup finely chopped celery
1½ tablespoons oil

1 pound frozen tofu, thawed and squeezed dry (see pages 17-18)
1 to 2 cloves garlic, minced
2 tablespoons soy sauce
2 to 3 teaspoons miso
2 to 3 tablespoons tomato paste
2 to 3 tablespoons tahini or sesame paste
3 to 4 tablespoons water
¾ cup bread crumbs
½ cup chopped parsley

Yield: 6 to 8 servings

*8 to 12 Japanese or small Italian
  eggplants*

1 medium onion, minced
1 to 2 tablespoons olive oil
*⅓ cup minced mushrooms
  (about 2 ounces)*
*4 to 5 fresh or reconstituted
  shiitake mushrooms, minced*

⅓ cup Rich Brown Sauce, page 78

French Moussaka

Served with rich brown sauce this is a superb creation. Plump little eggplants (the Japanese variety, if you can get them) are stuffed with a "meaty" mixture of tofu and walnuts and seasoned delicately with herbs and a hint of cinnamon. It takes a little time to make both the sauce and the dish, but if you make the sauce several days, or even weeks, ahead of time and freeze it, all goes fairly quickly and you and your guests will reap great rewards. For this delicacy, get out your best china, and adorn each plate as beautifully as you can with a few vegetables to balance the color of the purple eggplants. A delicate mousse or terrine to start the dinner would be nice, followed by a green salad or a light soup.

In selecting the eggplants, choose the plumpest ones available. If they are very small, you may want to serve two per person. Wash them and slice in half lengthwise. With a sharp knife, make a few deep gashes in the cut side. Sprinkle with salt and let drain, cut side down, in a colander for 20 to 30 minutes. Preheat the oven to 375°F. Rinse the eggplant under cold water and squeeze gently. Bake until soft, about 20 minutes.

While the eggplants bake, sauté the onions in the olive oil until tender. Place the mushrooms and shiitake in a thin cloth, and wring out their juices into a bowl (to add to the Brown Sauce later). The mushrooms should be very dry. Add them to the onions, and continue sautéing until soft.

If you are preparing the Rich Brown Sauce simultaneously, add the mushroom juices and simmer along with the rest of the ingredients. If the sauce has ben prepared ahead of time, add the mushroom juices while reheating it, and allow it to simmer for at least 15 minutes. Remove ⅓ cup of this to thicken so it will bind the filling. Make a roux by melting the margarine and adding the flour. To this add the ⅓ cup sauce, and cook until very thick, stirring constantly.

When the eggplants are tender and have been allowed to cool slightly, scoop out the pulp with a spoon, leaving the skins and a thin layer of pulp intact. Reserve the skins, as they will be stuffed with the mixture.

Add ⅔ of the chopped pulp to the onions and mushrooms, and combine with all of the other ingredients except the bread crumbs, cinnamon, and eggplant skins. Add enough of the bread crumbs to thicken and hold the filling together, and add a dash or two of cinnamon. Season with salt and pepper to taste, adjusting the seasonings as desired.

Preheat the oven to 350°F. Fill half the skins with this mixture, mounding it high, and top with the remaining skins to form "whole" eggplants. Place on a lightly oiled cookie sheet, and bake for 20 minutes until the filling looks brown, almost like ground meat.

Pour a generous serving of Rich Brown Sauce on each plate, then position a baked eggplant or two nicely in the center. Surround the eggplants with steamed green beans, asparagus, green peas, or other vegetables, and add a little grilled red bell pepper or tomato for color.

Per serving: Calories 340, Protein 15 g, Fat 12 g, Carbohydrates 48 g

1 tablespoon nonhydrogenated margarine
1 tablespoon flour
12 to 15 ounces firm tofu, frozen, thawed, squeezed dry, and crumbled finely (see pages 17-18)
⅓ cup finely ground walnuts
1 to 2 tablespoons tomato paste
1 tablespoon miso
½ teaspoon dried thyme
½ teaspoon dried rosemary
1 clove garlic, minced

½ cup or more dry bread crumbs
1 to 2 dashes cinnamon
Salt and pepper

Yield: 4 to 6 servings

1 pound frozen tofu, thawed
   (see pages 17-18)
1¼ cups red wine
5 tablespoons mirin
5 tablespoons soy sauce
2 to 3 tablespoons medium
   or light miso
2 cloves garlic, minced
2 tablespoons red wine vinegar
   or balsamic vinegar

½ cup unbleached white
   or whole wheat pastry flour
3 tablespoons oil

1 medium onion, finely chopped
12 ounces mushrooms, sliced
¾ cup frozen peas
Approximately ⅔ cup rich soy
   cream or soymilk
1 to 2 teaspoons arrowroot, kuzu,
   or cornstarch to thicken,
   if necessary

Tofu Bourguignon

This rich, tasty creation brims with mushrooms and chewy pieces of tofu in an aromatic red wine sauce. It will taste as if it took hours to prepare, although it can be whipped up in less than a half hour (not including the time needed for marinating the tofu). If possible, make your own fettuccine to serve with it. Although best with pasta, it can also be served with brown rice or crusty bread to soak up the delicious sauce.

After the tofu has thawed, press it gently between both hands to extract as much water as possible without breaking or tearing it. Cut it into slices about ⅜ inch thick x 1 inch x 1¼ inches. Mix the red wine, mirin, soy sauce, miso, garlic, and vinegar, and marinate the tofu in this mixture for at least 30 minutes (several hours if desired). Remove the tofu one piece at a time, and squeeze lightly to remove some, but not all, of the marinade it absorbed. If you press too hard, you will end up with a tasteless piece of tofu; if you don't extract any of the marinade, the tofu may taste too "winey." Measure the remaining marinade after doing this for all the pieces—you should have about 1½ cups. If you have too much, sprinkle some back onto the tofu; if not enough, squeeze the tofu a bit more. Flour the tofu lightly and sauté in 2 tablespoons of the oil on both sides until brown and crispy. Remove from the pan and set aside.

Shiso Steaks with Shiitake Béarnaise Sauce, page 165

Wipe out the skillet with a paper towel, and add the remaining tablespoon of oil. Add the chopped onion, cover, and sauté until tender, then add the mushrooms and cover again. Cook over low heat about 5 minutes until the mushroom juices begin to ooze out. Add the remaining marinade and simmer for another 10 minutes. Add the green peas and cook for another 2 minutes. Now add the soymilk or soy cream, and cook another minute or two to allow the flavors to blend. It should thicken, but if it does not, dissolve a teaspoon or two of arrowroot or kuzu in a little more milk and add to it, stirring constantly, until the sauce has some body. Add the tofu pieces, heat briefly until hot, then check the flavor, adjusting the seasonings and adding more soy cream, if necessary. Serve immediately over pasta, such as fettuccine cooked al dente.

Per serving: Calories 304, Protein 13 g, Fat 11 g, Carbohydrates 35 g

Gâteau de Crêpes, pages 138-39

1 medium head cabbage
(approximately 2 pounds)

12 ounces minced or
crumbled tempeh
3 tablespoons cider vinegar
2 teaspoons sweetener
3 to 5 tablespoons soy sauce
1 tablespoon sake (optional)
¼ teaspoon dry mustard, or
1 teaspoon prepared mustard
2 tablespoons oil
1 medium onion, minced
1 cup cooked brown rice
3 to 4 cloves garlic, minced
½ teaspoon dried thyme
¼ teaspoon rubbed sage
3 tablespoons tomato paste
2 ounces ground walnuts
1 tablespoon miso
Freshly ground pepper

HEARTY TEMPEH-STUFFED WHOLE CABBAGE

This will warm you on a cold winter day. It's also a fun dish to serve, because a beautifully sauced head of cabbage is cut open at the table to reveal a "meaty" filling. The tomato sauce is also fat free, although rich and tasty.

To core the cabbage, cut out a small cone at the core with a sharp knife. Fill a large pot that will hold the entire head of cabbage half full with water. Bring it to a boil, and add the cored cabbage. After the water reboils, simmer the cabbage for about 10 minutes. With two forks, start removing the leaves of the cabbage, being careful not to tear them too badly—some tearing is inevitable. They should come off easily. Remove 14 to 16 leaves, and set them aside to drain in a colander. Pierce the remaining cabbage (still cooking in water), and if it seems raw or undercooked, boil a few more minutes. If it is tender, remove it and set aside to cool. The cabbage should be tender but still slightly crisp, not mushy. When cool enough to handle, shred or chop it finely. Reserve 1¼ cups of the cooking water for later.

Mix the tempeh with the vinegar, sweetener, 3 tablespoons of the soy sauce, sake, and mustard, and sauté it in the oil until lightly browned. Add the minced onion and continue to sauté until tender, about 10 minutes. Add the remaining ingredients including the chopped cabbage, but not the leaves. Season to taste with plenty of freshly ground pepper and the additional 2 tablespoons of soy sauce, if desired.

Preheat the oven to 375°F.

Oil a glass or earthenware round casserole dish, and line it with 6 of the outer leaves, allowing the edges to extend beyond the rim of the dish so they can be folded over the top later. Trim the hard rib of the leaves if necessary, to make them more pliable. Pack half the tempeh filling into this, then neatly arrange about 4 leaves on top, again cutting away the rib, if desired. Pack the rest of the tempeh mixture in tightly, and arrange the remaining leaves over the top ones. Weight this down with a heavy plate or lid, and cover everything with aluminum foil. Bake for 1¼ hours.

While the cabbage bakes, mix all the ingredients for the sauce in a medium saucepan, cover, and simmer gently for 30 to 40 minutes. Purée in a blender or food processor, then return to the saucepan, and simmer for another 10 minutes, or until thick enough to coat the back of a wooden spoon. (Boil down if necessary.)

To serve, invert the cabbage onto a platter. You should have a shining, glimmering head of cabbage that will look delicious. Pour several tablespoons of the sauce on top, letting it dribble down like frosting on a cake. Cut the cabbage in wedges like a pie, and pass the remaining sauce around for individual servings.

Per serving: Calories 324, Protein 15 g, Fat 14 g, Carbohydrates 31 g

Tomato Sauce:

*1 pound very ripe tomatoes
   (may substitute canned)*
*1¼ cups water from boiling
   cabbage*
¾ cup red wine
2 tablespoons soy sauce
2 tablespoons mirin
½ tablespoon sweetener
½ tablespoon miso

Yield: 6 to 8 servings

1 pound tempeh

Marinade:

1 cup red wine
¼ cup soy sauce
1 tablespoon oil
1 tablespoon mirin
⅛ teaspoon allspice
1 tablespoon nutritional
    yeast flakes
Oil for deep frying

For the stew:

4 tablespoons oil or
    nonhydrogenated margarine
2 large onions, sliced or cut into
    chunks
½ cup unbleached white flour
    or whole wheat pastry flour
1 quart hot vegetable stock

Savory Tempeh & Vegetable Stew

*This is a deep, rich, flavorful stew that can be part of
a grand meal or the main course in a simple one,
accompanied by just salad, bread, and a good Cabernet.*

The stewed vegetables can be prepared several days in advance and refrigerated or frozen. In that case, prepare the tempeh the day of serving in order to have it as fresh as possible. Several hours or the day before, mix the marinade for the tempeh. Cut the tempeh into ¾-inch cubes, and marinate for several hours or overnight.

Heat the oil in a deep fryer or wok, and fry the marinated tempeh a few pieces at a time until well browned and crisp. Drain on absorbent paper. A second frying will produce a crispier surface, but is optional. If you prefer not to fry, the tempeh can be baked in a slow oven (300°F) until browned, about 40 minutes—but it may not have the same nutty flavor that many people enjoy.

To make the stew, heat the oil or margarine in a large Dutch oven or heavy-bottomed pot, and sauté the onions, covered, until soft. Add the flour, cook 2 minutes over low heat while stirring constantly, then add the stock. Cook until slightly thickened, stirring constantly, then add the remaining ingredients except the tempeh. Cover and simmer gently for 45 minutes. Add the tempeh and cook another 25 to 30 minutes. The stew should be extremely rich and flavorful, with a slightly thick consistency. Top with minced parsley, if desired.

Per serving: Calories 366, Protein 19 g, Fat 14 g, Carbohydrates 34 g

For the stew (cont.):

6 to 7 dried shiitake mushrooms, reconstituted and quartered
½ to ¾ pound mushrooms, quartered or thickly sliced
2 carrots, sliced ¼ inch thick
2 potatoes (preferably waxy), diced
2 large, very ripe tomatoes, chopped
1 head garlic, peeled and sliced
3 tablespoons tomato paste
2 tablespoons miso
1¼ to 1½ cups red wine
¼ cup soy sauce
3 tablespoons Rich Yeast Flavoring Powder, page 168,
*   or 2 tablespoons nutritional yeast flakes*
1 teaspoon dried thyme
1 teaspoon dried rosemary
½ teaspoon powdered sage
½ teaspoon dried savory
½ teaspoon allspice
¼ teaspoon cloves
2 bay leaves

Marinade:

3 tablespoons soy sauce

3 tablespoons water

2 teaspoons grated ginger

1 teaspoon dark sesame oil

1 tablespoon rice vinegar

⅓ cup tempeh, cut into short sticks ¼ inch x ¾ inch

1 tablespoon oil

Oriental Stuffed Eggplant

This is a very tasty, Japanese-inspired dish. If possible, use the slender, long Japanese eggplants in order to make attractive individual servings. To save time, you can cook them several hours or the day before. Serve with brown rice, miso soup, and some simple sautéed vegetables.

Combine the soy sauce, water, grated ginger, sesame oil, and rice vinegar to make the marinade. Marinate the tempeh sticks for several hours or the day before serving the dish. When ready to prepare the dish, remove the tempeh from the marinade, and sauté in a tablespoon of oil until browned. Add the remaining marinade and continue sautéing until the liquid has been completely absorbed.

Preheat the oven to 350°F. Split the eggplants in half lengthwise, and brush the cut surfaces lightly with oil. Bake for 10 to 15 minutes, depending on their size, until tender. When cool enough to handle, scoop out the insides, leaving a thin wall and being careful not to tear the skin. Lightly chop the removed pulp, and place in a bowl.

When preparing the sesame seeds, it's always preferable to start with untoasted hulled seeds and toast them yourself, since pretoasted ones quickly become rancid, and you won't get the necessary nutty flavor. Place the seeds in a small skillet, and cook over low heat, stirring constantly, until you hear them begin to crackle. Remove immediately and do not allow them to color at all; they will puff up slightly. Pound the toasted seeds in a suribachi (a Japanese mortar with grooves) until the seeds are finely ground and begin to show a gleam of oil. A regular mortar and pestle can be used, but it takes more effort. A food processor or blender can also be used, but be careful that the sesame seeds do not turn into butter or paste; you want to release the oil so that the seeds look slightly sticky, but do not turn into tahini. Mix in the miso, mirin, and the grated ginger/water mixture. Add the tempeh and eggplant pulp, and fold together gently but completely.

Preheat the oven to 350°F. Fill the eggplant skins and bake for 20 to 25 minutes until well browned. They can be served hot, warm, or at room temperature.

Per serving: Calories 224, Protein 8 g, Fat 9 g, Carbohydrates 27 g

3 long or 6 short, small eggplants (Japanese, if possible)
Oil for brushing onto eggplant surfaces

5 tablespoons hulled sesame seeds, lightly toasted
1 to 1½ tablespoons medium miso
2 tablespoons mirin
1 teaspoon grated ginger mixed with 1 tablespoon water

Homemade Gluten

Let me introduce you to seitan and other highly metamorphic concoctions! Homemade gluten has so many uses and can transform into such a variety of textures and flavors, that it is really worth spending two or three hours once or twice a month to make a big batch to have on hand in either the refrigerator or freezer. It is also a great deal of fun to make and always surprising the first time to see plain, whole wheat flour suddenly metamorphose into a stretchy, gum-like substance, which again transforms into protein. The protein is isolated by first mixing water and flour together to make a dough, then washing away the starch and bran. Raw gluten can be baked, fried, stewed, or boiled and will come to resemble ground meat, turkey, roasts, etc. If flavored properly, it is delicious and will surprise your guests.

The Chinese have used gluten in vegetarian cooking for centuries. In the United States, gluten products are now readily available at natural food stores and are usually called "seitan," a term that refers to cooked gluten. Try the variety of recipes on the following pages for gluten and seitan. And have fun! You will feel like a magician with gluten.

Basic Raw Gluten: The recipe here is for about 3 pounds of flour, but if your bowl will hold more, make more since the work is all the same. The important point to remember is to use a high-gluten whole wheat flour. Whole wheat pastry flour will not give you the same results. If you're in doubt, ask for the best flour for bread baking—it has the highest gluten content.

Place the flour in a large bowl, and add the water while stirring constantly. Add enough water to make a very firm dough, much firmer than bread dough. Allow this to set for at least 1 hour. No kneading or setting overnight is necessary.

Place the bowl containing the dough in the sink. Fill the bowl with tap water, and begin to massage the dough. The water will grow very white and milky at first as the starch rinses out. This liquid can be saved and used in place of arrowroot or cornstarch to thicken sauces and such. It will keep for about two weeks in the refrigerator. It you don't save it, discard the water as it gets cloudy, and fill the bowl with fresh water. Keep filling with fresh water, massaging the dough, and discarding the water for about 10 to 15 minutes until the water grows clear. During this process, the dough will shrink in size as the starch and bran are washed away. At one point the dough may appear to be falling apart completely. In the end it will all congeal into one stretchy mass. When it looks like you have a giant wad of well-chewed bubble gum, you have transformed flour into raw gluten. You can now prepare it into a number of delectable substances.

Although a bowl is all that is really necessary to produce raw gluten, a plastic or steel colander (not wire mesh) can be a great help, especially at the stage when the gluten feels as if it is disintegrating. The water can be poured off through the colander, and the colander will catch any loose bits of gluten.

Yield: almost 4 cups raw gluten

3 or more pounds high-gluten whole wheat flour
3 or more cups water

Yield: about 4 cups raw gluten

2½ cups vital wheat gluten
2 cups water

How to use vital wheat (instant) gluten flour: If you don't mind skipping the magic show of transforming wheat flour into gluten, you can greatly expedite the process by simply using vital wheat gluten. All you need to do is mix with water, and voilà! Instant raw gluten appears. Actually, there is even an advantage here, since seasonings and flavorings can be mixed right into the flour with the water, yielding a tastier product. (Instant gluten flour is available in natural food stores or by mail order. See page 234.)

To make raw gluten from instant gluten flour, simply combine the flour with the water. Mix well. Part of the water may be replaced by stock, soy sauce, miso, tomato paste, liquid aminos, or another liquid flavoring agent. Various herbs, spices, and other seasonings can be included in the liquid before you add it to the flour.

Basic Ground Seitan

Yield: 5 to 6 cups (6 to 8 servings)

This can be used either alone or in combination with tempeh to produce chewy sausages, burgers, etc. It will keep one week to ten days refrigerated, or it can be frozen for longer periods.

1 recipe Homemade Gluten,
   pages 156-58

Stretch out basic raw gluten into a circular shape approximately ½ inch thick. Place on a well-oiled cookie sheet. Bake in a preheated 350°F oven for about 30 minutes, or until puffed up and golden brown. Pierce with a sharp knife in several places, and allow to sit in the oven for another 15 minutes with the oven turned off to allow steam to escape. If you are pressed for time, you can pierce it the last 10 minutes of baking. Remove from the oven and cover with a damp cloth until cool. Tear it into chunks and grind in a food processor.

Per serving: Calories 349, Protein 38 g, Fat 2 g, Carbohydrates 44 g

Oven Roasted Seitan

Yield: 6 to 8 servings

Stewing gluten in an oven will produce a firm, chewy texture. The process alone is given below; the liquid used can be anything from plain stock to stock with wine, soy sauce, garlic, mushrooms, or herbs.

1 recipe Homemade Gluten,
   pages 156-58

Preheat the oven to 300°F. Place basic raw gluten in a Dutch oven or deep casserole dish. Pour in enough stock to fill the pot or dish nearly to the brim. Cover and bake for 1½ to 2 hours. The gluten will expand and become firm and springy to the touch. The resulting liquid will be very tasty and can be used in sauces or soups. The gluten itself can be sliced, sauced, and served, or can be sautéed and added to stir-fries, etc.

Per serving: Calories 299, Protein 33 g, Fat 2 g, Carbohydrates 37 g

1 to 2 medium onions, sliced
2 tablespoons oil
1 recipe Homemade Gluten,
    pages 156-58
Soy sauce
Garlic
Herbs
Nutritional yeast
Red wine
Shiitake mushrooms

STOVE-TOP SEITAN

Stewing gluten on top of the stove will result in a softer, spongier texture than oven-stewing. However, it will firm up in the refrigerator and can be used for sandwiches, etc. Again, it can be flavored a number of different ways by varying the amounts of stock, soy sauce, water, garlic, onions, etc.

Sauté the onions in the oil in a large Dutch oven or pot. While the onions are cooking, form the raw gluten into a fat log, and cut into ¼-inch slices. Place the slices in the pot, and add water or stock to fill the pot three-quarters of the way. Add any amount of the remaining ingredients you desire to flavor the stock. Other vegetables, such as celery and carrots, may also be added. Cover the pot and stew gently for 1 to 2 hours. The slices will swell and become spongy and chewy, and the liquid will grow quite flavorful.

The slices can be breaded and sautéed, deep-fried, or refrigerated to use in sandwiches. Use the liquid to make soups and sauces.

Per serving: Calories 349, Protein 33 g, Fat 6 g, Carbohydrates 41 g

Tempeh & Gluten Burgers

Homemade ground gluten and tempeh work excellently together to form juicy, chewy, light, and tasty burgers. This is very simple if you have the ground gluten (which can be stored frozen) on hand.

Mix all the ingredients together, form into patties, and sauté on both sides until browned. Serve them on a whole wheat bun or with a sauce.

Per burger: Calories 222, Protein 20 g, Fat 5 g, Carbohydrates 19 g

Yield: 6 to 8 burgers

2 cups tempeh, steamed and crumbled

2½ to 2¾ cups Basic Ground Seitan, page 159

1 to 2 cloves garlic, minced

½ large onion, finely chopped

2 tablespoons Rich Nutritional Yeast Flavoring, page 168, or nutritional yeast flakes with ½ teaspoon each of basil, thyme, and oregano

3 tablespoons tomato paste

2 tablespoons soy sauce

3 tablespoons peanut butter

⅛ teaspoon allspice

Marinade:

1 cup dried shiitake, soaked in
    2½ cups of water for several
    hours or overnight until soft
1½ cups red wine
½ cup soy sauce
2 tablespoons chopped garlic

Seitan:

2 cups water
2 to 3 tablespoons soy sauce
1 to 2 tablespoons chopped garlic
¼ cup red wine
2¾ to 3 cups vital wheat gluten
    (instant gluten flour)
3 to 4 tablespoons oil for sautéing

Have ready:

A large pot of boiling water or
    stock, at least 3 quarts

Seitan Medallions with Braised Japanese Mushrooms

These marinated steaks can be frozen for several months, so you may prepare the entire recipe and set some of the steaks aside for later use.

Begin preparing the marinade by removing the shiitake from the soaking liquid, reserving the mushrooms for later. Place the liquid in a small pot, and boil over medium-high heat to reduce to 1 cup. Combine the reduced shiitake stock with the wine, soy sauce, and garlic. Set aside.

To make the seitan, combine the 2 cups water, soy sauce, garlic, and wine. Add the vital wheat gluten, and mix to achieve a soft, pliable consistency. Divide into 1½ to 2-inch balls, and flatten out as much as possible, about ¼ inch. (Alternatively, you may divide into eight portions for large steaks). Heat a little oil in a nonstick pan, and sauté each piece on both sides until well browned. Transfer the seitan to the boiling water, and simmer for approximately 20 to 30 minutes (longer if the pieces are large). Remove from the water and cover with the marinade for a minimum of 1 hour or overnight. (This whole part can be prepared several days in advance and refrigerated.)

To cook the medallions, use 3 medallions (or 1 large steak) per serving. Heat a sauté pan. Add a little oil, or spray with nonfat cooking spray. Sauté the steaks on both sides over medium heat until browned. Remove from the pan and keep warm. Turn the heat up high. Add a splash more oil, then the mushrooms, and toss and cook until browned. It's okay if they stick to the pan. Deglaze the pan with ⅓ cup per serving of the marinade, scraping the bottom of the pan to loosen any cooked bits of mushroom. When it sizzles, add the dissolved arrowroot. Thin it with more shiitake marinade if too thick. Pour over the steaks and, if desired, sprinkle with chopped parsley. Serve immediately.

Per steak: Calories 284, Protein 45 g, Fat 1 g, Carbohydrates 15 g

For each serving, have prepared:

2 to 3 ounces mixed mushrooms per person (reconstituted shiitake from marinade, shimeji, enoki, oyster, or even regular button)

½ teaspoon arrowroot per serving, dissolved in a small amount of water

Rich stroganoff crème:

2 cups raw cashews

2 cups water

⅓ cup lemon juice

1 teaspoon salt

1 pound regular tofu

¼ cup canola oil (optional)

Seitan marinade:

2 cups wild mushroom broth or
      rich shiitake soaking stock

2 cups red wine

1 tablespoon chopped garlic

⅓ cup soy sauce

Per serving:

⅓ cup chopped onions

5 to 6 small chunks
      marinated seitan

2 cups sliced mushrooms

Small handful of oyster mushrooms

Salt and pepper

For 6 to 8 servings, use:

¾ to 1 full batch stroganoff crème

2 cups marinade

2 to 3 cups marinated seitan pieces

2 cups chopped onions

12 cups sliced mushrooms

Salt and pepper

SEITAN & MUSHROOM STROGANOFF

This was a highly popular dish at our restaurant. When we closed down, several customers asked for the recipe. Well, here it is! The crème can be used as a sour cream substitute in other dishes and will keep in the refrigerator for one week. I offer two versions here, one for making individual servings (you will have to make a batch of the crème, but that has other uses) and one for 6 to 8 servings.

Purée the cashews with the water in a blender until a thick crème results. Add the lemon juice, salt, and tofu, and purée until thick. If desired, oil can be added for super rich results.

Mix together the ingredients for the marinade, and marinate chunks of seitan overnight before using. Save the marinade sauce for the next step.

For each serving, steam or sauté the chopped onions in a little water or oil until tender. Add the marinated seitan chunks, and sauté until browned, then add the mushrooms and sauté for a minute or two. Pour in ⅓ cup of the seitan marinade, and simmer for several minutes. Stir in ½ to ⅔ cup rich stroganoff crème, and cook only to heat. Add salt and pepper to taste, and serve alongside fettuccine or rice.

Per serving: Calories 481, Protein 30 g, Fat 21 g, Carbohydrates 29 g

Shiso Steaks with Shiitake Béarnaise Sauce

This is similar in preparation to the braised seitan medallions but features a different sauce. The seitan can be prepared a day or two prior to serving, if desired, or even frozen in its marinade. The béarnaise sauce is best prepared the day you are serving it.

Begin preparing the marinade by removing the shiitake from the soaking liquid, reserving the mushrooms for later. Place the liquid in a small pot, and boil over medium-high heat to reduce to 1 cup. Combine the reduced shiitake stock with the wine, soy sauce, and garlic. Set aside.

To make the seitan, combine the 2 cups water, soy sauce, garlic, and red wine. Add the vital wheat gluten, and mix to achieve a soft, pliable consistency. Divide this into 1½- to 2-inch balls, and flatten out as much as possible. (You may also divide into eight portions for eight large steaks.) Heat a little oil in a nonstick pan, and sauté each piece on both sides until well browned. Add the seitan to the boiling water, and simmer for approximately 20 to 30 minutes (longer if the pieces are large). Remove from the water and cover with the marinade for a minimum of 1 hour or overnight. This whole part can be prepared several days in advance and refrigerated.

To cook the steaks, heat a tablespoon of oil in a sauté pan. Cook the steaks for several minutes on each side until browned. Place 2 shiso leaves on top of each hot steak. Top with béarnaise sauce and serve immediately.

Per serving: Calories 319, Protein 40 g, Fat 8 g, Carbohydrates 13 g

Yield: 8 to 10 servings

See photo facing page 148.

Red wine and shiitake marinade:

1 cup dried shiitake mushrooms, soaked in 2½ cups of water for several hours or overnight until soft
1½ cups red wine
½ cup soy sauce
2 tablespoons chopped garlic

Seitan mix:

2 cups water
2 to 3 tablespoons soy sauce
1 to 2 tablespoons chopped garlic
¼ cup red wine
2¾ to 3 cups vital wheat gluten (instant gluten flour)

1 recipe Shiitake Bearnaise Sauce, page 75, kept warm
16 green shiso leaves

Have ready:

At least 3 quarts boiling water or vegetable stock

Yield: 6 servings

Sauce:

2 tablespoons oil

10 shallots, peeled and minced

½ red bell pepper, diced

1 tablespoon chopped garlic

4 ounces capers

2 cups white wine

¼ cup lemon juice

2 tablespoons sweetener of choice

Salt and pepper

Filet:

½ cup flour

1 cup dry bread crumbs

1 cup soymilk

3 pieces nori, cut in half

6 slices Stove-Top Seitan, page 160, approximately 6 inches x 3 inches x ½ inch

¼ cup oil

Filet of Soul with Lemon Caper Sauce

Easy and elegant, here is a delicate vegetarian replica of food from the sea. This goes well with rice.

To make the lemon caper sauce, heat the oil in a pan. Over low heat, sauté the shallots and red bell pepper until tender. Add the garlic, capers, wine, lemon juice, sweetener, and salt and pepper to taste. Simmer for 15 minutes.

Place the flour, bread crumbs, and soymilk in three separate small bowls or soup bowls. Wrap a half piece of nori around each piece of seitan. Dredge the nori-seitan slices in flour to coat both sides. Dip each slice in the soymilk, then coat with bread crumbs on both sides. Heat the oil in a sauté pan, and cook on both sides for several minutes until golden brown. Drain on a paper towel. Serve immediately with the sauce poured on top.

Per serving: Calories 561, Protein 32 g, Fat 15 g, Carbohydrates 58 g

BEANS & "BACON" CASSEROLE

Simple to make, this tasty, homey casserole will comfort you on winter nights. Serve with Orange-Maple Yams or Minted Carrots (page 185) and some warm rolls.

Preheat the oven to 350°F.

Prepare the "bacon" and set aside. Combine all the other ingredients (the onions and mushrooms do not need to be precooked), and pour into a shallow, rectangular pyrex dish or casserole. Lay the "bacon" strips on top, and cover all with aluminum foil. Bake for about 1 hour. There should be a nicely flavored sauce bubbling away. Serve while hot.

Per serving: Calories 530, Protein 29 g, Fat 19 g, Carbohydrates 60 g

Yield: 6 servings

1 to 2 recipes Believable "Bacon,"
    page 33
Two 15-ounce cans kidney beans
    or one 28-ounce can, with
    approximately half its liquid
1½ onions, chopped
6 to 8 mushrooms, sliced
4 to 6 cloves garlic, minced
½ cup red wine
4 to 6 tablespoons soy sauce
2 tablespoons flour

Yield: 1¼ cups

1 cup water or stock
2 tablespoons dark miso
2 tablespoons soy sauce
½ teaspoon celery seeds
2 to 3 tablespoons nutritional
  yeast flakes (or Rich Yeast
  Flavoring Powder, below)
Freshly ground pepper
3 tablespoons cornstarch mixed
  with enough water to dissolve

Fat-Free Gravy

Combine all the ingredients except the cornstarch mixture, and bring to a simmer for 5 minutes. Add the cornstarch mixture a little at a time, stirring constantly until thickened.

Per ¼ cup: Calories 47, Protein 1 g, Fat 0 g, Carbohydrates 9 g

1 cup nutritional yeast flakes
3 tablespoons dried parsley
2 tablespoons salt
1½ tablespoons dill seeds
1½ tablespoons onion powder
1½ tablespoons dried basil
1½ tablespoons celery seeds
1 tablespoon dried thyme
2 teaspoons dried rosemary
1 tablespoon black pepper

Rich Yeast Flavoring Powder

This is similar to a beef stock flavoring.

Combine all the ingredients in a blender, and pulverize to a powder. Store in a jar in a cool place. Add to soups, loaves, burgers, and to recipes in this book where noted.

Light Yeast Flavoring Powder

This has a poultry-type flavor.

Pulverize all the ingredients in a blender until powdered. Store in a jar in a cool place.

1 cup nutritional yeast flakes

1 tablespoon salt

½ teaspoon ginger

½ teaspoon turmeric

1 teaspoon black pepper

1 teaspoon dried marjoram

1 teaspoon dried tarragon

1 teaspoon paprika

1 teaspoon dried rosemary

2 teaspoons dried sage

2 teaspoons celery seed

2 teaspoons dried thyme

2 teaspoons garlic powder

2 teaspoons onion powder

Vegetable Dishes & Salads

8 to 12 ounces Tofu "Cheese,"
    pages 42-43
Lemon juice (to marinate "cheese")
1 cup walnuts
2 red bell peppers
6 cups baby spinach

Sweet Balsamic Dressing

¼ cup seasoned rice vinegar
¼ cup balsamic vinegar
¼ cup extra-virgin olive oil
Freshly ground black pepper

Baby Spinach & "Chevre" Salad

Make tofu "chevre" (a slightly tangy mock goat cheese) by marinating the tofu "cheese" in enough lemon juice to cover for 2 to 3 hours.

Toast the walnuts in a 350°F oven for about 10 minutes, or until lightly browned. Break up into smaller pieces if desired, or leave as halves. Roast the red bell peppers under the broiler or directly over a gas flame, turning every few minutes, until the skin has blackened. Allow to cool until easily handled, and then peel off the blackened skin. Cut in half, scrape out the seeds and veins with a spoon, and cut into ¼-inch strips.

To make a sweet balsamic dressing, combine the vinegars, then whisk in the olive oil in a thin, steady stream. Season to taste with black pepper.

To assemble the salad, toss the spinach with the dressing. Place a mound of greens on individual salad plates, decorate with red pepper strips, walnuts, and "chevre." Serve immediately.

Per serving: Calories 98, Protein 0 g, Fat 10 g, Carbohydrates 1 g

Very Benevolent Caesar Salad

You would never believe that this wonderful replica of Caesar salad was actually free of cheese, eggs, anchovies, and low in fat to boot.

Prepare the lettuce and place in a large bowl. To make the dressing, combine the almond meal, garlic, mustard, and nutritional yeast to make a paste, then whisk in the remaining ingredients, except the croutons

To assemble the salad, top the lettuce with the croutons, and toss with the dressing. Serve immediately.

Per serving: Calories 94, Protein 9 g, Fat 3 g, Carbohydrates 11 g

Yield: 4 servings

1 small head romaine lettuce,
    washed, dried, and torn into
    large pieces

Dressing:

2 tablespoons almond meal
    (blanched ground almonds)
3 cloves garlic, pressed through
    a garlic press
3 tablespoons Dijon mustard
3 tablespoons nutritional yeast
    flakes
2 tablespoons soy sauce
3 tablespoons lemon juice
¼ cup water
1 tablespoon extra-virgin olive oil
    (optional)

Herb & Garlic Croutons, page 182

Dressing
  (for 8 servings):

½ *cup soy sauce*
½ *cup red wine vinegar*
1 *tablespoon fruit juice concentrate*
¾ *cup grapeseed or olive oil*
Freshly ground pepper

For each entrée serving of salad
  (prepare immediately before
  eating):
3 *cups baby spinach*
A dash of oil
2 *to 3 slivered fresh or*
  reconstituted shiitake
  mushrooms
¼ *bunch enoki mushrooms*
A few shimeji or oyster mushrooms
3 *tablespoons sake*
Pinch of salt
¼ *cup dressing*

Wilted Spinach Salad with Japanese Mushrooms

If the dressing is made ahead and kept refrigerated, this can become an easy and elegant first course or light entrée that can be whipped up in moments, even for one. The recipe for the dressing makes about eight servings, but the instructions given for the salad are for one individual entrée serving or two appetizer salads. Just double, triple, or quadruple the servings as necessary.

To prepare the dressing, whisk the soy sauce, vinegar, and fruit juice concentrate together. Dribble in the oil, whisking all the while. Season to taste with pepper. Keep refrigerated in a tightly covered jar.

Place the spinach in individual serving bowls.

Heat a sauté pan until hot. Add the oil, heat a moment, then add the mushrooms over high heat, stirring or tossing to prevent sticking. They should not crowd the pan, or they will become watery. When they begin to brown and stick to the pan, deglaze the pan with some sake, scraping the bottom of the pan to mix up any stuck bits of mushroom. Season with a pinch of salt, and allow to sizzle for a moment. Pour into the pan ¼ cup of the dressing, heat, and pour immediately over the spinach. Toss, cover with a plate or an inverted pan for about 20 seconds, then serve immediately. The spinach will wilt slightly but should not look completely cooked.

Do not try to make more than 2 or 3 servings of this dish at one time unless you have a very large sauté pan, as the mushrooms tend to get watery. If you are serving up to 8 people, you can still make the salad in less than 10 minutes by making 2 or 3 portions at a time.

Per entrée serving: Calories 171, Protein 7 g, Fat 12 g, Carbohydrates 13 g

Wakame Salad

Wakame salads started to appear on the Japanese culinary scene in the '80s as the Japanese began to adopt Western foods. They added soy sauce to a basic vinaigrette and made "Wa-Fu Dressing."(Wa-Fu literally means "Japanese-style.") Then they poured it on top of tender wakame and greens, and voilà, a new culinary tradition was established.

Using the most tender wakame you can find for this dish is of paramount importance. Often you will find chopped dried wakame marketed as "cut wakame" in Japanese food stores. Obviously tough-looking, stringy wakame in long strands will not do the job when it comes to eating it raw and fresh. Although the packs of finely chopped dried wakame contain only a few ounces, you don't need much for your salad; about 1 to 2 tablespoons per person will reconstitute into a healthy heap. Some Japanese grocery stores carry fresh wakame preserved in salt in the refrigerated section. If it looks tender to you, this works well too. Be sure to rinse it thoroughly, then soak and rinse again before using it, or you will choke on the salt.

Reconstitute the dried wakame in the water for 10 minutes. It will swell and and come to life. Drain.

Arrange the vegetables on a plate, top with the wakame, and pour on a generous serving of Wa-Fu Dressing. Devour immediately!

Per serving: Calories 60, Protein 2 g, Fat 0 g, Carbohydrates 10 g

Per serving:

Approximately 1 to 2 tablespoons chopped dried wakame, reconstituted in ½ cup water, or ¼ cup fresh wakame in salt (see instructions)

For the salad:

Any vegetables you like: lettuce, tomatoes, cucumbers, scallions, red onions, grated carrots, fresh corn kernels

Wa-Fu Dressing, page 181

Yield: 1 serving

Maple-Dijon Dressing
(makes 2 cups)

¾ cup Dijon mustard
¾ cup maple syrup
¼ cup balsamic vinegar
¼ cup canola or safflower oil
Freshly ground black pepper
(optional)

1 to 1½ cups pecans
Salt
½ cup maple syrup

Salad, per person:

Approximately 1½ cups organic
spring lettuce or mesclun mix
⅓ crisp, ripe pear, sliced
A few caramelized pecans
Approximately 1 tablespoon
dressing

Pear & Caramelized Pecan Salad with Maple Dijon Dressing

This delightful salad can be served as a leading course to an elegant or rich dinner—definitely not a side dish salad.

To prepare the dressing, combine the Dijon mustard with the maple syrup and balsamic vinegar. Whisk in the oil to emulsify. If desired, season with freshly ground black pepper.

Preheat the oven to 400°F.

Place the pecans on a cookie sheet, and sprinkle with some salt. Pour the maple syrup on top. Bake until the maple syrup is bubbly and the pecans appear brown, about 15 minutes. Do not burn! Pour immediately onto a greased cookie sheet or waxed paper. Place in the refrigerator or freezer to cool. When hard, break or cut up into small pieces.

To assemble the salad, toss the spring lettuce mix lightly with the dressing. Mound on a plate, top with the pear, and sprinkle pecans on top. Drizzle on a little extra dressing for effect.

Per serving: Calories 139, Protein 2 g, Fat 7 g, Carbohydrates 20 g

Balsamic Vinaigrette

Yield: Approximately 3 cups

In a large bowl, whisk together the fruit juice concentrate, garlic, and balsamic vinegar. Pour in the olive oil in a slow and steady stream, whisking constantly to emulsify. Season with salt and pepper to taste.

*2 tablespoons fruit juice
  concentrate*
1 tablespoon chopped garlic
1 cup balsamic vinegar
2 cups extra-virgin olive oil
Salt and pepper

Per tablespoon: Calories 81, Protein 0 g, Fat 9 g, Carbohydrates 0 g

Basil Onion Vinaigrette

Yield: Approximately 2¼ cups

*Nicely balanced and flavored with a slightly sweet touch.
If desired, the amount of sweetener can be reduced.
Using a red onion will yield a lovely pinkish color.*

Place all ingredients, liquids first, into a blender, and purée until thick and creamy.

1¼ cups extra-virgin olive oil
⅓ cup fruit juice concentrate
⅓ cup white or red wine vinegar
½ large onion, cut into chunks
½ teaspoon sea salt
1 cup packed fresh basil leaves

Per tablespoon: Calories 72, Protein 0 g, Fat 7 g, Carbohydrates 1 g

Yield: 1⅔ cups

⅓ cup freshly squeezed
    lemon juice
⅓ cup balsamic vinegar
1 tablespoon fruit juice
    concentrate or sugar
1 cup extra-virgin olive oil
1 teaspoon salt
Black pepper

Greek Vinaigrette

*Great on top of a vegan Greek salad with crispy romaine,
kalamata olives, and tofu "feta."*

Place all ingredients, liquids first, into a blender, and purée
until smooth.

Per tablespoon: Calories 73, Protein 0 g, Fat 8 g, Carbohydrates 1 g

Yield: 2½ cups

8 ounces frozen or fresh
    raspberries
½ cup water
⅓ cup white wine vinegar
⅓ to ½ cup fruit juice
    concentrate
1 teaspoon salt
2 tablespoons lemon juice
    concentrate
3 tablespoons balsamic vinegar

Raspberry Vinaigrette

A delicious and light fat-free dressing that is great on field greens.

Purée all the ingredients in a blender until creamy and
pink. Chill before serving.

Per tablespoon: Calories 8, Protein 0 g, Fat 0 g, Carbohydrates 2 g

Tarragon Garlic Vinaigrette

Wonderful for marinating grilled or roasted vegetables as well as various beans for an elegant bean salad.

Combine all the ingredients, except the tarragon, in a blender, and purée until thick and creamy. Add the tarragon and purée again only until chopped. Do not allow dressing to become green.

Per tablespoon: Calories 86, Protein 0 g, Fat 9 g, Carbohydrates 1 g

Yield: 1½ cups

1 cup extra-virgin olive oil
⅓ cup white wine vinegar
2 tablespoons fruit juice
   concentrate
1 teaspoon salt
2 tablespoons chopped
   fresh garlic
2 tablespoons dried tarragon
   or ¼ cup fresh

Ume Lime Dressing

Absolutely refreshing and unique, excellent on julienne daikon or jicama.

Mix all the ingredients well. If serving over julienne daikon or jicama, pour on immediately before serving, or you will lose the crunchiness of the vegetable quickly.

Per tablespoon: Calories 18, Protein 0 g, Fat 0 g, Carbohydrates 4 g

Yield: ⅔ cup

⅓ cup freshly squeezed
   lime juice
⅓ cup fructose or fruit juice
   concentrate
1 tablespoon ume paste

Yield: 2 cups

¾ cup fruit juice concentrate
½ cup tamari or soy sauce
½ cup freshly squeezed
  lemon juice
2 tablespoons ume paste
2 tablespoons sesame oil

Tamari Ume Dressing

Low in fat with an Asian touch, this slightly tangy dressing goes well over greens, sea vegetables, and salads with Asian pears.

Combine all the ingredients and whisk well. This can be stored in the refrigerator for several weeks.

Per tablespoon: Calories 24, Protein 1 g, Fat 1 g, Carbohydrates 4 g

Yield: 1½ cups

⅓ cup freshly squeezed lime juice
¼ cup fruit juice concentrate
  (either white grape, or pear-
  peach-pineapple combo)
1 large ripe mango, peeled
  and seeded
Salt and freshly ground pepper

Mango Lime Dressing

Whipped up in a flash, this fat-free dressing provides a refreshing and flavorful contrast to the usual vinaigrette. It is especially good on soft butter lettuce or spring lettuce mix.

Purée all the ingredients in a blender until smooth, adding salt and pepper as desired.

Per tablespoon: Calories 11, Protein 0 g, Fat 0 g, Carbohydrates 3 g

Baby Spinach & "Chevre" Salad, page 172

Orange-Soy Dressing

Yield: ½ cup

A wonderful, unusual combination perfect for tender leaves of Boston or butterhead lettuce tossed together with ripe avocado and perhaps a few roasted pecans. It is also excellent with Belgian endive, orange pieces, and pecans.

It's very important to squeeze the orange juice right before using, or it will lack the necessary aroma and flavor. Mix the juice, soy sauce, and vinegar together, then whisk in the safflower oil slowly until thickened.

¼ cup freshly squeezed orange juice

1½ tablespoons soy sauce

1 tablespoon rice vinegar
   (available at natural food stores
   or Japanese grocers)

¼ cup safflower or other light oil

Per tablespoon: Calories 67, Protein 0 g, Fat 7 g, Carbohydrates 1 g

California Salad

Although excellent over tender greens, this dressing can also be used over a mixture of shredded cabbage and carrots, diced avocados, orange pieces, and lightly toasted sunflower seeds. This is a nice, light alternative to cole slaw.

Wa-Fu Dressing

Yield: 1¾ cups

Here is a simple dressing that contains very little fat per serving. It is tasty over regular greens, shredded cabbage (a common component of Japanese salads), reconstituted wakame, or other delicate sea vegetables. At our restaurant, we served this over our popular wakame salad, which consists of romaine lettuce topped with delicate wakame, fresh corn, tomatoes, red onions, and cucumbers.

Whisk all the ingredients together.

Scant ½ cup soy sauce

⅓ cup fruit juice concentrate or
   FruitSource, or ¼ cup sugar

¾ cup rice wine vinegar

1 tablespoon sesame oil

1 tablespoon toasted sesame seeds
   (optional)

Per tablespoon: Calories 14, Protein 0 g, Fat 0 g, Carbohydrates 2 g

Chocolate Almond Raspberry Torte, pages 188-89

14 to 16 ounces firm silken tofu (no
    other kind will do for this)
4 tablespoons canola or safflower oil
2 tablespoons lemon juice
½ teaspoon salt

Tofu Sour Cream

Blend all the ingredients together until thick and smooth.

Per tablespoon: Calories: 38, Protein 1 g, Fat 4 g, Carbohydrates 1 g

3 to 4 slices stale French or
    sourdough bread, trimmed
    of crust and cubed (about
    1½ cups cubed)
Nonstick spray (for a not so
    low-fat version, use
    3 tablespoons olive oil)
1 tablespoon minced garlic
½ teaspoon dried rosemary
½ teaspoon dried marjoram
¼ teaspoon salt

Herb & Garlic Croutons

Preheat the oven to 250°F. Spray the cubes of bread with
the nonstick spray, or alternatively, toss with olive oil in a
bowl. Toss with the garlic, herbs, and salt. Place on a cookie sheet in a single layer, and toast until lightly browned,
about 25 minutes. The object is not to bake them, but to dry
them out. Remove from the oven; they will continue to
crisp as they cool.

Per serving: Calories 40, Protein 2 g, Fat 0 g, Carbohydrates 6 g

Roasted Vegetables

This simple technique works wonders with a variety of vegetables, amplifying their flavors and rendering them absolutely sweet and succulent. Some vegetables, such as asparagus, are utterly luscious prepared this way and will elicit questions such as, "Wow! How did you season these?" Simply with a little salt and olive oil, will be my answer. Expect each person to consume about one bunch of asparagus. Even unpopular veggies, such as turnips, will gain star status.

Roasted vegetables can be consumed as is, used to garnish a salad, served with a sauce (such as the Orange Coconut Curry, page 119), tossed with a vinaigrette or marinade as an appetizer, or as the star filling for a delicious sandwich.

Use vegetables either singly or in combination. Prepare them according to type and how you want to serve them: asparagus needs a little trimmed off the bottom only, and mushrooms can be kept whole or cut in half, but other vegetables should be sliced about ½ inch thick.

Preheat the oven to 400°F. In a bowl, toss the vegetables with a little salt and olive oil to coat lightly. Place on a baking sheet in a single layer, and bake for about 15 to 20 minutes, or until browned. Some vegetables will cook faster; check after 10 minutes and spear with a fork for tenderness. They should be tender, succulent, and lightly brown, although asparagus should not be allowed to become too brown or wrinkled.

Almost any vegetable: asparagus, beets, bell peppers, every variety of mushroom, eggplant, turnips, zucchini, onions, green beans, etc.

Salt

Extra-virgin olive oil

Freshly ground pepper (optional)

Yield: 4 to 6 servings

*2 large sweet potatoes or yams,
    steamed, baked, or micro-
    waved until soft*
3 teaspoons freshly grated ginger
2 to 3 teaspoons curry powder
2 teaspoons soy sauce
2 teaspoons ground coriander
Approximately ½ cup soymilk
Oil for frying
Coconut Crème Fraiche, page 83

CURRIED SWEET POTATO CAKES

*Try these slightly spicy and rich-tasting patties in place
of the traditional candied yams for Thanksgiving
or Christmas (or anytime, for that matter).*

Peel the cooked sweet potatoes, cut them up into chunks,
and process with the other ingredients in a food processor
until smooth. The mixture should be firm enough to handle
and shape. Form into patties and sauté on both sides in a
little oil until crispy on both sides. Serve with with Coconut
Crème Fraiche, if desired.

Per serving: Calories 105, Protein 2 g, Fat 0 g, Carbohydrates 23 g

Yield: 4 servings

1 medium eggplant
2 tablespoons olive oil
¼ pound small button mushrooms
½ cup red wine
2 to 3 tablespoons soy sauce
2 tablespoons mirin

EGGPLANT & MUSHROOMS
STEWED IN RED WINE

A dark and delicious concoction.

Cut the eggplant into ½-inch cubes, and sprinkle generously with salt. Let it drain in a colander for 20 to 30 minutes, then rinse and pat dry with paper towels. Heat the
olive oil in a pan, and sauté the eggplant until slightly tender. Add the mushrooms and continue sautéing for 3 to 4
minutes. Add the red wine, soy sauce, and mirin, cover
with a tightly fitting lid, and stew slowly until only a few
tablespoons of liquid remain in the pan and the vegetables
are nearly black in appearance.

Per serving: Calories 149, Protein 3 g, Fat 7 g, Carbohydrates 17 g

Orange-Maple Yams

Not overly sweet, this harmonious combination of flavors complements a holiday meal nicely. It can also be served at any other time of the year.

Scrub the yams well and bake in a 350°F oven until a fork pierces through easily (anywhere from 30 to 60 minutes, depending on size). If desired, the yams can be baked hours or even the day before serving. Allow to cool enough to handle, then peel. Mash the yams in a bowl, combine with the maple syrup and orange juice, and mix well. Place in a buttered casserole or baking dish, and if desired, season with salt and pepper. Cover with aluminum foil and bake at 350°F until heated through.

Per serving: Calories 309, Protein 5 g, Fat 0 g, Carbohydrates 76 g

Yield: 4 to 6 servings

3 pounds yams
6 tablespoons maple syrup
4 tablespoons frozen concentrated orange juice
Salt and pepper, to taste

Minted Carrots

This is one of my favorite ways to serve carrots; easy to prepare, with a very interesting and refreshing flavor. I like to serve them for Thanksgiving and Christmas.

Cut the carrots into slices or sticks as desired, and steam until tender. Toss with the remaining ingredients while the carrots are still hot, and serve immediately.

Per serving: Calories 73, Protein 1 g, Fat 4 g, Carbohydrates 8 g

Yield: 4 to 6 servings

1 pound carrots
2 tablespoons chopped fresh mint
2 tablespoons nonhydrogenated margarine
2 tablespoons orange juice
1 teaspoon sweetener, or more to taste
Salt and pepper

Desserts

Even the most committed dieter or natural food afficionado occasionally breaks down in front of a rich, decadent dessert. Unfortunately, "natural" substitutes (the colorless, dry concoctions that try to pass for sweet treats in health food stores) do not always satisfy that particular craving we mortals sometimes have for indulgence. The bottom line is that people eat desserts because they taste good, not for any nutritional benefit. This is not to say that they can't be nutritious, but simply that they shouldn't have to taste too "healthy." Here is a collection of desserts ranging from fruit dishes to richer mousses and tarts that make no apologies for the way they taste. They are, however, all good for you, and I do extend my apologies to anyone out there who might be disturbed by that and claim that I was destroying their ability to enjoy these treats.

A note about sweeteners: Most of the following recipes can be sweetened as desired. Barley malt, rice syrup, maple syrup, or concentrated fruit juice can be used interchangeably in many of the recipes, and are indicated where applicable. (See pages 13 to 14.) Evaporated cane juice or sugar can also be used. Again, personal taste will often dictate how sweet a dessert should be, so feel free to increase the amount of sweetener used.

Yield: 12 servings

See photo facing page 181 and on the back cover

For the layers:

½ cup nonhydrogenated margarine (preferably unsalted), or vegetable oil

⅔ cup white grape juice concentrate, maple syrup, or barley malt

3 tablespoons brandy

7 ounces almond meal (finely ground blanched almonds)

2 cups semidried okara (see instructions for drying on page 8 and the recipe on the facing page)

⅔ cup soymilk

6 tablespoons cocoa or carob powder

2½ teaspoons aluminum-free baking powder

Chocolate Almond Raspberry Torte

This rich, decadent, special-occasion treat contains no eggs, dairy products, or flour and is equally delicious made with chocolate or carob. Okara, the high-fiber part of the soybean that is a by-product of tofu processing, helps to produce a moist, delicate cake. Okara can either be made at home (see the recipe below right) or purchased from a local tofu manufacturer.

Preheat the oven to 350°F.

To prepare the layers, cream the margarine with the sweetener, then add the brandy, mixing well. Stir in the almond meal and okara, mixing well, then add the soymilk. Sift the cocoa with the baking powder, and mix in well. (This batter will resemble a very soft, moist cookie dough.) Line a cookie sheet with baking paper, divide the batter into two portions, and pat out two circles (about 7½ inches each) on the sheet. (Two 8-inch springform pans lined with baking paper may also be used.) Do not attempt to use regular cake pans, or the layers will crumble upon removal! Bake for 25 minutes until the edges are beginning to darken. They will expand by an inch or more in diameter. Allow to cool completely before handling.

While the layers are baking, prepare the raspberry filling. Set aside a few raspberries for garnish, and combine the rest with the sweetener or apple juice in a saucepan. Bring to a boil, reduce the heat, and simmer for about 10 minutes, stirring occasionally, until the raspberries have dissolved. Mix the cornstarch and water over low heat, and add to the raspberries to thicken. Set aside to cool.

To prepare the dark chocolate cream, melt the chocolate chips over (not in) hot water. Combine the remaining ingredients in a food processor, and blend until absolutely creamy. Taste for sweetness, adding more sweetener if desired. Use this soon after making, or it will stiffen too much to spread.

To assemble the cake, place one layer upside-down on a platter with the baking paper still intact. Peel off the paper and spread about ⅓ of the chocolate cream evenly over the layer. Place the other cake layer upside-down on top, and peel off the paper gently. Spread the raspberry "jam" on top. Trim the sides with a very sharp knife, and cover completely with most of the remaining chocolate cream, saving about ⅓ to ½ cup for decorating the top.

To decorate, pipe rosettes on top with a pastry bag or tube. Garnish with chocolate rolls or shavings, if desired, and dust lightly with cornstarch.

Per serving: Calories 498, Protein 13 g, Fat 23 g, Carbohydrates 55 g

Optional chocolate rolls or shavings

Melt the chocolate and pour onto a marble slab or similar cold, hard surface. Chill completely, then scrape with a vegetable peeler or knife to form rolls or shavings.

Homemade okara

Start with 1½ cups dry soybeans. Soak until doubled. Process 1 cup soaked beans at a time with 2½ cups water in a blender until it forms a fine slurry. Pour all the batches into a heavy bottomed pot or double boiler. Carefully bring to a boil, then simmer for 20 minutes. Drain the mixture into a colander lined with cheesecloth or nylon set atop a large pot. (The liquid you drain off is delicious homemade soymilk, which you can use for cooking or chill for drinking.) The pulp remaining in the colander is the okara you'll need for this recipe. To dry it, see the directions on page 9.

Raspberry filling:

8 ounces raspberries

⅓ cup white grape juice
*   concentrate*
*   or ½ cup frozen concentrated*
*   apple juice*

2 tablespoons cornstarch

2 to 3 tablespoons water

Dark Chocolate Cream:

6 ounces unsweetened chocolate or
*   carob chips*

20 ounces tofu (if firm, add
*   ½ cup soymilk)*

½ cup maple syrup or sugar,
*   or ¾ cup barley malt*

⅓ cup cocoa

1 teaspoon vanilla

2 tablespoons brandy

Chocolate rolls or shavings (for
*   garnish—optional):*

2 ounces bittersweet chocolate or
*   carob chips (if using chocolate,*
*   try a dairy-free, white sugar-free*
*   variety, if available)*

See photo facing page 212.

1 cup semisweet nondairy chocolate

2 pounds regular tofu

1 cup cocoa

1 cup sweetener of choice, either
   maple syrup, evaporated cane
   juice, FruitSource, or white
   grape juice concentrate

¼ cup arrowroot

2 teaspoons baking powder

2 teaspoons vanilla

Chocolate Soufflé Roll or Buche de Noël

Divinely rich and chocolatey, this flourless cake can be filled with a crème or icing and rolled up, or simply stacked like a traditional cake. It can also form the base for a beautiful holiday yule log (Buche de Noël), dusted with cocoa and powdered sugar and decorated with icing mushrooms.

Melt the chocolate either in the microwave, oven, or double boiler. If using a microwave, place the chocolate in a clean, dry glass bowl. Microwave on high for about 60 seconds; the chocolate should look very soft. Stir with a clean, dry spoon to see if it is melted completely; the residual heat is often sufficient to do this. If not, return to the microwave for another 15 seconds, then stir again until smooth. If using the oven or double boiler, the chocolate can be placed in either a glass or metal bowl. Either place on top of a small pot of simmering water, stirring occasionally until smooth and melted, or place in a 300°F oven for about 5 minutes, then stir. Do not overheat; the chocolate should never become hot to the touch, just warm enough to melt. Overheating can cause the chocolate to lose its smoothness and become grainy. Set the chocolate aside while proceeding with the remaining instructions.

Place the tofu, cocoa, sweetener, arrowroot, baking powder, and vanilla in the bowl of a food processor, and purée until relatively smooth. If only a blender is available, crumble the tofu in a large bowl, and combine it with the remaining ingredients with a whisk or potato masher. Process in several batches in the blender, stirring the batches together in a separate bowl to combine. Add the melted chocolate and continue to process until completely smooth.

Preheat the oven to 350°F. Line a 9 x 13-inch baking pan with parchment, and either spray the sides with nonstick spray or oil with vegetable oil. Spread the mixture in it evenly. Bake for 20 to 25 minutes until puffy and a "skin" has formed on top. It will be dry to the touch. Remove from the oven and allow to cool completely. If possible, chill overnight or for several hours in the refrigerator before filling and rolling.

To roll, dust a clean sheet of parchment heavily with additional cocoa powder. Flip the pan over, turning the cake out. Peel off the parchment paper, and discard. Spread with the icing of your choice. Holding the parchment sheet on the bottom of the soufflé, roll it up tightly. It will crack some. Transfer to a platter carefully, and using a sieve or sifter, dust all over with additional cocoa or homemade powdered sugar. To serve, slice with a serrated knife.

Per serving: Calories 314, Protein 10 g, Fat 12 g, Carbohydrates 41 g

Filling ideas:

For the richest, fluffiest filling, use Hip Whip (available in natural food stores). Chocolate Buttercreme, page 231, can also be used, or fill with Rich Tofu Crème, page 229

½ cup oil

1 cup fruit juice concentrate,
*   white grape juice concentrate,*
*   or maple syrup*

1 teaspoon vanilla

2¾ cups unbleached pastry flour,
*   or whole wheat pastry flour*

1 tablespoon baking powder

1 cup soymilk or rice milk

2 teaspoons apple cider vinegar

Basic Sponge Cake

Utterly simple to make, and yet so much like a "regular" sponge cake—light, airy, delicious! This versatile cake can form the base of many grand or everyday creations and can be flavored with extracts and zests to suit the occasion. It is fabulous for strawberry shortcake or can be decorated with chocolate buttercreme or any other icing of your fancy. I have found that fruit juice concentrate yields the lightest results. For the maple rum torte on page 198, use maple syrup.

Preheat the oven to 350°F.

In a bowl, whisk together the oil, sweetener, and vanilla. In a separate bowl, sift the flour with the baking powder. Add ⅓ cup milk to the oil mixture, and whisk well. Add about ⅓ of the flour, and whisk well again. Repeat with the milk and flour until everything has been added, then beat for about 60 seconds after the final addition of flour. Whisk in the vinegar.

Prepare two 8- or 9-inch round cake pans, a 9 x 13-inch rectangular baking pan, or a cookie sheet by covering with parchment and oiling the sides, or by oiling the entire pan and lightly dusting with flour. Pour in the batter. Bake for 20 to 25 minutes, depending on the thickness of the layers, or until barely golden brown on top. It should not be allowed to color too much, or it will be overbaked. Touching the middle of the cake should yield a springy feel. Alternatively, a toothpick inserted in the middle will come out clean.

Per serving: Calories 221, Protein 3 g, Fat 9 g, Carbohydrates 30 g

Lemon Cake

Add 1 teaspoon lemon oil or 2 teaspoons lemon extract and the grated zest of 1 lemon to the oil and sweetener.

Orange Cake

Add the grated zest of 1 orange to the oil and sweetener.

Spice Cake

Add 1 teaspoon cinnamon, ½ teaspoon cardamom, ¼ teaspoon nutmeg, ½ teaspoon ginger, and ¼ teaspoon mace to the flour.

Coconut Cake

Add 1 cup grated coconut to the sweetener and oil.

*Yield: two 9-inch layers or one
9 x 13-inch sheet pan
(16 servings)*

½ cup oil

1 cup white grape juice
   concentrate or maple syrup

2 teaspoons vanilla

2 cups white or whole wheat pastry
   or cake flour

¾ cup cocoa powder

1¼ teaspoons baking soda

1 cup water

1 teaspoon apple cider vinegar

Chocolate Sponge Cake

*It's hard to believe that such a simple recipe would yield
such light, delicate chocolate layers that can be used for
just about any chocolate cake.*

Preheat the oven to 350°F. Line two 9-inch round cake pans with parchment, or oil and flour well.

In a medium-sized bowl, combine the oil and sweetener with a whisk, then add the vanilla. Sift the flour, cocoa powder, and baking soda. Add ½ cup of the water to the liquid mixture, and mix well. Then whisk in half of the flour mixture, beating with the whisk until thoroughly combined. Add the rest of the water, and mix well. Add the remaining flour mixture, whisking for about 60 seconds until thoroughly combined. Add the cider vinegar and whisk for another 10 seconds.

Divide the batter between the two pans. Bake for 20 to 25 minutes, or until the tops feel springy.

Per serving: Calories 151, Protein 2 g, Fat 8 g, Carbohydrates 21 g

Chocolate Buttercreme Ganache Cake

With a serrated knife, split each chocolate layer into two layers to yield a total of four layers. Place one layer gently on a cake stand or plate. If desired, brush on a little liqueur. Ice with about a ¼-inch layer of buttercreme. Place another cake layer on top. Repeat the procedure until all layers are used. Cover the top and sides of the cake with icing. Chill the cake slightly. Prepare the ganache, allow to cool slightly, then pour over the cake (spreading lightly if necessary), and decorate as desired.

Chocolate Ganache

Place the chocolate chips in a dry glass or metal bowl over a small pot with an inch of water. Bring the water to a gentle simmer. Stir the chocolate with a dry spoon every couple of minutes until the chocolate melts. Add the soymilk and mix; it may be grainy at first, but it will eventually become very smooth. Allow to cool briefly before pouring over the cake.

Per serving: Calories 443, Protein 5 g, Fat 27 g, Carbohydrates 49 g

Yield: 16 servings

2 Chocolate Sponge Cake layers
1 recipe Chocolate Buttercreme, page 231
1 recipe Chocolate Ganache (below)
Optional: ¼ cup or more rum, brandy, Kahlua or other coffee liqueur, or Grand Marnier

Chocolate Ganache:

12 ounces semisweet vegan chocolate chips
1 cup rich, vanilla-flavored soymilk (less can be used for richer flavor, although it will be harder to pour)

½ cup fruit juice concentrate or
    maple syrup

¼ cup nonhydrogenated margarine

1 cup almond meal (pulverized or
    ground blanched almonds)

1 cup semidried okara
    (see instructions for drying on
    page 8 and the recipe on page
    189)

2 tablespoons flour

1¼ teaspoons aluminum-free
    baking powder

⅓ cup soymilk

2 tablespoons brandy or dark rum,
    or ½ tablespoon vanilla plus
    1½ tablespoons apple juice

½ cup sliced almonds (or more,
    if desired)

Almond Cake

*Here's a delicate, rich cake perfect for tea. The recipe can be doubled
to make two layers for the delicious Christmas tree cake at right.*

Heat the oven to 350°F. Oil and flour an 8-inch round cake
pan, preferably springform or with a false bottom.

Cream the sweetener and margarine. Add the almond meal
and okara. Sift the flour with the baking powder, and add
to the mixture, folding gently. Add the soymilk and brandy,
mixing gently but well.

Spread into the prepared pan. Cover the top with almond
slices, and bake for about 20 minutes. Allow to cool completely before removing from the pan.

Per serving: Calories 360, Protein 8 g, Fat 27 g, Carbohydrates 24 g

CHRISTMAS TREE CAKE

This batter is thick enough that it can actually be patted into any shape desired. To assemble a Christmas tree-shaped cake that will delight both children and adults, oil and flour a large cookie sheet. Double the recipe and form two trees on the sheet (triangles with a square stump—better to keep it simple). Bake for 20 minutes at 350°F. After the layers have cooled, put them together with an all-fruit jam. Make 3 recipes of the tofu crème, page 229, and add parsley juice to ⅔ of it to color it a bright green. (Mince the parsley in a food processor, and press it in a thin towel to squeeze out the juice.) Add carob powder to the remaining one-third of the tofu crème. Now frost the tree with the green crème, and use the carob crème to frost the trunk. Decorate with cranberries; if desired, pipe some plain white tofu crème around the borders. Very pretty! Try also making a Valentine cake, and use your imagination to create various shapes for birthdays and other special occasions.

Have ready:

Basic Sponge Cake, page 192, made with maple syrup as the sweetener and either baked as two layers or baked as one layer and split in two with a serrated knife.

Maple Buttercreme:

1¼ cups maple syrup

8 ounces firm tofu

1½ cups nonhydrogenated margarine (12 ounces)

1 teaspoon vanilla

Rum Syrup:

⅓ cup maple syrup

¼ cup water

2 to 3 tablespoons dark rum

1 recipe Chocolate Ganache, page 195

Maple Rum Torte

Rich and devastating.

To prepare the maple buttercreme, place the maple syrup in a 1- or 2-quart heavy bottomed pot. Bring the syrup to a boil, and simmer for 15 to 20 minutes until reduced and thickened, making sure to watch the heat so the syrup will not boil over or burn. If you place a few drops of the boiled syrup on an ice cube, it should form a soft to firm mass. Allow to cool for 5 minutes.

Purée the tofu in a food processor or blender until smooth. Add the maple syrup at once, and purée until smooth. Add the margarine and vanilla, and purée again until smooth. The mixture may be runny at this time. Chill until firm enough to spread.

To make the rum syrup, heat the maple syrup and water in a small saucepan, and bring to a simmer for a couple of minutes. Turn off the heat, and add the rum. Although this can be prepared ahead of time, it will need to be hot when it is brushed onto the layers.

To assemble the cake, Place one layer of the cake on a plate, brush generously with the warm rum syrup, and spread one-third of the buttercreme on top. Stack the other layer on top, brush on more syrup, and cover the sides and top of the cake generously with the remaining buttercreme. Chill the cake thoroughly by placing in the freezer for 1 hour.

Prepare the chocolate ganache and cool slightly. Pour on top of the chilled cake, allowing it to run down the sides. Chill the cake slightly again to allow the ganache to set before serving.

Per serving: Calories 540, Protein 6 g, Fat 32 g, Carbohydrates 58 g

CASHEW CHEESECAKE

Yield: 8 to 10 servings

This rich, creamy, no-bake cheesecake with a jelled orange topping was a favorite in my cooking classes.

Wrap the tofu in towels and refrigerate overnight, or press with a weighted plate for 1 hour to remove the water. Mash.

Combine the cashews, water, lemon zest, and juice in a blender or food processor until absolutely creamy and smooth. This is very important or you will have a grainy cheesecake. You may need to blend in batches, then combine. Add the sweetener, vanilla, orange liqueur, and tofu, and blend again until smooth.

Combine the agar with the orange juice in a small saucepan, cover, and simmer over medium to medium-high heat for 2 to 3 minutes, stirring frequently. Add to the mixture in the food processor, and blend again. Immediately pour this mixture into the prepared pie crust, and chill in the refrigerator for 20 to 30 minutes.

When the top feels relatively solidified, prepare the jelled orange topping. Combine the orange and apple juices, and dissolve the agar in the mixture. Pour this on top of the cheesecake, and allow to chill and set overnight in the refrigerator before unmolding and serving.

For a slightly different flavor, you can use a pineapple or berry-based juice in place of the orange juice for the topping. (The apple juice functions primarily as a sweetener.)

Per serving: Calories 412, Protein 13 g, Fat 20 g, Carbohydrates 48 g

1½ pounds regular tofu
1 cup raw unsalted cashews
½ cup water
Grated zest and juice of 2 lemons
⅓ to ½ cup fruit juice concentrate, FruitSource, or agave (see page 14)
1 teaspoon vanilla, or seeds from ½-inch vanilla bean pod
2 tablespoons Grand Marnier or other orange liqueur (optional)
1 bar or 1 teaspoon agar, or ¼ cup agar flakes
¾ cup orange juice

1 recipe Oatmeal Crust, page 208, baked in a 9-inch springform pan

Topping:
½ cup orange juice
½ cup apple juice
⅓ bar or ⅓ teaspoon powdered agar, or 1¼ teaspoons agar flakes

Yield: 10 servings

½ cup sultana raisins

½ cup chopped almonds

½ teaspoon grated orange zest

Juice and grated zest of 1 large
lemon

1 tablespoon flour

1⅝ pounds regular tofu, pressed
(see page 18)

½ cup fruit juice concentrate,
evaporated cane juice, or
FruitSource

3 tablespoons rum, or 1 teaspoon
rum flavoring

1 teaspoon vanilla

2 tablespoons arrowroot

1 Almond Pastry Crust,
page 203, patted onto the bottom
of a springform pan

½ cup sliced almonds

Italian Cheeseless Cake

This is similar to a cheesecake I had once in Italy that was full of raisins and nuts. I believe the original was made of ricotta and cream; this one substitutes no-cholesterol tofu to get very pleasant results.

Preheat the oven to 350°F.

Toss the raisins, almonds, and grated zest with the flour. Blend the tofu, sweetener, rum, vanilla, and arrowroot in a food processor or blender until smooth. If using a blender, combine the ingredients with a whisk or potato masher in a large bowl, and process in batches. Combine the batches in a separate bowl when finished. Mix in the raisin-almond-flour mixture. Pour over the crust, sprinkle the sliced almonds on top, and bake for 1 hour.

Chill overnight before removing from the pan and serving.

Per serving: Calories 431, Protein 13 g, Fat 25 g, Carbohydrates 38 g

LEMONY LEMON CREAM TART

Very zesty, creamy, and luscious.

Blend the cashews with the water, lemon juice, zest, and sweetener in a food processor or blender until absolutely smooth and creamy. Remove all but ½ cup of this mixture, place in a saucepan, and warm over gentle heat. When hot, dissolve the arrowroot, cornstarch, or kuzu in a small amount of water, and add to the saucepan, stirring constantly until thickened.

Crumble the tofu and add it to the remaining ½ cup of the lemon-cashew mixture in the blender. Process again until smooth and creamy. Mix this with the thickened mixture above, and transfer to a large bowl. Add the Grand Marnier.

In a small saucepan, dissolve the agar in the orange juice, cover, bring to a boil, and then allow it to simmer uncovered on medium to medium-high heat for 2 to 3 minutes, stirring frequently. Whisk well into the lemon-tofu-cashew mixture. Pour immediately into the prepared tart crust, and chill until firm. Decorate with thin lemon slices and Tofu Crème rosettes, if desired.

Per serving: Calories 298, Protein 6 g, Fat 13 g, Carbohydrates 43 g

Yield: 8 small tarts or one 9-inch tart

Scant ⅔ cup raw cashews
¾ cup water
½ cup lemon juice
Grated zest of 1½ lemons
⅔ cup fruit juice concentrate, sugar, or agave (see page 14)
2 tablespoons cornstarch or arrowroot, or 1 tablespoon kuzu

½ pound tofu
1 tablespoon Grand Marnier or other orange liqueur (optional)

¾ teaspoon agar powder, or ¾ bar agar or 3 tablespoons agar flakes
¼ cup orange juice

1 baked tart shell of your choice
Lemon slices, for garnish
Tofu Crème, for garnish

LEMON MOUSSE

Pour into wine or parfait glasses, alternating with fresh berries or other fruit in season, and top with Tofu Crème or Tofu Cashew Crème, page 229.

1 cup blanched almonds
   or almond meal
½ to ¾ cup water
   (use more water with whole,
   blanched almonds than almond
   meal)
3 to 5 tablespoons fruit or white
   grape juice concentrate, agave,
   or sugar (see page 14)
1 teaspoon vanilla
2 tablespoons kirschwasser,
   or 2 tablespoons water and
   several drops lemon juice
3 tablespoons arrowroot, kuzu,
   or cornstarch
Several tablespoons soymilk
4½ cups fresh, ripe, sweet
   strawberries in season
3 to 4 more tablespoons sweetener

Have ready:
1 recipe Almond Pastry, prebaked
   (page 203), or whole wheat pie
   crust

Fresh Strawberry Almond Tart

What can I say about this? If I were to choose one dessert for my Last Meal, this would be it. It is, simply put, just absolutely wonderful. Strawberries must be fresh, ripe, and sweet. Don't attempt this tart with frozen or unripe, unsweetened strawberries, or you'll be gravely disappointed.

Make an almond pastry cream by combining the almonds and water in a blender or food processor. (A blender will produce a smoother cream.) Process until smooth and creamy, adding more water if necessary. Add the sweetener, vanilla, and 1 tablespoon of the kirschwasser, and continue blending; it should be absolutely smooth. Pour it into a small saucepan, and place over low heat, stirring constantly. Dissolve 2 tablespoons of the arrowroot in a small amount of water, and when the almond cream comes to a boil, add the arrowroot, stirring constantly until the mixture thickens. Remove from the heat and allow to cool. Pour a thin layer of soymilk on top to prevent a skin from forming.

Wash and hull all the strawberries. In order to make the tart as visually appealing as possible, it is best if the strawberries are generally the same size; try to separate 3 cups of berries that are roughly equal in size. The remaining 1½ cups will be puréed to make a glaze, and hence can be assorted sizes and shapes, as well as slightly overripe. For the glaze, combine the 1½ cups of irregular strawberries and the 3 to 4 tablespoons of sweetener in a saucepan. Cover and cook for 10 to 15 minutes, or until their juices have been exuded and the sauce is a bright, beautiful red. Pour this into a blender, and purée until smooth. Pour back into the saucepan, reheat, and thicken with the remaining 1 tablespoon of arrowroot dissolved in the remaining kirschwasser or water with a few drops of lemon juice. It should be a light, clear, bright red sauce.

To assemble the tart, spread the almond pastry cream in the prebaked crust. Arrange the whole strawberries attractively over the pastry cream. (If they are large, you may want to cut them in half.) With a spoon or pastry brush, cover up the tart with the strawberry glaze while it is still hot. (The glaze will set as it cools.) Chill for 3 to 4 hours before serving. If you want to make this dessert the day before serving, it is best to use a shortbread crust so it will stay crisp. The delicate almond pie crust tends to soften if left too long in the refrigerator (24 hours).

Per serving: Calories 409, Protein 15 g, Fat 23 g, Carbohydrates 41 g

Almond Pastry (Almond Short Crust)

Yield: 1 crust (8 servings)

Delicious as a crust for the strawberry almond tart and other fresh fruit tarts, as well as for cheesecake.

Combine the flour, almond meal, and salt in a bowl. With a pastry cutter or mixer on low speed, cut in the margarine until it resembles coarse meal. Mix in the sweetener and the brandy to hold it all together. Chill several hours or overnight before rolling out, or you will have a sticky mess.

Preheat the oven to 350°F. After rolling out the pastry, place in a lightly oiled tin. Bake for 13 to 15 minutes, and allow to cool before filling with pastry cream, custard, fresh fruit, or other filling of your choice.

Per serving: Calories 237, Protein 5 g, Fat 18 g, Carbohydrates 15 g

¾ cup whole wheat pastry flour
¾ cup blanched almond meal or powder (this should be very fine)
Pinch of salt
6 tablespoons unsalted nonhydrogenated margarine, chilled and cut into little cubes
1½ tablespoons maple syrup or other sweetener
1 tablespoon brandy or dark rum, or 1 teaspoon vanilla and 2 teaspoons water

Flaky Pie Crust, page 207 or
Almond Pastry, page 203

Pastry cream:

1¾ cups soymilk

⅓ cup macadamia nut butter or
raw cashew butter

½ cup maple syrup or evaporated
cane juice

2 teaspoons vanilla

Pinch of salt

1 to 2 tablespoons brandy or
Grand Marnier (optional)

4 tablespoons cornstarch

⅓ cup water

Ripe fresh fruit and berries:
strawberries, blueberries,
peaches, apricots, nectarines,
pineapple, kiwi, melon, and
other soft fruit

About ⅔ cup jam or jelly of your
choice, traditionally apricot,
although raspberry or another
with a pretty hue will do

¼ cup water

Fresh Fruit Tart or Tartlettes

*By far, this is one of the most attractive and favorite desserts of all.
Serve these at a party, and they will be quickly devoured.*

Preheat the oven to 375°F. Prepare the pie crust according
to the instructions, and either roll out as a single crust in a
10-inch tart pan, or use 10 to 18 small tartlette tins to make
individual tarts. (These can just be pressed in with your fingers rather than being rolled out.) Prick the bottoms with a
fork, and bake for about 10 to 12 minutes, or until the pastry is white, slightly puffy, and light. (They will be overbaked if they are brown.) Allow to cool.

To make the pastry cream, combine the soymilk and nut
butter in a blender, and purée until thick and creamy. Pour
into a thick-bottomed saucepan, and add the sweetener,
vanilla, and salt. Over low heat, bring the mixture to a simmer, stirring frequently, whisking immediately and thoroughly if you feel any lumps forming. Dissolve the cornstarch in the water, and add to the saucepan in a thin
stream, whisking constantly. Continue heating until the
mixture is thick and glossy. Add the brandy or Grand
Marnier, if using, and allow to cool.

Spread the cooled pastry cream into the baked crust. Place
the fruit on top in a decorative pattern, or simply throw
them on—any way you do it, it will look beautiful.
(Strawberries can be sliced, cut in half, or left whole; all
other berries should be left whole. Other fruit should be
sliced thinly and peeled if appropriate or desired.) Place
the jam and water in a small saucepan, and heat to a gentle
simmer to make the glaze. Cool slightly. With a pastry
brush, spread the glaze over the fruit. Chill briefly before
serving. Consume this the day it is made, or the crust can
get soggy.

Per serving: Calories 339, Protein 5 g, Fat 13 g, Carbohydrates 48 g

Pumpkin Pie

Yield: 8 servings

*So tasty, you won't miss the cream or eggs. Top with tofu crème or
tofu cashew crème, page 229, for a special treat.*

Preheat the oven to 425°F. Blend all the ingredients until
smooth in a food processor or in batches in a blender. Pour
into the unbaked pie crust, and bake for 10 minutes.
Reduce the heat to 350°F, and continue baking for an additional 40 minutes, or until the pie has risen and feels firm.

This is delicious either hot or cold. It can be baked several
days in advance and reheated before serving, if desired.

Per serving: Calories 233, Protein 6 g, Fat 8 g, Carbohydrates 36 g

*One 9-inch unbaked whole
 wheat pie crust*
*1 pound cooked, mashed
 pumpkin (about 3 cups)*
10 ounces firm tofu
*½ cup sweetener of choice
 (or more to taste)*
*¼ cup raisin syrup, or 2
 tablespoons molasses (optional)*
1½ to 2 teaspoons cinnamon
1 to 1½ teaspoons ginger
¼ teaspoon cloves
¼ teaspoon nutmeg
¼ teaspoon salt
*2 tablespoons arrowroot or
 cornstarch*
*½ teaspoon grated orange zest
 (optional—gives it a less
 traditional but refreshing taste)*

Yield: one 9- or 10-inch pie, big
enough for 12 servings

¾ cup raw cashew pieces

½ cup water

Dash salt

1 teaspoon vanilla

½ cup arrowroot

1¾ cups maple syrup (This is the
only sweetener that will work,
since it needs to caramelize.)

8 ounces pecans (2½ cups chopped)

Frozen, unbaked, deep-dish 9-inch
pie shell, or medium 10-inch
pie shell, either homemade or
store-bought

PECAN PIE

*Eggless and dairyless, and yet every bit as sweet and rich as
the best in the South. It is important that the pie shell you use be
frozen, so if you make your own crust, be sure to freeze it before
making the pie, or it may burn before the filling has congealed.*

Preheat the oven to 325°F. Spread the pecans on a cookie
sheet, and toast for about 10 minutes. The oven can remain
on while the filling is prepared.

Purée the cashews and water in a blender until white,
creamy, and absolutely smooth. Add the salt, vanilla, and
arrowroot, and purée again. Bring the maple syrup to a boil
in a 2-quart pot, and simmer for 5 minutes, making sure
that it does not boil over. Add to the cashew mixture, and
blend to combine all the ingredients. Pour the mixture into
the frozen pie shell. Top with the pecans and stir lightly.
Bake for about 30 minutes, or until the top has risen and is
dry to the touch.

Per serving: Calories 390, Protein 4 g, Fat 20 g, Carbohydrates 48 g

Dessert Crêpes

Blend the water and tofu in a blender, then add the remaining ingredients, and blend for 60 seconds. Allow the mixture to rest for 1 to 2 hours so the crêpes will hold together better when cooked. Prepare according to the directions on page 138.

2¾ cups water

2 ounces tofu

1 tablespoon oil

¼ cup sweetener of choice

2 cups unbleached flour

½ to 1 teaspoon salt

2 teaspoons baking powder

Per crêpe: Calories 87, Protein 2 g, Fat 1 g, Carbohydrates 17 g

Flaky Pie Crust

Yield: enough for 3 to 4 crusts
(24 servings)

Excellent for all pies and pastries, sweet and savory. The tahini replaces egg yolk to produce a rich crust that holds together well.

Combine the flour and salt in a large bowl. With a pastry cutter or a mixer on low speed, cut in the margarine to make little beads. (The more you blend, the mealier and less flaky the crust becomes.) Combine the tahini with a little chilled water, then add enough additional chilled water to make ⅔ cup and mix well. Add to the flour mixture, and mix gently. Combine into a ball and chill for at least 1 hour before rolling out.

18 ounces unbleached or whole
   wheat pastry flour
   (approximately 4 cups)

1 teaspoon salt

10 ounces nonhydrogenated
   margarine, chilled well and cut
   into little cubes (1¼ cups)

2½ tablespoons creamy tahini

Approximately 10 tablespoons
   chilled water

Per serving: Calories 157, Protein 3 g, Fat 10 g, Carbohydrates 16 g

Whole Wheat Pie Crust

Yield: 2 crusts (8 servings)

2 cups whole wheat pastry flour
½ teaspoon salt
½ cup oil (corn oil is best)
⅓ to ½ cup chilled apple juice

Simple to make and very tasty. Unlike most pie crusts, this one can be rolled out immediately or even patted into the pie tin.

Mix the flour and salt, and stir in the oil with a fork. Add the apple juice and mix well. At first, it may seem very wet, but it will dry out almost immediately. Form into a ball and roll out between sheets of waxed paper or on a pastry cloth, or simply pat into a pie plate with your hands.

Per serving: Calories 230, Protein 4 g, Fat 14 g, Carbohydrates 23 g

Oatmeal Crust

Yield: 1 crust (8 servings)

1½ cups rolled oats
½ cup whole wheat pastry flour
Pinch of salt (optional)
5 tablespoons corn or safflower oil
2 tablespoons maple syrup or
    other sweetener of choice
2 to 3 tablespoons brandy, rum,
    or apple juice

A sweet, crunchy, cookie-like crust that is great for cream pies and cheesecakes. And it's hard to mess this one up—it's so very easy!

Preheat the oven to 375°F. Mix the oats, flour, and salt in a bowl. In a separate bowl, mix the oil and sweetener well. Add to the oat-flour mixture, and combine thoroughly. Mix in the liquor or apple juice, adding enough to moisten the mixture and hold it all together. Pat into an oiled 9 x 10-inch pie tin or springform mold, as indicated in the particular recipe to be used. Bake for about 12 to 15 minutes until a light golden brown. Do not allow it to brown too much, or it will be dry. The crust will become crispy as it cools. Fill when cool.

Per serving: Calories 230, Protein 5 g, Fat 11 g, Carbohydrates 28 g

Sweet Tahini Almond Cakes

A Greek bakery in Santa Fe inspired these cookies, even though the original ones contained no tahini, as far as I know. They are rich and sweet with an unusual flavor.

Cream the tahini and margarine. Work the sweetener into the almond paste in a separate bowl, then add to the creamed ingredients. Add the flour ½ cup at a time, making sure that the dough does not become too stiff. (A little less than 1½ cups may be required.) It should have some resilience.

Preheat the oven to 350°F. Shape the dough into flat cakes about 1½ x 2½ inches. Press some of the chopped nuts onto the tops. Bake on an oiled cookie sheet for 10 to 15 minutes until they are a delicate brown.

While the cakes are baking, dilute the sweetener with the water. Add a little vanilla and heat over a low flame until the sweetener is completely dissolved. When the cakes come out of the oven, transfer them to a plate, then pour a teaspoon or two of the sauce on each while the cakes are still warm.

Per cake: Calories 113, Protein 3 g, Fat 5 g, Carbohydrates 16 g

Yield: 24 cakes

1 cup tahini
⅓ cup nonhydrogenated margarine
½ cup maple syrup or FruitSource
¼ cup almond paste
1½ cups whole wheat pastry flour
⅓ cup finely chopped walnuts,
*   pecans, or almonds*
¼ to ⅓ cup extra liquid sweetener
*   for sauce*
2 to 3 tablespoons water
Vanilla extract

Yield: 2 dozen squares

*1 pound (4 cups) unbleached
   pastry flour or whole wheat
   pastry flour (a matter of taste
   and nutritional concern)*
½ teaspoon salt
*¾ cup oil (corn oil is good,
   or use canola)*
*½ cup maple syrup or grape
   juice concentrate*
2 teaspoons vanilla

Shortbread

Hooray! Rich, flaky shortbread (either as cookies or as a base for bars or pies) can be made with oil and natural sweeteners. This is especially good dipped in chocolate, as in the recipe on page 212.

Combine the flour and salt in a bowl. Mix in the oil with a fork; the mixture will become very crumbly. Combine the vanilla with the sweetener, and mix in, combining well. The mixture should be moist but not wet. If it is too dry and crumbly, add an additional 2 tablespoons or so of the sweetener you are using. Handle lightly—do not knead.

The dough can now be formed in a variety of ways. For traditional shortbread, pat or roll out onto an oiled cookie sheet ½ inch thick. Alternatively, it can be rolled out slightly thinner, and cut with a cookie cutter for cookies. You may also roll or pat it out ½ inch thick to form a shortbread pie crust.

To make the traditional ½-inch thick shortbread, bake at 325F° for about 20 minutes until it is white and dry on top. Some people prefer to bake it a little longer until golden brown on top, although it will become a little less flaky. Remove from the oven. While still warm, cut with a sharp knife into rectangles or squares. Do not attempt to remove the shortbread from the pan while warm, however, as it will crumble hopelessly.

Per square: Calories 143, Protein 2 g, Fat 7 g, Carbohydrates 18 g

Tahini Shortbread

Yield: 2 dozen squares

I created this and the sweet tahini almond cakes in college when I tried to get the student co-op to order tahini. No one knew what it was or how to use it, so I had to convince a few people of its merits, then order about twenty pounds of it for myself in order to meet the required minimum. Then I had to create numerous delectable ways to use the stuff up! A teacher informed me a few years ago that my tahini recipes were still circulating within the co-op. It is very important to use the smooth, Middle-Eastern style tahini and not the grainy, raw type. Both are usually found in natural food stores.

1 cup tahini
¼ cup vegetable oil or
    nonhydrogenated margarine,
    preferably unsalted
¼ teaspoon salt (optional)
⅓ cup FruitSource or other
    sweetener of choice
1 cup whole wheat pastry flour
¼ cup cornstarch or arrowroot

Cream the tahini and margarine, then add the salt and sweetener, and mix thoroughly. Sift the flour with the cornstarch, and add to the tahini mixture, gently mixing it in with your hands. Preheat the oven to 325°F. Press the mixture into an 8-inch pan so that it is ⅓ to ½ inch thick. Bake for 15 to 30 minutes, depending on the thickness. Do not allow it to brown or it will become dry and crumbly.

Per square: Calories 84, Protein 2 g, Fat 5 g, Carbohydrates 9 g

Pecan Shortbread

Yield: 2 dozen squares

A wonderful combination! This is a favorite at holiday time.

1 recipe Shortbread, page 210
Pecan Pie, page 206, without the
    frozen crust

Prepare the shortbread and spread out ½ inch thick on an oiled cookie sheet. Chill for several hours, or place in a freezer for 1 hour. (Since it is very thick, you will not need to freeze it, but chilling helps.)

Preheat the oven to 325°F. Prepare the pecan pie filling, and pour on top of the shortbread. Bake for 30 minutes. When completely cool, cut into squares.

Per square: Calories 301, Protein 3 g, Fat 14 g, Carbohydrates 39 g

Have ready:

1 recipe Shortbread, page 210

1 cup nondairy chocolate chips

Chocolate Dipped Shortbread

Prepare the shortbread as for the recipe on page 210.

Melt the chocolate either in a microwave, oven, or double boiler. If using a microwave, place the chocolate in a clean, dry glass bowl. Microwave on high for about 60 seconds; the chocolate should look very soft. Stir with a clean, dry spoon to see if it is melted completely—the residual heat is often sufficient to do this. If not, return to the microwave for another 15 seconds, then stir again until smooth. If you are using the oven or a double boiler, the chocolate can be placed in a glass or metal bowl. Either set on top of a small pot of simmering water, stirring occasionally until smooth and melted, or place in a 300°F oven for about 5 minutes, then stir. Do not overheat; the chocolate should never become hot to the touch, just warm enough to melt. Overheating can cause the chocolate to lose its smoothness become grainy.

After cutting the shortbread into squares and cooling completely, remove one square at a time and dip half of the square in the melted chocolate. Place each square on waxed paper or parchment, and chill until the chocolate has hardened.

Per square: Calories 179, Protein 2 g, Fat 9 g, Carbohydrates 22 g

Left: Buche de Noël, pages 190-91,
Right: Maple Rum Torte, page 198

Spice Slices with Jam Dots

Beat the margarine and sweetener until smooth and creamy, then add the vanilla. Sift the flour with the spices, and add to the margarine mixture. Mix well but do not overbeat. Roll into 1½-inch logs and chill until they can be cut neatly.

Preheat the oven to 350°F. Slice the logs into ¼-inch pieces. Make an indentation in the middle of each slice with your finger, and fill with ½ teaspoon of the jam. Bake for 7 to 8 minutes.

Per cookie: Calories 48, Protein 1 g, Fat 2 g, Carbohydrates 7 g

Yield: 4 dozen cookies

*½ cup nonhydrogenated margarine
   or vegetable oil*
½ cup sweetener of choice
1 teaspoon vanilla
2⅓ cups whole wheat pastry flour
2 teaspoons cinnamon
1 teaspoon cardamom
½ teaspoon ginger
¼ teaspoon cloves
¼ teaspoon nutmeg
¼ teaspoon allspice
*Approximately ½ cup sugar-free,
   all-fruit jam of your choice*

Baked Apples Filled with Chestnut Purée, pages 218-19

Yield: 40 kisses

½ *cup nonhydrogenated*
  margarine or vegetable oil
½ *cup maple syrup or other*
  sweetener
2 *heaping tablespoons grain*
  coffee substitute, or 1 teaspoon
  instant coffee
5 *tablespoons cocoa or carob*
  powder
4 *ounces walnuts, ground in a*
  blender (½ cup)
1 *cup whole wheat pastry flour*
  plus ¼ cup (optional—a little
  extra flour will produce a
  firmer cookie. The less flour, the
  more delicate these will be.)

Chocolate or Carob Walnut Kisses

Rich and delicious without being overly sweet.

Preheat the oven to 350°F. Mix the margarine, sweetener, grain coffee substitute, and the cocoa or carob powder until well blended. Add the walnuts and flour, and mix until completely blended, but do not overmix or beat. Pipe out into fat kisses on an oiled baking sheet, then bake for 12 to 13 minutes. They will be very soft when they come out of the oven but will become delicately crisp as they cool on a rack. Store in an airtight container.

Per kiss: Calories 56, Protein 1 g, Fat 3 g, Carbohydrates 7 g

Chocolate Chip or Chocolate Chocolate Chip Cookies
with Carob Variation

The addition of ground walnuts to this recipe produces rich, satisfying cookies. Forget Tollhouse!

Preheat the oven to 350°F. Mix the margarine with the sweetener until smooth. Add the cinnamon and vanilla, then the walnuts, flour (or flour, carob, and grain coffee), and baking powder. (Either sift the baking powder with the flour, or mix it into the flour well before adding it to the other ingredients.) Add the carob chips and optional chopped nuts last, then bake for 10 to 15 minutes until golden brown.

Per cookie: Calories 72, Protein 1 g, Fat 4 g, Carbohydrates 9 g

Yield: 4 dozen cookies

½ cup nonhydrogenated margarine or oil

¾ cup maple syrup or other sweetener of choice

3 scant teaspoons cinnamon

1 teaspoon vanilla

4 ounces walnuts, ground in a blender (½ cup)

For Chocolate or Carob Chip Cookies:

1⅓ cups whole wheat pastry flour

for Chocolate Chocolate or Carob Carob Chip Cookies:

1 cup whole wheat pastry flour

⅓ cup cocoa or carob powder

2 tablespoons grain coffee substitute , or 1 teaspoon instant coffee

1 teaspoon aluminum-free baking powder (optional)

1 cup chocolate or carob chips

¾ cup chopped nuts, such as pecans (optional)

1 cup peanut butter

⅓ cup oil

½ cup FruitSource, maple syrup,
   or sweetener of choice

2 teaspoons cinnamon

1 teaspoon vanilla

1¾ to 2 cups whole wheat
   pastry flour

½ cup currants or raisins
   (optional)

PEANUT BUTTER COOKIES

I like the addition of currants in these cookies.

Preheat the oven to 350°F. Mix the peanut butter with the oil and sweetener until smooth and creamy. Add the cinnamon and vanilla, then mix in the flour and currants, adding a tad more flour if the mixture seems extremely sticky. Drop by spoonfuls onto an oiled cookie sheet, and flatten out with the back of a fork. Bake for 12 minutes.

Per cookie: Calories 91, Protein 3 g, Fat 6 g, Carbohydrates 10 g

Lemon Almond Wafers

Delicate lemony wafers with the crunch of almonds.

Mix the margarine, sweetener, and tahini until well blended. Add the lemon rind and lemon juice, then add the flour and mix thoroughly, but do not overbeat. Roll into a log 1½ inches in diameter, and chill for at least 2 hours, preferably overnight. Slice ¼ inch thick and place the slices on an oiled cookie sheet. Preheat the oven to 350°F.

For the topping, place the sweetener and lemon juice in a small saucepan, and bring to a boil for 1 minute. Remove from the heat. Brush the slices with this mixture, then sprinkle generously with the almond slices. Bake for 10 to 12 minutes until the almonds are golden brown and the cookies have spread out a little.

Per cookie: Calories 69, Protein 1 g, Fat 4 g, Carbohydrates 8 g

Yield: 4 dozen wafers

½ cup nonhydrogenated
  margarine or vegetable oil
⅓ cup fruit juice concentrate,
  FruitSource, or sugar
1 tablespoon tahini
Grated zest of 1 lemon
1 tablespoon lemon juice
2½ cups whole wheat pastry flour

Topping:

4 tablespoons fruit juice
  concentrate, FruitSource,
  or sugar
2 tablespoons lemon juice
Approximately 1 cup sliced
  almonds

1 pound fresh chestnuts,
    1½ cups canned or bottled
    chestnuts, or 4 ounces dried
    chestnuts, cooked

⅓ cup soymilk
⅓ cup apple juice
5 to 6 tablespoons maple syrup
    or barley malt
1 teaspoon cinnamon
¼ teaspoon nutmeg
⅓ cup currants or raisins

6 to 8 crisp, sweet apples (Fuji are
    good)
A few tablespoons lemon juice
A little extra cinnamon

1 stick cinnamon
¾ cup white wine or apple juice

1 recipe Oat or Brown Rice
    Crème, page 230
Mint leaves and thin orange slices
    for decorating (optional)

Baked Apples Filled with Chestnut Purée

An entirely satisfying and warming dessert for crisp, cool fall and winter days.

If you are using fresh chestnuts, place them in a large pot with plenty of water, and cook for about 20 minutes—the time will vary slightly according to size. Run them under cold water, cut off the flat part with a sharp knife, and scoop out the meat with a spoon. If you are using canned or bottled chestnuts, heat them in their liquid until hot. (Try to purchase a brand that does not use heavy syrup.) If using dried chestnuts, cook them according to the instructions on the package until tender (usually 20 to 30 minutes on the stove top).

Drain the cooking liquid and purée the chestnuts while still hot in a food processor or high-speed mixer with the soymilk, apple juice, 4 tablespoons of the maple syrup or barley malt, cinnamon, and nutmeg, adding more spices if desired. Add the raisins by hand.

Peel the apples and remove the core from the top, leaving the bottom intact. Then, with a grapefruit spoon or metal measuring spoon, scoop out most of the inner apple, leaving a ½-inch wall. (Strangely enough, stainless steel measuring spoons with their thin, sharp sides work well for this.) Chop as much of the edible scooped-out apple meat as possible, and add this to the chestnut mixture. Brush lemon juice onto the outside of the apples to prevent discoloration, and sprinkle the insides with a little cinnamon.

Fill the apples with the chestnut mixture. Preheat the oven to 350°F. Arrange the apples and cinnamon stick in a buttered baking dish, and pour the white wine or apple juice and remaining syrup or barley malt around them. Bake for 30 to 40 minutes until tender, basting occasionally with the liquid in the pan. The liquid in the dish should be cooked down to a light syrup; if it seems watery, cook down on the stove over high heat until it thickens slightly. Pour this over the apples and serve. Pass a dish of the oat or cashew crème.

Optional: To make this dish a little more elegant, the apples can be placed on individual croûtes. To make croûtes, trim 6 to 8 slices of bread, and cook both sides until browned in melted oil or margarine in a skillet. Brush on the wine-apple syrup, and place an apple on each croûte.

Per serving: Calories 449, Protein 9 g, Fat 5 g, Carbohydrates 91 g

Glistening Poached Pears

Delightfully easy to make and a joy to eat, these jewel-like glistening pears will make a fine, light dessert after a rich meal.

Wash the pears and place them in a large pot. Add the juice, wine, sweetener, and lemon. Cover and simmer about 30 minutes until the pears are tender.

Dissolve the kuzu, cornstarch, or arrowroot in a small amount of water, and add to the liquid in the pot over low heat, stirring constantly, until it thickens to a light glaze.

Serve hot, or allow to cool slightly to just warm, and decorate with a sprig of mint, if desired.

Per serving: Calories 297, Protein 1 g, Fat 0 g, Carbohydrates 71 g

Yield: 6 servings

6 Bosc pears, medium firm
  (do not use mushy ones)
1 quart cherry juice
1 cup red wine
⅓ cup fruit juice concentrate,
  light agave, or sugar
  (see page 14)
½ lemon, sliced
2 tablespoons kuzu,
  or 3 tablespoons cornstarch or
  arrowroot

Jellied Peach Jewels

Yield: 4 servings

¾ bar or ¾ teaspoon powdered
agar, or 3 tablespoons agar flakes
1 pint apple juice
1 large peach, peeled and
chopped into ½-inch chunks
Juice of ½ lemon
2 tablespoons fruit juice
concentrate, agave, evaporated
cane juice, or sugar (see page 14)

So light, refreshing, and easy to make. Peeling a peach is simple if you plunge it in boiling water for 20 seconds—the skin slips right off.

Dissolve and heat the agar in the apple juice as described on pages 2-3. Add the peach to the apple juice, and continue to boil for another 30 seconds. Add the lemon juice and sweetener, and cook another moment (long enough to dissolve the sweetener). Pour into individual parfait or wine glasses. Chill until set.

If desired, make a half-recipe of cashew cheesecake, page 199, pour it in the bottom of individual dishes, then pour the jellied peaches on top for a two-layer summer treat.

Per serving: Calories 103, Protein 0 g, Fat 0 g, Carbohydrates 26 g

Fresh Figs Stewed in Red Wine

Yield: 4 servings

Juice and zest of 1 lemon
8 large fresh figs
1½ cups red wine
¼ cup currants
4 tablespoons agave, or ¼ cup
concentrated apple or
white grape juice (see page 14)
1 cinnamon stick or 5 whole
cloves (optional)

Fresh figs are rarely seen in the United States, a shame since they are among the most luscious of fruit. Although rather unattractive on the outside, a really ripe, fresh fig will reveal beautifully succulent purple flesh once split open with your fingers. This dessert is simple and can be a delicious ending for a summer meal.

To prepare the lemon rind, simply peel the thin, yellow surface—there's no need to grate it. Combine all the ingredients in a saucepan with a tight fitting lid, and simmer gently for 20 minutes. Serve warm or chilled. If desired, a little tofu cashew crème, page 229, may be served alongside.

Per serving: Calories 229, Protein 1 g, Fat 0 g, Carbohydrates 48 g

Christmas Pudding

A real traditional once-a-year treat that is well worth the trouble. Serve with Brandy Sauce, Grand Marnier Sauce, Citrus Brandy Sauce, pages 232-33 or unaccompanied. If tightly wrapped, it will keep well for many, many weeks, so it can be made ahead of time, if desired.

Mix all but the sweetener, margarine, brandy, and egg replacer in a large bowl. Cream the sweetener with the margarine and brandy, and work it into the first mixture with your hands. Add the egg replacer or tahini-arrowroot mixture to bind all the ingredients. Pat the mixture into a well-oiled 2-quart ceramic or metal bowl, cover with a double layer of aluminum foil, and place in a large pot. Fill the pot halfway up the bowl with hot water, cover, and simmer for 7 to 9 hours. Be sure that the pot does not run out of water; otherwise, you can pretty much leave it alone.

Allow to sit for at least 1 hour before inverting onto a plate. Pour some more brandy on it, if desired, and light it with a match as you carry it into the dining room. The flame will die down in moments and the alcohol will burn off, but this creates a spectacle. Slice, serve, and pass the brandy or Grand Marnier sauce, if desired.

Note: If you're making this several days or even weeks in advance, leave in the bowl and resteam in the pot for an hour before serving. Let it sit for 15 minutes before inverting onto a platter.

Per serving: Calories 486, Protein 7 g, Fat 15 g, Carbohydrates 83 g

1 pound good-quality whole grain bread, coarsely pulverized into bread crumbs (cake and cookie crumbs can also be used to replace part of the bread)

¼ cup whole wheat pastry flour

1 to 1⅓ cups currants

1 to 1⅓ cups sultana raisins

1 pound raisins

Grated zest of 1 lemon

1 teaspoon salt

2 teaspoons mixed spices (cinnamon, nutmeg, allspice, cloves) in the proportion you prefer

½ to 1 teaspoon ginger

½ cup maple syrup or fruit juice concentrate

8 ounces nonhydrogenated margarine

3 tablespoons brandy or dark rum, or 1 teaspoon rum flavoring

Egg replacer equivalent to 2 eggs, or 4 tablespoons tahini creamed with 2 tablespoons arrowroot and ⅓ cup water

Brandy Sauce, Grand Marnier Sauce, or Citrus Brand Sauce, (pages 232-33)

¾ cup espresso

½ cup sweetener of choice, but
  not fruit juice concentrate
  (maple syrup is good)

½ cup raw cashews

One 12.3-ounce box firm
  silken tofu

⅓ cup Kahlua

1½ teaspoons agar powder, or
  2 tablespoons agar flakes

½ cup water

KAHlUA BRULÉE

A delicate dessert with a flan-like consistency.

Purée the espresso, sweetener, and cashews in a blender until smooth. Add the tofu and Kahlua, and purée again until smooth. In a small pot, combine the agar and water. Bring to a boil and simmer for 3 minutes, stirring occasionally, until completely dissolved. Turn the blender on and pour in the agar mixture in a steady stream. Blend for a minute, then pour this mixture into espresso cups or metal molds. Chill for several hours before serving. If you have used molds, they can be dipped for a moment in hot water to release the dessert, then inverted onto a plate. Serve as is or with a chocolate sauce.

Per serving: Calories 215, Protein 6 g, Fat 7 g, Carbohydrates 28 g

Pumpkin Mousse

In a blender, combine the pumpkin, cinnamon, nutmeg, ginger, salt, Grand Marnier, maple syrup, lemon and orange zests, orange juice, and tofu. Blend until absolutely smooth, and pour into a bowl. In the same blender, purée the cashews with the ⅔ cup water to form a thick cream. Combine with the pumpkin mixture. Pour about 1 cup of this mixture back into the blender. In a small pot, dissolve the agar in the orange juice or water, and bring to a boil. Simmer for 2 minutes, then add the dissolved arrowroot to thicken. Pour this into the mixture in the blender, and blend for a moment. Pour immediately into the mixture in the bowl, and whisk well. Pour into molds or wine glasses. Chill for at least 4 hours before serving. Top with the tofu whipped cream of your choice, and enjoy!

Per serving: Calories 187, Protein 4 g, Fat 5 g, Carbohydrates 31 g

Yield: 8 servings

One 15-ounce can pumpkin
1½ teaspoons cinnamon
¼ teaspoon nutmeg
1 teaspoon freshly grated
*   ginger root*
Dash salt
2 tablespoons Grand Marnier
*   (optional)*
¾ cup maple syrup
1 teaspoon grated lemon zest
Grated zest of ½ orange
Juice of 1 orange (½ cup)
6 ounces firm silken tofu
⅓ cup raw cashew butter,
*   or ⅔ cup raw cashews*
⅔ cup water
1½ teaspoons agar powder,
*   or 1½ tablespoons flakes*
½ cup orange juice or water
2 tablespoons arrowroot dissolved
*   in a small amount of water*

½ cup raw cashews

½ cup water

1¼ cups nondairy bittersweet or
  semisweet chocolate chips

Two (12.3-ounce) packages firm
  silken tofu (Mori-Nu or similar
  brand in aseptic packages works
  well)

6 tablespoons Dutch cocoa

2 teaspoons vanilla

6 tablespoons liquid FruitSource,
  maple syrup, or evaporated cane
  juice

CHOCOLATE DREAM MOUSSE

This cholesterol-free mousse has the same richness and texture as the classic variety while avoiding the usual eggs, butter, cream, or sugar.

Purée the cashews and water in a blender until thick, white, and absolutely smooth and creamy. Remove the mixture from the blender, and set it aside in a bowl. Place the chocolate chips in a dry glass or metallic bowl, and place the bowl over a small pot of hot water over low heat. Stir occasionally until the chips have melted completely. The chips should not be allowed to become too hot, or they can become grainy; they merely need to be warm to melt. Be sure not to get even a drop of water in the chocolate, as this will also make the melted chocolate grainy.

Combine the tofu, melted chocolate, cocoa, vanilla, and sweetener of choice in the same blender (no need to wash it out after the cashews), and purée until smooth, scraping down the sides as necessary. Pour this chocolate mixture into the cashew purée, and fold with a whisk until combined thoroughly. Pour into eight wine glasses, and chill for several hours before serving.

Per serving: Calories 251, Protein 8 g, Fat 13 g, Carbohydrates 25 g

Orange Bavarian

Creamy, sweet, delightful.

Yield: 4 servings

1 large orange
1 lemon
¼ cup plus 2 to 3 tablespoons
    agave or fruit juice concentrate
    (see page 14)
3 tablespoons cornstarch or kuzu
One 12.3-ounce package firm silken
    tofu
3 tablespoons canola or safflower oil
2 tablespoons Grand Marnier or
    other orange liqueur
½ bar or ½ teaspoon powdered
    agar, or 2 teaspoons agar flakes
½ cup orange juice

Grate the orange zest, and juice both the orange and lemon. Combine the zest, the two juices, and ¼ cup of the sweetener in a small saucepan, and place it over medium heat. Dissolve the cornstarch or kuzu in a small amount of water. When the juice mixture comes to a boil, add the cornstarch mixture in a steady stream while stirring constantly. Lower the heat and continue cooking until clear and very thick, stirring all the while. Remove from the heat.

Place the tofu, oil, orange liqueur, and the remaining sweetener in a food processor or blender, and process until smooth and creamy. Add the orange custard to this, and blend for only a few moments at low speed to combine gently. (Do not overblend!)

Dissolve the agar in the orange juice, using the method described on pages 2-3, and add to the mixture in the food processor. Once again, blend for another few moments, only long enough to combine gently. **Do not overblend or the texture will be destroyed.** Pour into wine or parfait glasses, and chill for 3 to 4 hours or overnight until set. If desired, top with Tofu Crème or Tofu Cashew Crème, page 229.

Per serving: Calories 323, Protein 6 g, Fat 13 g, Carbohydrates 44 g

DESSERTS 225

2 pints fresh strawberries,
   washed and hulled
½ cup blanched almonds or
   almond meal (almond meal
   purées faster)
½ cup water
2 tablespoons oil (optional, for
   richer flavor)
2 tablespoons kirschwasser,
   or ½ tablespoon lemon juice
   and 1 tablespoon rum
⅓ cup agave, fruit juice
   concentrate, or sugar (see page
   14—you may need more,
   depending on the sweetness of
   the strawberries)
12 ounces tofu, pressed (see page
   18)
½ bar or ½ teaspoon powdered
   agar, or 2 tablespoons agar flakes
2 tablespoons arrowroot,
   cornstarch, or kuzu, dissolved
   in 1 to 2 tablespoons water
1 recipe Tofu Crème of choice,
   page 229

Strawberry Mousse Parfait

Delicate, sweet, rich, and pretty.

Reserve 6 to 8 nicely shaped strawberries for decorating the top. (The hulls can be left on these, if desired).

In a blender, make an almond cream by puréeing the almonds, water, oil, and kirschwasser until absolutely smooth. (A blender works better than a food processor for this.) Pour into a large bowl.

In the same blender, purée 1 pint of the strawberries with the sweetener and tofu until smooth. Add to the almond cream, and combine well with a whisk.

Rinse out the blender. Purée the other pint of strawberries with a small amount of water. You should have about 1 cup of juice. Pour this into a saucepan, and dissolve the agar in it as described on pages 2-3. After it has been dissolved, turn the heat down low, and add the arrowroot-water mixture in a steady stream, stirring constantly until thick and clear. Pour the tofu-almond mixture back into the blender, and add the agar mixture, blending well.

Spoon this in alternating layers with the Tofu Crème in tall wine glasses or champagne flutes, ending with a dollop of the Tofu Crème, and top with a whole strawberry. Chill for several hours before serving.

Per serving: Calories 352, Protein 13 g, Fat 16 g, Carbohydrates 41 g

A Different Pumpkin Ice Cream

A wonderful tofu-based ice cream with an unusual, complex character. The undertones of orange and spice make this special; serve it in champagne glasses with a sprig of mint on top.

Combine all the ingredients except the orange juice and agar in a food processor or blender, and mix until very smooth and creamy. Dissolve the agar in the orange juice as described on pages 2-3, and add it to the ingredients in the blender, processing once again. If you have an ice cream maker, follow the manufacturer's instructions for churning. Otherwise, pour into a bowl and place in the freezer until completely frozen. Remove from the freezer, allow to soften slightly, then chop into large chunks, and process in the food processor until perfectly creamy and homogenized. It can be served immediately or refrozen.

Per serving: Calories 326, Protein 9 g, Fat 18 g, Carbohydrates 31 g

Yield: 4 servings

14 ounces tofu

1 cup canned pumpkin, cooked butternut squash, or Japanese pumpkin (kabocha), preferably the latter

4 tablespoons canola or safflower oil

4 tablespoons or more agave, fruit juice concentrate, or sugar, depending on the sweetness of the pumpkin or squash used (see page 14)

2 tablespoons Grand Marnier or other orange liqueur

2 teaspoons grated orange zest

½ teaspoon grated lemon zest

Scant ½ teaspoon cinnamon

Scant ¼ teaspoon nutmeg

½ cup freshly squeezed orange juice

½ bar or ½ teaspoon powdered agar, or 2 tablespoons agar flakes

Yield: 4 servings

12 ounces tofu

3 ripe bananas
   (should be spotty brown)

1 cup grated or flaked
   unsweetened coconut

½ cup soymilk

2 teaspoons vanilla

1 tablespoon dark rum (optional)

4 tablespoons canola oil (optional)

A few tablespoons sweetener of
   choice (such as agave, fruit
   juice concentrate, or maple
   syrup; amount depends on
   sweetness of bananas and
   coconut—see page 14)

TROPICAL COCONUT BANANA
ICE CREAM OR SAUCE

Blend all the ingredients together in a food processor until smooth. If you have an ice cream maker, follow the manufacturer's instructions for freezing. Otherwise, place the mixture in a bowl in a freezer until semihard. Then homogenize it by creaming it in a food processor, and freeze again until firm.

Per serving: Calories 267, Protein 9 g, Fat 11 g, Carbohydrates 38 g

COCONUT BANANA SAUCE

*This is great for banana bread, pound cake,
leftover cake, or brownie chunks.*

Use only half the amount of tofu, coconut, and banana. Delete the oil and sweeten to taste as for ice cream. Purée everything in a blender or food processor, and serve immediately.

Tofu Crème

Here are several versions of light toppings made from tofu. All of them can be used interchangeably, and you may find that you prefer one to the other. Although regular tofu can be used for any of these, you will find that the crèmes are smoother and lighter if made with silken tofu.

Drain the tofu in towels by wrapping and refrigerating for 3 to 4 hours or pressing under a weighted plate for 1 hour. Process all the ingredients in a food processor or blender until thick and smooth. Chill before serving, if desired. This will thicken slightly upon refrigeration.

Per serving: Calories 127, Protein 6 g, Fat 7 g, Carbohydrates 11 g

Tofu Cashew Crème

Process the cashews with the water and sweetener in a blender until smooth. Add the tofu, drained as in the tofu crème recipe, and blend again until smooth. Flavor as desired with vanilla, brandy, Grand Marnier, or lemon juice.

Per serving: Calories 126, Protein 5 g, Fat 7 g, Carbohydrates 13 g

Tofu Coconut Crème

Drain the tofu as in the tofu crème recipe. Blend with the coconut milk, lemon juice, and some sweetener until smooth and creamy.

Per serving: Calories 102, Protein 6 g, Fat 5 g, Carbohydrates 3 g

Yield: 4 to 8 servings

1 pound firm silken tofu

3 tablespoons agave, maple syrup, fruit juice concentrate, or sugar (see page 14)

1 teaspoon vanilla

1 to 2 tablespoons canola oil

1 tablespoon Grand Marnier or brandy, or 1 teaspoon vanilla

1 tablespoon tahini (optional)

Tofu Cashew Crème:

½ cup cashews

½ cup water

3 tablespoons agave, maple syrup, fruit juice concentrate, or sugar (see page 14)

One 12.3-ounce package firm silken tofu

Vanilla, brandy, Grand Marnier, or lemon juice

Tofu Coconut Crème:

1 pound firm silken tofu

½ cup coconut milk (freshly made or canned)

2 tablespoons lemon juice

Agave, maple syrup, fruit juice concentrate, or sugar (see page 14)

1 cup rolled oats or cooked
    brown rice

4 cups apple juice

2 to 4 tablespoons cashew or raw
    almond butter, or tahini
    (optional, for richer flavor)

2 teaspoons vanilla

2 tablespoons brandy or dark
    rum, or ½ to 1 teaspoon
    cinnamon, or both

1 to 2 tablespoons maple syrup
    (optional)

Up to 1 cup soymilk, if necessary

OAT OR BROWN RICE CRÈME

*You would never imagine that whole grains could cook up
into such creamy, sweet sauces.*

Combine the oats or brown rice, apple juice, and tahini or nut butter in a large saucepan. Bring to a boil, then lower the heat, cover, and simmer for at least 20 minutes. Turn off the heat, add the remaining ingredients, and purée in a blender or food processor until smooth and creamy. If too thick, thin it out with more apple juice or soymilk.

Per serving: Calories 145, Protein 3 g, Fat 2 g, Carbohydrates 27 g

CAROB FONDANT

The above recipe will transform into a nutritious substitute for fondant, the sugary semihard icing used on cakes and petit fours. To the above recipe, add several tablespoons carob powder and a tablespoon of grain coffee substitute before puréeing. (The amount of carob powder can be increased or decreased according to how "chocolatey" you want it to be.) Delete the cinnamon and add the brandy. This can be poured over cakes or petit fours and will harden slightly, giving a smooth, slick appearance when chilled.

Chocolate Buttercreme

Although by no means low in fat, this is very smooth, light, and delicious.

In a blender, combine the cashews and water. Blend until absolutely smooth and creamy. Add the oil a little at a time (almost drop by drop) while continuing to blend until thick and creamy. Add the tofu, melted chocolate or carob chips, vanilla, and liqueur if using, and blend again until creamy and smooth. Chill briefly, then whip with an electric mixer at high speed until light and fluffy.

Per serving: Calories 115, Protein 3 g, Fat 9 g, Carbohydrates 8 g

Mocha Buttercreme

In place of water, use ⅓ cup espresso, very strong grain coffee substitute, or decaffeinated coffee. If desired, add 1 to 2 tablespoons Kahlua.

Yield: enough to fill and frost 1 large cake or 2 medium cakes (16 servings)

½ cup cashews

¼ cup water

⅓ cup canola oil

One 12.3-ounce package firm silken tofu

12 ounces chocolate or carob chips, melted (see tips for melting, pages 4-5)

2 teaspoons vanilla

1 to 2 tablespoons brandy or rum (optional)

1⅓ cups orange juice

3 to 4 tablespoons agave, sugar,
    FruitSource, or fruit juice
    concentrate (see page 14)

2 tablespoons kuzu,
    or 3 to 4 tablespoons cornstarch
    or arrowroot (dissolve both in
    2 tablespoons water)

⅓ cup almond or cashew milk
    or soymilk

1 teaspoon vanilla

4 tablespoons Grand Marnier

GRANd MARNiER SAucE

*Serve this warm or chilled over cake, ice cream,
or Christmas pudding, page 221.*

Heat the orange juice and sweetener until almost boiling,
then slowly add the dissolved kuzu or cornstarch, stirring
constantly with a wooden spoon or wire whisk until thickened. Add the milk and vanilla, heat for another minute,
and add the Grand Marnier. Allow to cool slightly before
serving.

Per 2 tablespoons: Calories 55, Protein 2 g, Fat 1 g, Carbohydrates 9 g

Yield: 1½ cups

One 8-ounce basket fresh
    raspberries (about 1½ cups)

2 tablespoons agave, sugar,
    FruitSource, or fruit juice
    concentrate (see page 14)

2 tablespoons kirschwasser or
    brandy

1 to 2 tablespoons cornstarch or
    arrowroot, dissolved in a little
    water

RAspbERRy SAucE

*A brilliant, deep red sauce that can be served with cake,
ice cream, cheesecake, or mousses.*

Liquefy the raspberries in a blender. Pour into a small
saucepan. (If you prefer, you can strain out the seeds by
pouring through a sieve first.) Add the sweetener and
kirschwasser, and heat. Add the cornstarch and simmer
until thickened. Serve chilled.

Per 2 tablespoons: Calories 3, Protein 0 g, Fat 0 g, Carbohydrates 6 g

Brandy Sauce

Yield: 1½ cups

Unlike the traditional sweet, buttery-rich brandy sauces, this is much lighter. Serve over warm puddings.

Combine the milk, apple juice, and sweetener in a saucepan, and heat over a low flame. Do not bring to a boil, or it will curdle. Add the dissolved kuzu or cornstarch, stirring constantly, and heat until thickened. Add the vanilla and brandy, and simmer another moment. If desired, swirl in the unsalted margarine for a little extra richness.

Per 2 tablespoons: Calories 34, Protein 1 g, Fat 0 g, Carbohydrates 4 g

1 cup cashew or almond milk
or soymilk

¼ cup frozen concentrated
apple juice

2 tablespoons sweetener of
choice (optional)

2 tablespoons kuzu,
or 2 tablespoons cornstarch
or arrowroot (dissolved in 2
tablespoons water)

1 teaspoon vanilla

4 tablespoons brandy or cognac

1 to 3 tablespoons unsalted
nonhydrogenated margarine
(optional)

Citrus Brandy Sauce

Yield: 1 cup

Goes great with Christmas pudding, page 221.

Heat the sweetener, orange juice, and zests in a small saucepan. Add the brandy and simmer for 2 to 3 minutes. Thicken with the dissolved cornstarch, and cook for another minute.

Per 2 tablespoons: Calories 92, Protein Fat 0 g, Carbohydrates 22 g

½ cup agave, sugar, or fruit
juice concentrate (see page 14)

⅓ cup frozen concentrated
orange juice

Grated zest of 1 orange and
1 lemon

2 to 3 tablespoons brandy

2 teaspoons cornstarch or
arrowroot, dissolved in
1 tablespoon water

Mail Order Sources

If you have difficulty finding any of the more unusual ingredients called for in these recipes, many of them can be order by mail.

For nutritional yeast, instant gluten powder for making seitan, agar, arrowroot, tamari, tempeh starter, organic sweeteners, carob, and many other vegetarian products:

The Mail Order Catalog for Healthy Eating
P.O. Box 180
Summertown, TN 38483
1-800-695-2241
www.healthy-eating.com

Index

A

agar 1-3
agave 14
Aïoli, Tofu 87
Aïoli Spread, Tofu 46
almond milk 7
    Almond Sauce 69
    Brandy Sauce 233
    Shiitake Bisque 98
    Sweet White Wine Sauce 73
    Tangy White Wine Sauce 72
    White Sauce or Béchamel 68
almond paste
    Sweet Tahini Almond Cakes 209
Almond Scones, Orange 24
almonds
    Blintzes 25
    Cake 196
    Chocolate Raspberry Torte 188-89
    Eggplant & Tofu Pâté 50
    Lemon Wafers 217
    Pastry or Short Crust 203
    Sauce, Nutty 69
    Strawberry Mousse Parfait 226
    Strawberry Tart 202-03
    Tomatoes Almondine 40
appetizer pastries and tarts, about 55
apples
    Baked 218-19
    Chestnut Soup 103
    Cream of Watercress Soup 105
    Spice Muffins 27
arrowroot 3
asparagus
    & Oyster Mushroom Crêpes 118
    Garden Scramble 30
    Vegetable Aspic Terrine 52-53
aspic
    Vegetable Terrine 52-53

Aurora Sauce, Mushroom 77
Avocado & Cucumber Soup 107

B

"bacon," vegetarian 33
    Beans & "Bacon" Casserole 167
Baked Apples 218-19
Balsamic Dressing, Sweet 172
Balsamic Vinaigrette 177
Banana Coconut Ice Cream or Sauce 228
Banana-Nut Pancakes 22
bars. See cookies
Basic Muffins 26
Basic Quiche 59
Basic Vegetable Stock 90-91
basil
    Basil Onion Vinaigrette 177
    Mediterranean Potato Soup 102
    Pesto Sauce 84
    Pesto Vegetable Soup 97
    Portobello & Polenta Lasagne 136-37
    Spinach Mousse 49
    Stuffed Pasta 134
Bavarian, Orange 225
Beans & "Bacon" Casserole 167
Béarnaise Sauce, Shiitake 75, 165
Béchamel Sauce 68
Believable "Bacon" 33
bell peppers
    & Quinoa Charlotte 130-31
    Bisque, Roasted 99
    Gâteau de Crêpes 139
    Portobello & Polenta Lasagne 136-37
    Spinach & "Chevre" Salad 172
Bisque, Herbal Shiitake 98
Bisque, Roasted Red Bell Pepper 99
black mushrooms (shiitake) 9-10

Blintzes 25
Blueberry Muffins 26
Blueberry Pancakes 22
Bourguignon, Tofu 148-49
"Boursin," Tofu 44
Brandy Sauce 233
bread crumbs
    Stuffed Onions 38
Broccoli & Potato Chowder 101
brown rice
    Crème 230
    Stuffed Onions, Savory 120-21
brown rice syrup 13, 14
Brown Sauce
    Easy Mushroom 81
    Quick 80
    Rich 78
    Suprême 79
Brulée, Kahlua 222
Buche de Noël 190-91
Burgers, Tempeh & Gluten 161
Burgers, Tofu 145

C

Cabbage, Tempeh-Stuffed 150-51
Cabbage Rolls, Chestnut-Filled 122-23
Caesar Salad 173
cakes
    Almond 196
    Buche de Noël 190-91
    Cashew Cheesecake 199
    Chocolate Almond Raspberry Torte 188-89
    Chocolate Buttercreme Ganache 195
    Chocolate Soufflé Roll 190-91
    Chocolate Sponge 194
    Christmas Tree 197
    Italian Cheeseless Cake 200
    Maple Rum Torte 198
    Sponge 192-93

Cakes, Curried Sweet Potato 184
California Salad 181
Canapés, Smoked Tofu, Mushroom
    & Garlic 56-57
Caper Sauce, Lemon 166
Caponata 37
carob 3-5
    Chip Cookies 215
    Fondant 230
    Walnut Kisses 214
carrots
    & Cashew Mousse 48
    & Orange Soup 109
    Curried Fruit Soup 110
    Flan 54
    Minted 185
    Quiche, Curried 60
    Vegetable Aspic Terrine 52-53
cashew milk 7
    Brandy Sauce 233
    Sweet White Wine Sauce 73
cashews
    Carrot Mousse 48
    Cheesecake 199
    Chocolate or Mocha
      Buttercreme 231
    Coconut Crème Fraiche 83
    Crème Sauce 82
    Lemon Cream Tart 201
    Mayonnaise 82
    Pecan Pie 206
    Pumpkin Mousse 223
    Seitan & Mushroom Stroganoff
      164
    Sour Crème 83
    Stuffed Onions, Savory 120-21
    Tofu Cashew Crème 229
Casserole, Beans & "Bacon" 167
Casserole, Herbed Soybean 124
Cauliflower & Fennel Soup 101
Charlotte, Tri-Colored Pepper &
    Quinoa 130-31
Cheese, Herb-Garlic 44
"Cheese," Tofu 42-43
cheesecake
    Cashew 199
    Italian Cheeseless Cake 200

Cheese Puffs, Herb 45
chestnuts
    Baked Apples 218-19
    Cabbage Rolls 122-23
    Soup 103
"Chevre," Tofu 172
Chicken-Free Stock 92
Chocolate
    Almond Raspberry Torte 188-89
    Buttercreme 231
    Buttercreme Ganache Cake 195
    Chip Cookies 215
    Dipped Shortbread 212
    Dream Mousse 224
    Ganache 195
    rolls or shavings 189
    Soufflé Roll 190-91
    Sponge Cake 194
    Walnut Kisses 214
chocolate chips 224
    Chocolate Cream, Dark 189
    Chocolate Dream Mousse 224
    Cookies 215
Chowder, Fresh Corn 100
Christmas Pudding 221
Christmas Tree Cake 197
Chutney, Mango 65
Citrus Brandy Sauce 233
Coconut Cake 193
coconut milk 5
    Coconut Crème Fraiche 83
    Orange Coconut Curry 119
    Tofu Coconut Crème 229
Concassé, Grilled Tomato 86
Consommé, Shiitake 93
cookies and bars
    Chocolate Chip 215
    Chocolate Walnut Kisses 214
    Lemon Almond Wafers 217
    Peanut Butter 216
    Pecan Shortbread 211
    Shortbread 210
    Spice Slices with Jam Dots 213
    Tahini Almond Cakes 209
    Tahini Shortbread 211

Corn Chowder, Fresh 100
Corn Soup, Cream of 114
Cranberry Walnut Muffins 26
Cranberry Walnut Scones 24
Cream Sauce, Red Wine 74
creamed soups. See soups,
    creamed
Crème Fraiche, Coconut 83
Crème Sauce, Cashew 82
crêpes 140
    Asparagus & Oyster Mushroom
      118
    Blintzes 25
    Deep Sea 117
    Dessert 207
    Gâteau de Crêpes 138-40
    Sushi 62
    Wild Rice 116
Croutons, Herb & Garlic 182
Cucumber Avocado Soup 107
Cucumber Vichyssoise 106
currants
    Christmas Pudding 221
Curried
    Carrot & Fruit Soup 110
    Carrot Quiche 60
    Mushroom Filo Triangles 65
    Sweet Potato Cakes 184
Curry, Orange Coconut 119

D

Deep Sea Crêpes 117
Dessert Crêpes 207
dessert sauces. See sauces, dessert
Dijon Dressing, Maple 176
Dijon Mustard Sauce 84
Dill Quiche, Spinach & 61
dressings
    Balsamic 177
    Basil Onion 177
    Greek 178
    Mango Lime 180
    Maple Dijon 176
    Orange-Soy 181
    Raspberry 178

dressings (cont.)
Sweet Balsamic 172
Tamari Ume 180
Tarragon Garlic 179
Ume Lime 179
Wa-Fu 181

E

eggplant
& Mushrooms, Stewed 184
& Tofu Pâté 50
Caponata 37
Filling, Zucchini & Fennel 39
Gâteau de Crêpes 138-40
Gratin, Mediterranean Tofu 143
Moussaka 146-47
Oriental Stuffed 154-55

F

Fat-Free Gravy 168
Fennel Filling, Zucchini, Eggplant & 39
Fennel Soup, Cauliflower & 101
Figs, Fresh Stewed 220
Filet of Soul 166
filo
French Onion Pie 135
Triangles, Curried Mushroom 65
Flaky Pie Crust 207
flan
Carrot 54
Kahlua Brulée 222
Flavoring Powders 168-69
Florentine Pasta 133
French Moussaka 146-47
French Onion Pie 135
French Onion Soup 95
French Toast 23
Fresh Corn Chowder 100
Fresh Marina 85
Fresh Tomato & Bread Soup 96
frostings and icings
Carob Fondant 230
Chocolate Buttercreme 231

frostings and icings (cont.)
Chocolate Ganache 195
Dark Chocolate Cream 189
Maple Buttercream 198
Mocha Buttercreme 231
fruit desserts
Apples, Baked 218-19
Banana Ice Cream, Coconut 228
Christmas Pudding 221
Figs, Stewed Fresh 220
Fruit Tart, Fresh 204
Lemon Cream Tart 201
Orange Bavarian 225
Peach Jewels, Jellied 220
Pears, Poached 219
Strawberry Mousse Parfait 226
fruit juice
Curried Carrot & Fruit Soup 110
fruit juice concentrate 13, 14
FruitSource 13, 14

G

Ganache, Chocolate 195
garbanzo beans
Neat Loaf 144
Garden Scramble 30
garlic
& Herb Croutons 182
Smoked Tofu & Mushroom Canapés 56-57
Soup 94
Tarragon Vinaigrette 179
Tofu Aïoli 87
Tofu Aïoli Spread 46
Gâteau de Crêpes 138-40
Gazpacho 108
Gluten, homemade 156-58
& Tempeh Burgers 161
See also seitan 159-165
Grand Marnier Sauce 232
grape juice concentrate 14
Gratin, Mediterranean Eggplant & Tofu 143
Gravy, Fat-Free 168
Gravy, Holiday 127

Gravy, Instant Seitan 87
Greek Olive & Basil Quiche 61
Greek Vinaigrette 178
Green Onion Pancakes 63
Green Pea Soup, Cream of 114
Grilled Tomato Concassé 86
Ground Seitan 159

H

Herb & Garlic Croutons 182
Herb Cheese Puffs 45
Herb-Garlic Cheese 44
Herbal Shiitake Bisque 98
Herbed Soybean Casserole or Stew 124
Holiday Pumpkin 126-27
Huevos Florentine 31

I

Ice Cream, Coconut Banana 228
Ice Cream, Pumpkin 227
icings. *See* frostings
Italian Cheeseless Cake 200

K

Kahlua Brulée 222
kidney beans
Beans & "Bacon" Casserole 167
kuzu-ko or kudzu 5

L

Lasagne, Portobello & Polenta 136-37
Lemon
Almond Wafers 217
Cake 193
Caper Sauce 166
Cream Tart 201
Mousse 201
Pepper Sauce 118
Light Yeast Flavoring Powder 169
limes
Mango Dressing 180
Ume Dressing 179
Loaf, Jeff's Favorite Neat 144

M

Madeira Mushroom Sauce 76
Mango Chutney 65
Mango Lime Dressing 180
maple syrup 13, 14
    Maple-Dijon Dressing 176
    Maple Rum Torte 198
    Orange Yams 185
    Pecan Pie 206
Marinara, Fresh 85
Marinated Tofu 141
Marinated Tofu, Smoky 142
Mayonnaise, Cashew 82
Mediterranean Potato Soup 102
Mediterranean Stuffed Tomatoes 36
Minted Carrots 185
mirin 5-6
miso 6-7
    Herb Cheese Puffs 45
    Tofu Aïoli Spread 46
    Tofu "Boursin" 44
    Tofu "Cheese" 42-43
    Tofu "Feta" Cheese 43
Mocha Buttercreme 231
"Mornay" Sauce 71
Moussaka 146-47
mousses, about 47
    Carrot & Cashew 48
    Chocolate Dream 224
    Lemon 201
    Pumpkin 223
    Spinach & Basil 49
muffins 26-28
mushrooms
    & Eggplant, Stewed 184
    Asparagus & Oyster Mushroom
        Crêpes 118
    Aurora Sauce 77
    Béarnaise Sauce, Shiitake 75, 165
    Bisque, Shiitake 88
    Brown Sauce 81
    Brown Sauce, Rich 78
    Brown Sauce Suprême 79
    Creamy Mushroom & Red Wine
        Soup 104

mushrooms (cont.)
    Curried Filo Triangles 65
    Deep Sea Crêpes 117
    Garden Scramble 30
    Garlic Soup, Clear 94
    Madeira Sauce 76
    Pâté 51
    Pesto Vegetable Soup 97
    Portobello & Polenta Lasagne
        136-37
    Quiche 60
    Sauce, Quick 74
    Seitan Medallions 162-63
    Seitan Stroganoff 164
    shiitake, about 9-10
    Shiitake Consommé 93
    shimeji (oyster), about 9
    Smoked Tofu & Garlic Canapés
        56-57
    Spinach Salad, Wilted 174
    Stuffed Shiitake Mushrooms 41
    Tempeh & Vegetable Stew 152-
        53
    Tofu Bourguignon 148-49
    Vegetable Aspic Terrine 52-53
    Vol-au-Vent 121
    Wild Rice Crêpes 116
Mustard Sauce, Dijon 84

N

Napoleons, Spinach 58
Neat Loaf 144
nori
    Filet of Soul 166
nut milks 7-8
nutritional yeast 8
Nutty Almond Sauce 69

O

Oat Crème 230
Oatmeal Crust 208
okara
    about 8-9
    Almond Cake 196
    Chocolate Almond Raspberry
        Torte 188-89

okara (cont.)
    Homemade 189
Olive & Basil Quiche 61
omelet, tofu (Zenmlet) 32
onions
    Basic Quiche 59
    Basil Vinaigrette 177
    Brown Sauce, Rich 78
    Brown Sauce Suprême 79
    Green Onion Pancakes 63
    Pie, French 135
    Savory, with Cashew-Rice
        Filling 120-21
    Soubise Sauce 70
    Soup, French 95
    Stuffed 38
oranges and orange juice
    Almond Scones 24
    Bavarian 225
    Cake 193
    Carrot Soup 109
    Citrus Brandy Sauce 233
    Coconut Curry 119
    Grand Marnier Sauce 232
    -Soy Dressing 181
    -Maple Yams 185
    Pumpkin Mousse 223
Oriental Stuffed Eggplant 154-55
Oven-Roasted Seitan 159
oyster mushrooms (shimeji) 9

P

Paella 125
Pancakes 22-23
Pancakes, Green Onion 63
Paprika Sauce 68
parsnips
    Chicken-Free Stock 92
Pasta, Homemade Tofu 132-33
Pasta, Summer Florentine 133
Pasta Stuffed with "Ricotta" &
    Sun-Dried Tomatoes 134
pastries, appetizer
    Curried Mushroom Filo
        Triangles 65

pastries, appetizer (cont.)
  Provençale Spinach Tarts 57
  Smoked Tofu, Mushroom &
    Garlic 56-57
  Spinach Napoleons 58
pastry crusts. *See* pie crusts
pâtés, about 47
  Eggplant & Tofu 50
  Mushroom 51
Peach Jewels, Jellied 220
Peanut Butter Cookies 216
Pear & Caramelized Pecan Salad
  176
Pears, Poached 219
Pea Soup, Cream of 114
pecans
  Pear Salad 176
  Pie 206
  Scones, Cranberry 24
  Shortbread 211
  Tofu "Boursin" 44
peppers
  & Quinoa Charlotte 130-31
  Caponata 37
  Sauce, Roasted Red Bell 86
Pesto Sauce 84
Pesto Vegetable Soup 97
pie crusts
  Almond 203
  Flaky 207
  Oatmeal 208
  Whole Wheat 208
pies
  French Onion 135
  Pecan 206
  Pumpkin 205
pine nuts
  Pesto Sauce 84
Pineapple Salsa 63
Polenta, Ume-Shiso 64
Portobello & Polenta Lasagne 136-
  37
Potato & Broccoli Chowder 101
Potato Soup, Mediterranean 102
pressed tofu 18

Provençale Spinach Tarts 57
puddings
  Chocolate Dream Mousse 224
  Christmas 221
  Kahlua Brulée 222
  Lemon Mousse 201
  Orange Bavarian 225
  Pumpkin Mousse 223
  Strawberry Mousse Parfait 226
pumpkin or squash
  Great Holiday Pumpkin
    (stuffed) 126-27
  Ice Cream 227
  Mousse 223
  Pie 205
  Soup, Cream of 113

Q

quiches, about 55
  Basic 59
  Curried Carrot 60
  Greek Olive & Basil 61
  Lorraine 60
  Mushroom 60
  Spinach & Dill 61
Quinoa Charlotte, Pepper & 130-31

R

raisins
  Blintzes 25
  Christmas Pudding 221
  Italian Cheeseless Cake 200
  Walnut Muffins 28
raspberries
  Chocolate Almond Torte 188-89
  Sauce 232
  Vinaigrette 178
red bell peppers
  Bisque, Roasted 99
  Sauce, Roasted 86
red wine
  Brown Sauce, Rich 78
  Brown Sauce Suprême 79
  Cream Sauce 74
  Creamy Mushroom Soup 104

red wine (cont.)
  Eggplant & Mushrooms, Stewed
    184
  Madeira Mushroom Sauce 76
  Marinated Tofu 141
  Sauce 123
  Seitan & Mushroom Stroganoff
    164
  Seitan Medallions 162-63
  Shiitake Consommé 93
  Shiso Steaks 165
  Smoky Marinated Tofu 142
  Stewed Fresh Figs 220
  Tempeh & Vegetable Stew 152-
    53
  Tofu Bourguignon 148-49
rice
  Great Holiday Pumpkin 126-27
  Paella 125
  Rich Tofu Crème 229
Rich Yeast Flavoring Powder 168
"Ricotta," Stuffed Pastry with 134
Roasted Red Bell Pepper Bisque 99
Roasted Red Bell Pepper Sauce 86
Roasted Vegetables 183

S

saffron
  Clear Garlic Soup 94
  Paella 125
sake 9
salads
  Caesar 173
  California 181
  Pear & Caramelized Pecan 176
  Spinach & "Chevre" 172
  Wakame 175
  Wilted Spinach 174
Salsa, Pineapple 63
Salsa, Roasted Tomato 31
sauces, dessert
  Brandy 233
  Citrus Brandy 233
  Coconut Banana 228
  Grand Marnier 232

sauces, dessert (cont.)
    Oat or Brown Rice Crème 230
    Raspberry 232
    Tofu Crèmes 229
sauces, savory
    Almond 69
    Béchamel 68
    Brown, Quick 80
    Brown, Rich 78
    Brown, Suprême 79
    Cashew Crème 82
    Dijon Mustard 84
    Lemon Caper 166
    Lemon Pepper 118
    Madeira Mushroom 76
    Marinara, Fresh 85
    Mushroom, Quick 74
    Mushroom Aurora 77
    Mushroom Brown 81
    Paprika 68
    Pesto 84
    Red Bell Pepper, Roasted 86
    Red Wine 123
    Red Wine Cream 74
    Shiitake Béarnaise 75
    Soubise 70
    Soubise Suprême 70
    Sweet and Sour 129
    Sweet White Wine 73
    Tangy White Wine 72
    Teriyaki 71
    Tofu "Mornay" 71
    Tomato Concassé, Grilled 86
    White 68
    Wine 72-73
Scones 24
seitan
    & Mushroom Stroganoff 164
    Basic Ground 159
    Filet of Soul 166
    Gravy 87
    Medallions 162-63
    Oven Roasted 159
    Shiso Steaks 165
    Stove-Top 160
    Tempeh & Gluten Burgers 159

sesame paste or butter 14
sesame seeds
    Oriental Stuffed Eggplant 154-55
    Teriyaki Sauce & Marinade 71
shallots
    Lemon Caper Sauce 166
shiitake (black) mushrooms 9-10
    Béarnaise Sauce 75
    Bisque 98
    Clear Garlic Soup 94
    Consommé 93
    Madeira Mushroom Sauce 76
    Mushroom Pâté 51
    Seitan Medallions 162-63
    Shiso Steaks 165
    Stuffed 41
    Wilted Spinach Salad 174
shimeji (oyster) mushrooms 9
Shiso Polenta, Ume- 64
Shiso Steaks 165
Shortbread 210
    Chocolate Dipped 212
    Pecan 211
    Tahini 211
Smoked Tofu, Mushroom & Garlic
    Canapés 56-57
Smoky Marinated Tofu 142
Soubise Sauce 70
Soubise Sauce Suprême 70
soups, chilled
    Avocado & Cucumber 107
    Carrot & Orange 109
    Cream of Watercress & Apple 105
    Cucumber Vichyssoise 106
    Curried Carrot & Fruit 110
    Gazpacho 108
    Spiced Autumn 111
soups, creamed
    Avocado & Cucumber 107
    Bell Pepper Bisque, Roasted Red 99
    Cauliflower & Fennel 101
    Chestnut 103

soups, creamed (cont.)
    Corn 114
    Corn Chowder, Fresh 100
    Cucumber Vichyssoise 106
    Green Pea 114
    Mushroom & Red Wine 104
    Potato, Mediterranean 102
    Potato & Broccoli Chowder 101
    Pumpkin 113
    Shiitake Bisque 98
    Watercress & Apple 105
soups, hot
    French Onion 95
    Garlic, Clear 94
    Pesto Vegetable 97
    Tomato & Bread Soup, Fresh 96
sour cream, soy 12
Sour Crème, Cashew 83
Sour Crème, Tofu 182
soy cream 11
    Red Wine Cream Sauce 74
    Sweet White Wine Sauce 73
    Tangy White Wine Sauce 72
soy sauce 11-12
soy sour cream 12
soy yogurt 12-13
Soybean Casserole or Stew 124
soymilk 10-11
    Almond Sauce 69
    Avocado & Cucumber Soup 107
    Béchamel Sauce 68
    Brandy Sauce 233
    Carrot & Orange Soup 109
    Cauliflower & Fennel Soup 101
    Chestnut Soup 103
    Cream of Watercress & Apple Soup 105
    Creamy Mushroom & Red Wine Soup 104
    French Toast 23
    Fresh Corn Chowder 100
    Fresh Fruit Tart 204
    Green Onion Pancakes 63
    Mediterranean Potato Soup 102
    Pancakes 22

soymilk (cont.)
    Potato & Broccoli Chowder 101
    Red Wine Cream Sauce 74
    Soubise Sauce 70
    Soubise Sauce Suprême 70
    White Sauce 68
Spice Cake 193
Spice Slices with Jam Dots 213
Spiced Autumn Soup 111
spinach
    & Basil Mousse 49
    & "Chevre" Salad 172
    & Dill Quiche 61
    Florentine Pasta 133
    Huevos Florentine 31
    Napoleons 58
    Salad, Wilted 174
    Tarts 57
Sponge Cake, and variations 192-93
Sponge Cake, Chocolate 194
squash or pumpkin
    Great Holiday Pumpkin 126-27
    Spiced Autumn Soup 111
Stew, Herbed Soybean 124
Stew, Savory Tempeh & Vegetable 152-53
Stock, Chicken-Free 92
Stock, Vegetable 90-91
Stove-Top Seitan 160
strawberries
    Almond Tart 202-03
    Mousse Parfait 226
Stroganoff, Seitan 164
Stuffed
    Eggplant, Oriental 154-55
    Onions (appetizer) 38
    Onions, Savory (main dish) 120-21
    Pasta 134
    Shiitake Mushrooms 41
    Tomatoes, Mediterranean 36
Sushi Crêpes 62
Sweet & Sour Tofu 128-29
Sweet Balsamic Dressing 172

Sweet Potato Cakes, Curried 184
Sweet White Wine Sauce 73
sweeteners 13-14

T

tahini 14-15
    Almond Cakes 209
    Shortbread 211
tamari 15
Tamari Ume Dressing 180
Tangy White Wine Sauce 72
Tarragon Garlic Vinaigrette 179
tarts
    Crust 203
    Fresh Fruit 204
    Lemon Cream 201
    Spinach 57
    Strawberry Almond 202-03
tempeh 15
    & Gluten Burgers 161
    Savory Vegetable Stew 152-53
    Stuffed Eggplant 154-55
    Stuffed Whole Cabbage 150-51
Teriyaki Sauce & Marinade 71
terrines, about 47
    Vegetable Aspic 52-53
tofu, frozen 17-18
    Bourguignon 148-49
    Burgers 145
    Mediterranean Eggplant Gratin 143
    Moussaka 146-47
    Neat Loaf 144
    Stuffed Shiitake Mushrooms 41
tofu, regular 16-17
    Aïoli 87
    Aïoli Spread 46
    Aki's Tofu Eggs 29
    "bacon," vegetarian 33
    Blintzes 25
    "Boursin" 44
    Carrot Flan 54
    Cashew Cheesecake 199
    Cashew Crème 229
    Cashew Sour Crème 83

tofu, regular (cont.)
    "Cheese" 42-43
    "Chevre" 172
    Chocolate Cream, Dark 189
    Chocolate Soufflé Roll 190-91
    Cream Cheese Spread 46
    Cream of Corn Soup 114
    Cream of Green Pea Soup 114
    Cream of Pumpkin Soup 113
    Crème, Rich 229
    Eggplant Pâté 50
    "Feta" Cheese 43
    French Onion Pie 135
    French Toast 23
    Herb Cheese Puffs 45
    Huevos Florentine 31
    Lemon Cream Tart 201
    Marinated 141, 142
    "Mornay" Sauce 71
    Mushroom & Garlic Canapés, Smoked 56-57
    omelet (Zenmlet) 32
    Pasta 132-33
    pressed 18
    Pumpkin Ice Cream 227
    Pumpkin Pie 205
    quiches 59-61
    Scones 24
    scrambled 29, 30
    Smoky Marinated 142
    Sour Crème 182
    Spinach & Basil Mousse 49
    Spinach & "Chevre" Salad 172
    Stuffed Pasta with "Ricotta" 134
    Stuffed Tomatoes 36
    Sweet & Sour 128-29
    Zenmlet 32
tofu, silken 16
    Chocolate Dream Mousse 224
    Chocolate or Mocha Buttercreme 231
    Coconut Crème Fraiche 83
    Kahlua Brulée 222
    Orange Bavarian 225
    Pancakes 22

tofu, silken (cont.)
    Pumpkin Mousse 223
    Sour Cream 182
    Tofu Cashew Crème 229
    Tofu Coconut Crème 229
    Tofu Crème 229
tomatoes
    Almondine 40
    & Bread Soup, Fresh 96
    Caponata 37
    Concassé, Grilled 86
    Gâteau de Crêpes 138-40
    Gazpacho 108
    Marinara, Fresh 85
    Mediterranean Eggplant & Tofu 143
    Paella 125
    Pesto Vegetable Soup 97
    Salsa, Roasted 31
    Stuffed 36
tomatoes, sun-dried
    Florentine Pasta 133
    Mediterranean Potato Soup 102
    Portobello & Polenta Lasagne 136-37
    Stuffed Pasta with "Ricotta" 134
Torte, Chocolate Almond Raspberry 188-89
Torte, Maple Rum 198

U

Ume-Shiso Polenta 64

V

Vegetable Aspic Terrine 52-53
Vegetable Soup, Pesto 97
Vegetable Stew, Tempeh 152-53
Vegetable Stock, Basic 90-91
vegetables, grilled or roasted
    Orange Coconut Curry 119
    Roasted 183
Vichyssoise, Cucumber 106
vinaigrettes
    Balsamic 177
    Basil Onion 177
    Greek 178
    Raspberry 178
    Tarragon Garlic 179
vital wheat gluten 158
Vol-au-Vent with Three Mushrooms 121

W

Wafers, Lemon Almond 217
Wa-Fu Dressing 181
Wakame Salad 175
walnuts
    Apple Spice Muffins 27
    Banana-Nut Pancakes 22
    Blintzes 25
    Chocolate or Carob Chip Cookies 215
    Chocolate or Carob Kisses 214
    Cranberry Muffins 26
    Eggplant & Tofu Pâté 50

walnuts (cont.)
    Muffins 28
    Mushroom Pâté 51
    Spinach & "Chevre" Salad 172
    Tofu "Boursin" 44
Watercress & Apple Soup, Cream of 105
Wheat-Free Pancakes 23
White Sauce 68
white wine
    Shiitake Béarnaise Sauce 75
    Soubise Sauce Suprême 70
    Sauce, Sweet 73
    Sauce, Tangy 72
Whole Wheat Pie Crust 208
Wild Rice Crêpes 116

Y

yams
    Orange-Maple 185
    Spiced Autumn Soup 111
yogurt, soy 12

Z

Zenmlet 32
zucchini
    Eggplant & Fennel Filling 39
    Gâteau de Crêpes 139
    Garden Scramble 30

Purchase these vegetarian cookbooks from your local bookstore or natural foods store, or you can buy them directly from:

Book Publishing Company

P.O. Box 99

Summertown, TN 38483

1-800-695-2241

Please include $3.50 per book for shipping and handling.

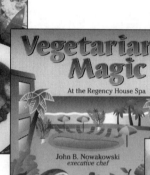
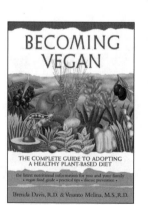

To find your favorite vegetarian and soyfood products online, visit:

www.healthy-eating.com